War, Media, and Propaganda

War, Media, and Propaganda

A Global Perspective

Edited by
Yahya R. Kamalipour
and Nancy Snow

ROWMAN & LITTLEFIELD PUBLISHERS, INC.
Lanham • Boulder • New York • Toronto • Oxford

ROWMAN & LITTLEFIELD PUBLISHERS, INC.

Published in the United States of America
by Rowman & Littlefield Publishers, Inc.
A wholly owned subsidiary of The Rowman & Littlefield Publishing Group, Inc.
4501 Forbes Boulevard, Suite 200, Lanham, Maryland 20706
www.rowmanlittlefield.com

PO Box 317, Oxford
OX2 9RU, UK

British Library Cataloguing in Publication Information Available

Library of Congress Cataloging-in-Publication Data

Kamalipour, Yahya R.
  War, media, and propaganda : a global perspective / Yahya R. Kamalipour and
Nancy Snow.
    p. cm.
  Includes bibliographical references and index.
  ISBN 0-7425-3562-2 (cloth : alk. paper) — ISBN 0-7425-3563-0
(pbk. : alk. paper)
    1. Mass media and war—United States. 2. Mass media and propaganda—United
States. 3. Iraq War, 2003—Mass media and the war. 4. Iraq War, 2003—Propaganda.
I. Snow, Nancy. II. Title.
P96.W352U554 2004
070.4'4935502—dc22

                                                                    2004006822

∞™ The paper used in this publication meets the minimum requirements of American
National Standard for Information Sciences—Permanence of Paper for Printed Library
Materials, ANSI/NISO Z39.48-1992.

In memory of the innocent victims of the September 11, 2001, attacks on the United States and the retaliatory U.S.–U.K. attacks on Afghanistan and Iraq.

Every gun that is made, every warship launched, every rocket fired signifies, in the final sense, a theft from those who hunger and are not fed, those who are cold and not clothed.

—Dwight D. Eisenhower

What difference does it make to the dead, the orphans, and the homeless, whether the mad destruction is wrought under the name of totalitarianism or the holy name of liberty and democracy?

—Mahatma Ghandhi

We have to face the fact that either all of us are going to die together or we are going to learn to live together and if we are to live together we have to talk.

—Eleanor Roosevelt

There never was a good war or a bad peace.

—Benjamin Franklin

The affairs of our world are largely based on Who gets what? Against whom? How? And At what price?

—Anonymous

Contents

Foreword

Ben H. Bagdikian—Author of The Media Monopoly

It was Senator Hiram Johnson who, in 1917, arguing before the Senate against the United States' entry into World War I, said, "The first casualty when war comes is truth."

It was I. F. Stone who told a group of aspiring journalists, "The first thing you need to understand in covering politics is that all governments lie."

And more than fifty years ago, it was Gordon Allport, with his Harvard associates in the study of riots, who found that when there are rumors, panic, or propaganda that induce anxiety and fear, the best antidote is not silence or mere comforting words or propaganda from the authorities but, to the contrary, as much solid and accurate information as possible.

The truths of Senator Johnson, I. F. Stone, and Professor Allport, and the demonstration of what happens when their statements are not only ignored but turned on their heads, was demonstrated in 2002, when President George H. W. Bush told the American people that it was urgently necessary to invade Iraq. This was urgent, he said, because Saddam Hussein possessed a fearsome arsenal of weapons of mass destruction. He listed the terrifying inventory of the weaponry. He added that Iraq was importing uranium and would soon have nuclear weapons that could devastate the United States and intimidate the Middle East.

The painful message of this book was further demonstrated when, too late, the public discovered that Iraq did not possess weapons of mass destruction. And that when President Bush claimed that Iraq was well on the way to creating a nuclear weapon by importing uranium from Niger, it was known by United States intelligence agencies (and agencies of other countries) that the uranium allegation was based on a forged document.

But another message of this book was yet another failure of a major element in American public information. The absence of Iraqi weapons of mass destruction and the fraudulence of the uranium importation were known and knowable to the standard news media of the country at the time. But there has been a reflex throughout the history of modern news: when the country goes to war, so do the major news organizations. They consider it "patriotic." But it is dubious patriotism that abandons citizens in unnecessary ignorance of critical information.

Only later, when the fantasies of the official weapons of mass destruction had been exposed on the battlefields of Iraq, did the major news media inform the public what they should have told the public before the debacle—and could have at the time the government frightened the country with imminent danger from vast Iraqi weaponry.

There is another systemic reason that the major U.S. news media failed to report the falsity of the uranium claim at the time the president made it. In their attempt to achieve "objectivity," the standard practice of the newspapers and news broadcasters is to take their governmental and corporate news almost exclusively from men and women with high titles—Cabinet secretaries, agency heads, congressional committee chairs, CEOs, chairs of boards, and top officers in major law and investment firms.

The knowledge and opinions of such leaders are important. But these titled people do not always tell the truth and nothing but the whole truth about information that might embarrass them and their organizations. A great many do not know the whole truth. The same applies to top government officials.

What does this mean as we go forward into a twenty-first century of massive changes in global demographics and power? What can we expect in the years to come?

All the major media of this country are controlled by five or six massive media conglomerates, who dominate every medium—printed, broadcast, and filmed—on which the majority of the American public say they depend. These multinational corporations are in turn oriented to, first, maintain their power and domination and, second, satisfy the stock market by doing whatever will increase the value of their corporate shares.

When Wall Street demands "better performance" (higher stock prices) from the media conglomerates, these conglomerates, powerful as they are, do whatever cost-cutting and mutual aid with each other that will produce obedience to the dictates of that special tribe, the "Wall Street analysts" (these are the analysts that were so perceptive and reliable that they happened to miss—and profit by—the fraudulent bookkeeping and other crimes of Enron and others in the 1990s).

Is there no hope? Must we remain ignorant and deluded about our own politics and economy? Fortunately, there is a glimmer of hope.

Though the major media failed in the prelude of the Iraqi war and remain wedded to high official sources, there are growing segments of the public, including a new generation of young men and women skilled in uses of the Internet. They are sophisticated in political organization and moved by progressive ideals, and they were surprisingly successful in using the Internet to produce large-scale public demonstrations against the impending Iraqi war. A significant portion of civilians—activists with more-than-average involvement in social and national policies—who look to progressive and specialized issue organizations, such as the environment and political websites and alternative publications, to learn more about candidates for public office. More of official "disinformation" (a euphemism for deliberates lies) is looked at skeptically and against a background of facts or at least from sources the main news media consider "too liberal." (In the early twenty-first century, "too liberal" refers to politics that thirty years earlier was considered the center.)

In the immediate aftermath of the Iraqi war, important portions of the standard news media were chastened, at least momentarily, by the failures of their prewar performance. Such media segments are learning how to cooperate with like-minded groups in exposing the costly pitfalls of the failure to expose the unholy trinity of "war, media, and propaganda." Unfortunately, in modern history the chastening effect has been felt only after the damage has been done, as in Vietnam and Iraq.

The before-and-after picture of U.S. officialdom presents a stark lesson of the tragedies of war and propaganda repeated in the major media, a lesson described in the famous dictum of George Orwell:

> One ought to recognize that the present political chaos is connected with the decay of language, and that one can probably bring about some improvement by starting at the verbal end. . . . Political language—and with variations this is true of all political parties from Conservatives to Anarchists—is designed to make lies sounds truthful and murder respectable, and to give an appearance of solidity to pure wind.

Acknowledgments

In completing this book, we have benefited from the kind support and cooperation of many people throughout the world. We would especially like to offer our gratitude to Ben Bagdikian, for writing the foreword to this book, and to the contributing authors. Without their genuine interest, hard work, and support, this timely project could not have materialized.

We are also indebted to the following individuals for their valuable support and encouragement throughout this project: Nabil Ibrahim, vice chancellor for academic affairs, and Dan Dunn, dean of the School of Liberal Arts and Social Sciences, at Purdue University, Calumet; Rick Pullen and Fred Zandpour, dean and associate dean, respectively, of the College of Communications at California State University, Fullerton; and Geoffrey Cowan, dean of the Annenberg School for Communication, University of Southern California. We thank Heather M. Cook, a graduate student in the Department of Communication at Purdue University, Calumet, for reformatting all the articles for uniformity in style and layout.

At Rowman & Littlefield, we are grateful to Brenda Hadenfeldt, for her enthusiasm and support throughout this project, and we are also appreciative of the interest and support of those in editorial, production, marketing, and everyone else involved in the process of publishing this volume.

Of course, we are indebted to our respective families, for their unconditional love, emotional support, and understanding.

Introduction

Yahya R. Kamalipour

Human beings are parts of a body, created from the same essence.
When one part is hurt and in pain, the other parts remain restless.
If the misery of others leaves you indifferent,
you cannot be called a human being . . .

—Sa'adi Shirazi, Persian poet-philosopher and author (1204–1292)

December 2003—As the manuscript for this book was nearing completion, people throughout the world were witnessing on their television screens the video footage of the U.S. soldiers' arresting the once-powerful Iraqi president, Saddam Hussein ("Butcher of Baghdad"), who was reportedly dragged out of the "rat hole" where he was hiding and subsequently videotaped. The footage, repeatedly broadcast on every television channel, shows Hussein being examined, in total humiliation, by an American military physician, who is looking into Hussein's mouth and searching through his unkempt hair—perhaps for bugs. This prompted a senior Vatican official, Cardinal Renato Martino, to criticize the United States for releasing the video footage in which the former Iraqi president was, as he put it, "handled like a cow" (*New York Times*, December 16, 2003). However, President George W. Bush and his cohorts were shown in a celebratory mood as they gleefully claimed a major victory against terrorism and for democracy and freedom in Iraq.

Significantly, the premise for the war on Iraq—articulated repeatedly by George W. Bush and Tony Blair—was that Hussein was pursuing a program of weapons of mass destruction (WMD). Not only based on the falsity of that premise but subject to continual and highly orchestrated propaganda techniques were the deaths of thousands of innocent Iraqis, the deaths of hundreds of American/Allied forces, and the destruction of the Iraqi infrastructures—all

1

of which were seemingly forgotten. Furthermore, the main perpetrators of the September 11, 2001, attacks on America, Osama bin Laden and al Qaeda, were pushed out of the arena of public opinion.

It was against that backdrop that the manuscript for *War, Media, and Propaganda: A Global Perspective* was being prepared for publication—at a juncture in the history of the civilized world when breakdown in communication, civility, international law, human rights, freedom, lack of humanity-based progress, and global–social justice indelibly mark the dawn of the third millennium. And at a time when such concepts as human rights, dialogue of civilizations, and clash of civilizations were being debated side by side with global terrorism, unilateralism, globalism, imperialism, and preemptive strike. Indeed, the looming turmoil in the global village, with the difficulties posed in intercultural communication, international communication, and international relations, render this book an essential platform for discussing, debating, and understanding the complexities of our global affairs.

Undoubtedly, the September 11, 2001, terrorist attacks on the World Trade Center and the Pentagon will be forever etched into the memories of the people who personally experienced, witnessed, or viewed the images of that unimaginable tragedy on television screens throughout the world. At the dawn of the third millennium, it has become quite apparent that we as human beings have made no progress toward elevating humanity to its potential level of civility. Rather, we have marched backward into the savageries of the Stone Age and succumbed to a vicious circle of violence that continues to plague our lives, curtail our freedoms, alter our way of life, damage our relationships, and distort our perceptions of one another.

In the name of an ideology of one kind or another, we do anything imaginable, including suicide bombings to ourselves and to our fellow human beings. A Slobodan Milosevic of Yugoslavia murders, tortures, and buries thousands of Muslims alive while the world watches. A General Augusto Pinochet of Chile kills his own people and builds mountains by piling up human skulls. A Mohamed Suharto of Indonesia kills millions of his people in East Timorese. A Hitler burns thousands of Jews alive for just being Jews. A Hutu tribe murders millions of Tutsis in Rwanda. A Saddam Hussein kills and even poisons his own people and thousands of Iranians with chemical weapons and subsequently erects victory monuments in Baghdad to display his savagery. An Osama bin Laden masterminds terrorist acts against America and American installations around the world. The American forces rain missiles and bombs on the millions of innocent peoples in Iraq, Sudan, Libya, Tanzania, Japan, and Vietnam. For the past fifty years, the Israelis and Palestinians have been killing each other, almost daily, in a land where the

three monolithic religions of the world—Christianity, Islam, and Judaism—
have historically and physically converged and are destined to coexist. We
are caught up in a complex web of our own making. We have lost our common sense and our perspectives on what this short journey called life is all
about. We have become beasts and evildoers. We use our fists more readily
than we do our heads. We destroy one another by thousands and even millions without blinking an eye.

OBJECTIVES OF THIS BOOK

In the post-9/11 terrorist attacks on the United States, this book presents a
multifaceted, global discussion and analysis of war, media, and propaganda.
The scholars and media professionals contributing to this book have investi-
gated and written on ways in which global media coverage of conflicts affect
human affairs, communication, and cultural–political implications in the
United States and around the world. This volume is intended to address the
following objectives:

- to present a multifaceted analysis of the consequences of war, media, and
  propaganda from diverse global perspectives;
- to describe some of the consequences and influence of regional and
  transnational media on popular opinion in various countries;
- to analyze the three themes of the book (war, media, propaganda) from
  academic and nonacademic perspectives; and
- to provide a platform for working toward the establishment of a relative
  state of peace throughout the world.

ORGANIZATION OF THIS BOOK

War, Media, and Propaganda: A Global Perspective will be a significant addition to the literature devoted to the study of media's role in global conflicts
and international communication.

The book consists of twenty-four original and invited essays, including an
introduction and a foreword, contributed by prominent authors, journalists,
scholars, and researchers from throughout the world. Rather than divide the
book into sections, we have organized the chapters logically—progressing
from the theoretical perspectives to the regional and national perspectives and
ending with articles that offer recommendations or solutions to the problems
posed in various chapters.

Despite widespread attraction to war, media, and propaganda, no similar book—with the same scope, diversity, breath, and accessibility—is available on the market.

WHO SHOULD READ THIS BOOK?

As globalization proceeds, the impact of information and communication technologies on our daily lives becomes ever more apparent. Becoming noticeably evident is the need for a book that addresses the ramifications of a complex and increasingly violent global environment on everyday life for people throughout the world. Hence, this book is intended for scholars, researchers, and students of media and international studies; as well as media professionals, instructors, researchers, and (most important) the general international public.

More specifically, this book will be beneficial to the following individuals, groups, and organizations:

- mass media, international, intercultural, and political communication scholars, researchers, and students—graduate and undergraduate;
- propaganda and persuasion studies scholars, researchers, and students;
- policy makers and stakeholders concerned with international communication and globalization issues;
- broadcast and print media professionals, educators, and students;
- U.S. and international developmental agencies, departments, and professionals; and
- internationally concerned independent writers, critics, researchers, and readers.

This book should also be appealing to members of cultural groups and organizations and to those interested in international, cross-cultural communication, especially that regarding war and propaganda.

DIVERSE PERSPECTIVES

To present a diverse and relatively balanced perspective about any issue with global dimensions and ramifications, it is essential to rely on researchers, authors, and scholars who have in-depth knowledge, personal experience, and keen interest in the subject matter. According to John Stuart Mill:

The only way in which a human being can make some approach to knowing the whole of subject is by hearing what can be said about it by persons of every variety of opinion and studying all modes in which it can be looked at by every character of mind. No wise man ever acquired his wisdom in any mode but this.

Accordingly, one of the key advantages of an edited volume, such as this book, is that it offers readers broad and multidimensional perspectives about war, media, and propaganda that are normally absent in a singularly authored textbook. You will note that the chapters in this book are diverse in content, approach, and style. Any perspective depends on where an individual stands and how she or he looks at a given situation—that is, where is this person from? What is this person's orientation and affiliation? And from what angle and through what lens does this person see a given context? In other words, diverse authors should be given an opportunity to express their diverse perspectives in their own words. This, in my view, is not necessarily a disadvantage but a strong advantage of a carefully planned and edited book, such as the one that you are holding.

A FINAL THOUGHT

In a message to the World Summit on the Information Society, the secretary general of the United Nations, Kofi Annan, said: "A technological revolution is transforming society in a profound way. If harnessed and directed properly, Information and Communication Technologies (ICTs) have the potential to improve all aspects of our social, economic and cultural life" (Geneva, December 10–12, 2003, www.itu.int/wsis). Accordingly, this book is intended to promote a constructive dialogue and, ideally, a set of solutions about issues related to war, media, and propaganda as they affect our lives throughout the world.

Globalism is upon us, and so is terrorism—an evil and destructive force to be reckoned with. Reckon, we must. But to do so, we must first focus on establishing a relative state of stability, peace, freedom, and humanity throughout the world. Nations of the world must put their differences aside and cooperate with one another on denouncing, condemning, and eradicating terrorism in any form or shape, regardless of where it takes place. This is a prime opportunity for the United Nations, NATO, the European Union, and other regional and global bodies to respond to the cries of help from the survivors of the victims of terrorism by devising and implementing a brand new approach toward eradicating this global cancer. This eradication can be achieved only through international cooperation, not by military might and war.

The ultimate goal of this book is to provide a reasonable and sufficient platform for generating meaningful discussions that would result in an increased awareness and understanding of the myriad of global problems that face humanity. It is hoped that such discussions would ultimately lead to action and positive change—peaceful coexistence, mutual respect, less conflict, increased cultural sensitivity, and better cooperation among the peoples and nations of the world. As the American Indian Chief Seattle once said, "Man did not weave the web of life, he is merely a strand in it. Whatever he does to the web, he does to himself."

1

Information Dominance: The Philosophy of Total Propaganda Control?

David Miller

The concept of information dominance is the key to understanding the United States' and the United Kingdom's respective propaganda strategies, and it is a central component of the United States' aim of "total spectrum dominance." Information dominance redefines our notions of spin and propaganda and of the role of the media in capitalist society. To say that it is about total propaganda control is to force the English language into contortions that the term *propaganda* simply cannot handle. Information dominance is not about the success of propaganda in the conventional sense with which we are all familiar. It is not about all those phrases "winning hearts and minds," about truth being "the first casualty," about "media manipulation," about "opinion control," or about "information war." Or, to be more exact—it is about these things, but none of them can quite stretch to accommodate the integrated conception of media and communication encapsulated in the phrase *information dominance.*

Information dominance is a concept of elegant simplicity yet at the same time complex interconnectedness. It plays a key role in United States' military strategy and foreign policy. The now quite well-known statement of this is contained in the Pentagon's *Joint Vision 2020,* where the key term is *full spectrum dominance,* which "implies that U.S. forces are able to conduct prompt, sustained and synchronized operations with combinations of forces tailored to specific situations and with access to and freedom to operate in all domains—space, sea, land, air and information."[1]

The inclusion of information on the list is not surprising, but it has not attracted much attention in public debate, even in the antiwar movement. The question is, How central is information? The U.S. Army regards it as important enough to issue a 314-page manual on it in November 2003. Titled *Information Operations: Doctrine, Tactics, Techniques, and Procedures*, the first sentence states unambiguously, "Information is an element of combat power."[2] The army defines *information operations* as "the employment of the core capabilities of electronic warfare, computer network operations, psychological operations, military deception, and operations security, in concert with specified support- ing and related capabilities, to affect or defend information and information sys- tems, and to influence decision making."

This already suggests a range of activities wider than those traditionally as- sociated with propaganda—a suggestion reinforced by the aim of information operations, which is to secure "information dominance." The U.S. military is not terribly open about this agenda, and it tends not to speak about it in pub- lic. It doesn't feature in the "approved for public release" manual on *Infor- mation Operations*. But internally there has been a long-term debate about in- formation dominance. To the outsider, discussions about how *information dominance* differs from *information superiority* might seem arcane, but they are nonetheless revealing. For example, in a paper written in 1997, Jim Win- ters and John Giffin, of the U.S. Space and Information Operations Direc- torate, argued that information superiority was insufficient: "At some base point 'superiority' means an advantage of 51–49, on some arbitrary metric scale. That is not enough of an advantage to give us the freedom of action re- quired to establish 'Full Spectrum dominance.'" Dominance implies "a mas- tery of the situation," superiority "only an edge." According to Winters and Giffin, "We think of dominance in terms of 'having our way'—'Overmatch' over all operational possibilities. This connotation is 'qualitative' rather than 'quantitative.' When dominance occurs, *nothing done, makes any difference. We have sufficient knowledge to *stop anything we don't want to occur, or do anything we want to do*" (my emphasis).[3] This could hardly be any clearer about the agenda of the U.S. military. There are two new elements to infor- mation dominance when compared to traditional conceptions of propaganda. The first is the integration of propaganda and psychological operations into a much wider conception of information war. The second is the integration of information war into the core of military strategy.

Traditional conceptions of propaganda involve crafting the message and distributing it via government media or independent news media. Current con- ceptions of information war go much further and incorporate the gathering, processing, and deployment of information—by way of computers, intelli- gence, and military information systems (command and control). The key pre- occupation for the military is *interoperability,* where information systems talk to and work with each other. Interoperability is a result of the computer revo- lution, which has led to a so-called revolution in military affairs. Now, propaganda and psychological operations are simply part of a larger information armory. As Colonel Kenneth Allard has written, the 2003 attack on Iraq "will be remembered as a conflict in which information fully took its place as a weapon of war." Allard tells a familiar story in military writings on such matters: "In the 1990s, the Joint Chiefs of Staff began to promote a vision of future warfare in which C4ISR (command, control, communications, computers, intelligence, surveillance and reconnaissance) systems would be forged into a new style of American warfare in which interoperability was the key to information dominance—and information dominance the key to victory."[4]

According to Lieutenant General Keith B. Alexander, the U.S. Army deputy chief of staff for intelligence, the way forward for integrating intelligence and information across the military is the creation of "information dominance centers." There are already fifteen of these in the United States and in Kuwait and Baghdad.[5] Information dominance is not something dreamt up by the Bush gang in the White House—or even by their ideologues in the Project for a New American Century. It is mainstream U.S. military doctrine. In fact it is even used by the Democrats in pronouncements on "progressive internationalism."[6] Although it originates in the United States, information dominance is also embraced in the United Kingdom. Given the close integration of United States' and the United Kingdom's global propaganda during the attack on Iraq, it could hardly be otherwise.[7] However the thinking underlying U.K. propaganda operations has transformed in the past decade, and both the Ministry of Defence and the Foreign and Commonwealth Office have staff assigned to "information operations." In future conflicts, according to the British Army, "maintaining moral as well as information dominance will rank as important as physical protection."[8] Or as John Spellar, M.P., the Minister for the Armed Forces, put it in a speech in January 2000, "We shall depend increasingly, not on simple numerical superiority in firepower, but on information dominance."[9]

The interoperability of the various types of "weaponized information"[10] has far-reaching, if little noticed, implications for the integration of propaganda and media institutions into the war machine. The experience of Iraq in 2003 shows how the planned integration of the media into instruments of war fighting is developing. It also shows the increased role for the private sector in information dominance, a role that reflects wider changes in the armed services in the United States and the United Kingdom.[11] Information dominance (ID) provides the underpinning rationale for all information-related work. As applied to traditional media management activities, the key to dominance is that "nothing done makes any difference." In practice this means that the United States and the United Kingdom can tolerate dissent in the media and alternative accounts on the Internet. Dissent only matters if it interferes with their plans. As U.S. military authors

Winters and Giffin put it, "Achieving ID involves two components: 1) building up and protecting friendly information; and 2) degrading information received by your adversary." Both of these refer not simply to military information systems but also to propaganda and the news media.

INTEGRATING THE MEDIA

The System of Embedding

Seen in the context of information dominance, embedding is a clear means of building up and protecting "friendly" information. The Faustian Pact allows journalists better access to the fighting than that given in any conflict since Vietnam. But the access is on military terms, and it can be rescinded if it does not meet the interests of the military. Although rarely highlighted in discussions of embedding, the Pentagon issued a fifty-point document titled "Public Affairs Guidance," listing what could and could not be reported.[12] They also insisted that all embeds sign a contract—one that does not mince its words, noting as it does that reporters must "follow the direction and orders of the Government."[13] In fact the tendency among reporters was to become fully integrated into military command structures, as this comment from embedded reporter Richard Gaisford, on BBC News 24, confirms: "We have to check each story we have with [the military]. And if they're not sure at the immediate level above us—that's the Captain who's our media liaison officer—he will check with the Colonel who is obviously above him and then they will check with Brigade headquarters as well."[14] The key phrase here is "the level above us."

Furthermore the system of embedding made the journalists dependent on the military for transport, food, and crucially physical protection. BBC reporter Ben Brown relates his experience:

> There was an Iraqi who . . . jumped up with an RPG and he was about to fire it at us because we were just standing there and this other Warrior just shot him with their big machine gun and there was a big hole in his chest. That was the closest I felt to being almost too close to the troops . . . because if he hadn't been there he would have killed us and . . . afterwards I sought out the gunner who had done that and shook his hand.[15]

Others journalists got closer and crossed the line from reporting to engaging in combat. Clive Myrie of the BBC has admitted:

> There was bullets flying everywhere. We get out of the Land Rover and we hide in a ditch. One of the marines said: why don't you make yourself useful? And

he's throwing these flares at me. And he's throwing the flares at me and I'm throwing them at the guy who's got to light them and send them off into the sky, and I'm thinking, why, what am I doing here?[16]

Perhaps most strikingly, Gavin Hewitt of the BBC has admitted picking out targets for the military:

I shouted across to the Captain "that truck over there—I think these guys are going to attack us." . . . Within seconds a Bradley fighting vehicle was opening up—tracers were flying across the field . . . eventually the truck went up— boom—like this. . . . And of course all the unit were delighted. From then on the bonding grew tighter.[17]

By all official accounts on both sides of the Atlantic, embedding was a great success.[18] The secretary of the D Notice Committee (the "voluntary" joint media–official censorship committee of the U.K. Ministry of Defense) reported:

despite the hundreds of embedded journalists and unilaterals in theatre, there had not been a single serious breach of security by any part of the U.K. media. The system and the advice in the five standing DA-Notices had proved entirely adequate, and as able to fulfil their role in such operations as in other conflicts and in peace.[19]

The U.K. Ministry of Defence even engaged a private firm to assess how successfully embedding had worked to manipulate coverage. According to the results of the exercise, "Commercial analysis of the print output . . . produced during the combat phase shows that 90% of embedded correspondents" reporting was either positive or neutral."[20]

"Deny, Degrade, Destroy"

The second part of achieving information dominance is the "ability to deny, degrade, destroy and/or effectively blind enemy capabilities."[21] Enemy or adversary capabilities in the philosophy of information dominance do not distinguish between actions of declared adversaries and those of independent media. The "unfriendly" information must be destroyed, wherever it comes from. This is perhaps best illustrated by the attack on an Al-Jazeera office in Kabul in 2001, which the Pentagon justified by claiming al Qaeda activity in the Al-Jazeera office. As it turned out, this referred to broadcast interviews conducted by Al-Jazeera with Taliban officials.[22]

The various attacks on Al-Jazeera in Kabul, Basra, and Baghdad should be seen in this context,[23] as should the killings of unilateral journalists and the attempt to discredit other critics. For example, the British minister of defense attempted to discredit the leading independent reporter Robert Fisk, when Fisk uncovered missile fragments fired by the United States into a crowded marketplace in Baghdad, killing over sixty civilians. These efforts are consistent with the doctrine of degrading or destroying enemy information capability. It is not critical information and commentary that is feared by the United States and the United Kingdom; rather, it is information that might hamper their ability to "do anything we want to do." If anything, the evidence suggests that the targeting of independent media and critics of the United States is widening. The Pentagon is reportedly coordinating the production of an "Information Operations Roadmap," drafted by the Information Operations Office of the Joint Chiefs of Staff. According to Captain Gerald Mauer, the assistant deputy director of the office, the roadmap noted that information operations would be directed against an "adversary." He went on to say that when the paper got to the office of the Under Secretary of Defense for Policy (Douglas Feith), it was changed to say that information operations will attempt to "disrupt, corrupt or usurp adversarial decision making."

"In other words," notes retired U.S. Army colonel Sam Gardiner, "We will even go after friends if they are against what we are doing or want to do."[24] No doubt the misinformation campaign against the French government in the U.S. press in 2003 is the result of such decisions.

"Towards Freedom"

Interoperability is central to the postconflict phase of "reconstruction" in Iraq. Here I note the integration of the media into the propaganda apparatus of the United States. The collapse of distinctions among independent news media, public relations work, and psychological operations is striking. The "reconstruction" of Iraqi media began on April 10, with the first broadcast of "Towards Freedom," a joint U.S.–U.K. television project broadcast on the same frequency as the former Iraqi state television service. The service included U.S. programming supplied by ABC, CBS, FOX, and PBS networks. The United Kingdom element was produced by the private company already contracted by the Foreign Office to provide satellite propaganda around the world. CBS president Andrew Heyward reportedly became convinced that "this is a good thing to do . . . a patriotic thing to do" after conversations with "some of the most traditional minded colleagues" at CBS.[25] Only CNN refused to join in. A spokesperson noted that "we didn't think that as an independent, global news organisation it was appropriate to participate in a United States government video transmission."[26] And of course that is what it was,

transmitted into Iraq by means of *Commando Solo*, the psychological operations aircraft used to broadcast U.S. propaganda.

But "Towards Freedom" was a stopgap, to be replaced by a new television
service for Iraq. In keeping with the philosophy of information dominance,
this was paid for by the Pentagon and supplied not by an independent news
organization but by a defense contractor, Scientific Applications International
Corporation (SAIC). Its expertise in the area—according to its website—is in
"information operations" and "information dominance."[27] The SAIC effort
quickly ran into trouble however. Its Iraq Media Network (IMN), which cost
$20 million over three months, was not obsequious enough for the Coalition
Provisional Authority. Within weeks, "occupying authority Chief L. Paul
Bremer III placed controls on IMN content and clamped down on the independent media in Iraq, closing down some Iraqi-run newspapers and radio
and television stations."[28] According to *Index on Censorship,* "Managers
were told to drop the readings from the Koran, the 'vox-pop' man-in-the-
street interviews (usually critical of the U.S. invasion) and even to run their
content past the wife of a U.S.-friendly Iraqi Kurdish leader for a pre-broadcast
check. The station rejected the demands and dug in their heels."[29] But this did
not stop Bremer, and further incidents have shown the preoccupation with
control, culminating in a nine-point list of "prohibited activity" issued by Bremer in June 2003.

It decreed that publishing material that "is patently false and is calculated
to provoke opposition to the CPA or undermine legitimate processes towards
self government" would henceforth be prohibited. This is not too dissimilar
to the Nazi press law introduced in Germany in 1933. It stated that journalists must "regulate their work in accordance with National socialism as a philosophy of life and as a conception of government."[30]

As *Index on Censorship* notes, "Bremer will 'reserve the power to advise'
the IMN on any aspect of its performance, 'including any matter of content'
and the power to hire and fire IMN staff. Thus the man in absolute authority
over the country's largest, richest, and best equipped media network is also
his own regulator and regulator of his rivals, with recourse to the U.S. Army
to enforce his rulings."

In particular, the assault on Al-Jazeera continues. In September the Iraqi
governing council voted to ban reports from Al-Jazeera and Al-Arabiya on
the grounds that they incite violence. As evidence of this, one member of the
Iraqi National Congress who voted for the ban noted that the television stations describe the opposition to the occupation as "the resistance." He said,
"They're not the resistance, they are thugs and criminals."[31] (The Iraqi National Congress, or INC, was set up by the public relations agency the Rendon Group and was funded by the U.S. government.) This is a statement

pregnant with irony, since the head of the INC, Ahmed Chalabi, is a convicted fraudster. In November, as casualties mounted, thirty media organizations, led by the Associated Press, complained to the Pentagon that they had "documented numerous examples of U.S. troops physically harassing journalists." The letter was signed by representatives from CNN, ABC, and the *Boston Globe*, among others.[32]

INFORMATION DOMINANCE ACHIEVED?

It is evident that the United States and its ally, the United Kingdom, are intent on ruling the world and that information control has become central to that effort. The key to understanding information dominance is to be clear that it is not dissent in itself that the U.S. planners object to; rather, it is dissent that hampers their ability to do whatever they want that matters. As the military itself puts it: "When dominance occurs, nothing done, makes any difference." In other words, it is not the expression of dissent that is a problem but the expression of dissent, which is part of a movement that challenges U.S. dominance. As the experience of the Iraqi Media Network shows, dominance does not always occur where there is resistance. Resistance from journalists, resistance from nation-states, direct resistance to occupation, and resistance in the form of the antiwar movement. All of these are obstacles in the way of information dominance. Although the U.S. and U.K. regimes have massive resources at their disposal to pursue information dominance, they are faced at every turn by resistance—and that in the end is the only thing that can stop the United States from achieving final information, or full spectrum dominance.

NOTES

1. Retrieved from www.dtic.mil/jointvision/jvpub2.htm.

2. Headquarters, Department of the Army, *Information Operations: Doctrine, Tactics, Techniques, and Procedures*, FM 3-13(FM 100-6), November 2003, iii. Retrieved from www.adtdl.army.mil/cgi-bin/atdl.dll/fm/3-13/fm3_13.pdf.

3. Jim Winters and John Giffin, *Issue Paper: Information Dominance vs. Information Superiority*, April 1, 1997. Retrieved from www.iwar.org.uk/iwar/resources/info-dominance/issue-paper.htm.

4. Col. Kenneth Allard, "Battlefield Information Advantage," *CIO Magazine,* Fall/Winter 2003. Retrieved from www.cio.com/archive/092203/allard.html.

5. Dawn S. Onley, "Army Exec Insists on Data Sharing to Give Soldiers 'Full Power,'" *Government Computer News* 22, no. 30 (October 13, 2003). Retrieved from www.gcn.com/22_30/dodcomputing/23815-1.html.

6. "Idea of the Week: Progressive Internationalism," *New Dem Daily*, October 31, 2003. Retrieved from www.ndol.org/ndol_ci.cfm?kaid=131&subid=207& contentid=252147.

7. See D. Miller, "The Propaganda Machine," in *Tell Me Lies: Propaganda and Media Distortion in the Attack on Iraq*, edited by D. Miller (London: Pluto, 2004).

8. "Operational Trends," chap. 2 of *Soldiering—The Military Covenant*. Last reviewed May 10, 2002. Retrieved from www.army.mod.uk/servingsoldier/usefulinfo/valuesgeneral/adp5milcov/ss_hrpers_values_adp5_2_w.html.

9. Address to the Seapower Conference, January 13, 2000. Available at http://news.mod.uk/news/press/news_press_notice.asp?newsItem_id=724.

10. Selwyn Clyde M. Alojipan, "A War for Information Dominance," *Metropolitan Computer Times*, March 31, 2003. Retrieved from www.mctimes.net/2003/Hyperdrive/200300331-A_War_for_Information_Dominance.html.

11. Ian Traynor, "The Privatisation of War," *Guardian*, December 10, 2003. Retrieved from www.guardian.co.uk/military/story/0,11816,1103649,00.html.

12. "Public Affairs Guidance (PAG) on Embedding Media during Possible Future Operations/Deployments in the U.S. Central Command's (CENTCOM) Area of Responsibility (AOR)," February 2003. Retrieved from www.militarycity.com/iraq/1631270.html.

13. U.S. Department of Defense, "Release, Indemnification, and Hold Harmless Agreement and Agreement Not to Sue," embedding release for Iraq 2003. Retrieved from www.journalism.org/resources/tools/ethics/wartime/embedding.asp.

14. BBC News 24, March 28, 2003 (01:37 GMT).

15. Justin Lewis, Terry Threadgold, Rod Brookes, Nick Mosdell, Kirsten Brander, Sadie Clifford, Ehab Bessaiso, and Zahera Harb, *The Role of Embedded Reporting during the 2003 Iraq War: Summary Report*. Report prepared by a research team at the Cardiff School of Journalism, Media, and Cultural Studies, and commissioned by the BBC. November 2003, 6.

16. "War Spin," *Correspondent*, BBC2, May 18, 2003. Retrieved from http://news.bbc.co.uk/nol/shared/spl/hi/programmes/correspondent/transcripts/18.5.03 1.txt.

17. Gavin Hewitt address to conference to mark World Press Freedom Day, City University, London, May 2, 2003.

18. See D. Miller, "The Propaganda Machine."

19. Record of a meeting held in the Ministry of Defence on May 15, 2003. Retrieved from www.dnotice.org.uk/records.htm.

20. Ministry of Defence, "The Information Campaign," chap. 10 in *Operations in Iraq: Lessons for the Future*. Retrieved from www.mod.uk/publications/iraq_futurelessons/chap10.htm.

21. Jim Winters and John Giffin, *Information Dominance Point Paper* (1997). This point paper has been drafted with the development of a revised information operations (IO) concept that focuses on information dominance (ID). Retrieved from www-tradoc.army.mil/dcscd/spaceweb/informat.htm.

22. Phillip Knightley, "History or Bunkum?" in *Tell Me Lies: Propaganda and Media Distortion in the Attack on Iraq*, edited by D. Miller (London: Pluto, 2004).

23. See Faisal Bodi's "Al Jazeera's War" and Tim Gopsill's "Target the Media," both in *Tell Me Lies: Propaganda and Media Distortion in the Attack on Iraq,* edited by D. Miller (London: Pluto, 2004).

24. Sam Gardiner, "Truth from These Podia: Summary of a Study of Strategic Influence, Perception Management, Strategic Information Warfare, and Strategic Psychological Operations in Gulf II," October 8, 2003. Retrieved from www.usnews.com/usnews/politics/whispers/documents/truth.pdf.

25. Henry Michaels, "American 'Free Press' in Action: U.S. Networks Agree to Serve as Pentagon Propaganda Tool in Iraq," World Socialist website, April 15, 2003. Retrieved from www.wsws.org/articles/2003/apr2003/med-a15.shtml.

26. Michaels, "American 'Free Press' in Action."

27. Retrieved from www.saic.com/natsec/dominance.html.

28. Alex Gourevitch, "Exporting Censorship to Iraq: The Press System We Allow the Iraqis Is Far from Free," October 1, 2003. Retrieved from www.prospect.org/print/V14/9/gourevitch-a.html.

29. Rohan Jayasekera, "Gives with One Hand, Takes Away with the Other." *Index on Censorship,* June 11, 2003. Retrieved from www.indexonline.org/news/20030611_iraq.shtml.

30. Oron J. Hale, *The Captive Press in the Third Reich* (Princeton, N.J.: Princeton University Press, 1964), 86.

31. Richard Lloyd Parry, "Iraqi Council Bans Al-Jazeera Reports," *Times,* September 23, 2003. Retrieved from www.timesonline.co.uk/article/0,,7374-827520,00.html.

32. "30 Media Outlets Protest Treatment in Iraq," November 13, 2003. Retrieved from www.independent-media.tv/item.cfm?fmedia_id=3794&fcategory_desc=Under%20Reported.

2

From Bombs and Bullets to Hearts and Minds: U.S. Public Diplomacy in an Age of Propaganda

Nancy Snow

From 1992 to 1994, I was employed as a government propagandist by the U.S. Information Agency (USIA) and the State Department in Washington, D.C. Of course, we didn't call what we did then *propaganda*, which was too loaded a term and one associated with dastardly regimes, such as Stalin and Hitler. Our euphemism was *public diplomacy*. The task then was to "tell America's story to the world," and in the context of the post–Cold War environment of freedom, peace dividends, economic prosperity, and a united pro-Western front, our task seemed simple enough. President Clinton was pushing the Clinton doctrine, which placed U.S. competitiveness and integration of the world economy at the heart of foreign policy. USIA's mission was linked to NAFTA and the World Trade Organization, with the belief that remaking the world in the image of a U.S.-led free market economy would end ideological clashes.

By the mid-1990s, USIA had lost its mission compass and, without a domestic constituency to save it, was sacrificed on the political altar. Officially abolished as an independent agency in 1999, USIA was folded back into its State Department origins, where it existed in obscurity until September 11, 2001. In a split second, it was clear that the propaganda war was underway and that the U.S. government needed to get back into the business of promoting and articulating U.S. positions. Further, the United States needed to do a better job of confronting its poor global image, which in the post-Saddam era has reached its nadir. We are now a nation very much in isolation from the rest of the world, with a reputation more for mistrust than honesty, hostility than goodwill. What went wrong?

To counter Osama and Saddam, the United States deployed food drops, initiated shortwave radio broadcasts, and tasked a recently departed Madison

Avenue advertising veteran who formerly sung the praises of Uncle Ben's
Rice to do the same for Uncle Sam. What's not to like about us? We give the
world superstars and super missiles, blockbuster films and bunker-busting
bombs, not an easy campaign for the slogan engineers at J. Walter Thompson.
However, in fall 2002, a $15 million paid media ad campaign to the Muslim
world failed miserably. It was promoted under the moniker "Shared Values,"
and it was fronted by a group called the Council of American Muslims for
Understanding (CAMU), a group financed by the U.S. State Department. The
one formal press conference that undersecretary of public diplomacy Charlotte Beers gave—at the National Press Club in Washington, D.C., December
18, 2002—featured six American protesters who disrupted Beers's address
with a slogan of their own: "You're selling war, but we're not buying."

The omnipresent post-9/11 question "Why does the world hate us since
9/11?" has spawned a lot of speculation, perhaps none more famous than the
remark by Representative Henry Hyde (R-IL), who asked rhetorically, "How
is it that the country that invented Hollywood and Madison Avenue has allowed such a destructive and parodied image of itself to become the intellectual coin of the realm overseas?"

Polling data over the last year (Council on Foreign Relations, Pew Center,
Gallup) indicate that the majority of the world now sees the United States as
brand aggressor to the world and the biggest threat to world peace. A May
2003 poll of more than fifteen thousand people in twenty countries (including the Palestinian Authority) was conducted by the nonpartisan, U.S.-based
Pew Research Center (PRC), and it shows that global alliances such as NATO
and the United Nations are fraying. As expected, the Pew Center poll supported the fear that many of us noncombatant U.S. citizens had, that the U.S.
war in Iraq would inflame anti-American sentiment. PRC director Andrew
Kohut reports that anti-Americanism has not only deepened in the Muslim
world but has also widened to the far reaches of Africa and Asia. One year
earlier, a Gallup survey, the largest in history and one conducted in nine Muslim countries, found that a majority surveyed have a poor opinion of the
United States, do not believe Arabs carried out the September 11 attacks, and
consider the U.S. war in Afghanistan morally unjustifiable.

More recent polling in Europe suggests that most British, French, Italians,
and Germans think that the United States is motivated by its own interests in
the war on terrorism and ignores the concerns of its allies. On *60 Minutes* in
January 2003, young South Koreans said that they feared President Bush
more than Kim Jong Ill, the dictator of North Korea. An April 1, 2003, article in the *Economist* reported that once the war in Iraq began, the public in
the United States, Great Britain, and Australia—the three main "coalitions of
the willing" (to use the rhetoric of the administration)—rallied around its

leadership. In these countries (and in Denmark, whose navy provided support to allied operations in the Gulf), a majority supported the war. But in the rest of the world, there was a clear majority against it—Canada, New Zealand, France, Portugal, Spain, India, Pakistan—even among Western allies such as the Japanese. Two traditional allies of both America and Britain—Canada and New Zealand—decided not to join in the war. In both of the latter countries, there were more who opposed the war than favored it. In Spain, where conservative Jose Maria Aznar signaled firm support for the coalition, over 90 percent of the public registered opposition to the war. On Sunday, March 30, 2003, two hundred thousand people marched in Rabat, Morocco, where the U.S. flag was burned. In Jakarta, Indonesia, one hundred thousand marched chanting "American imperialist, number one terrorist." In April, UN secretary Kofi Annan said that in this war, there will be no winners.

Once the Iraqi war effort was in full swing, there seemed little hope of winning Muslim public opinion, despite government protestations. To quote Tony Blair's op-ed in *Al-Ahram* (the progovernment Egyptian newspaper), "Our quarrel is not with the Iraqi people but with Saddam, his sons and his barbarous regime which has brought misery and terror to their country." Like President Bush, Blair insisted that administrations in Washington and London had wanted to avoid military action and that by using military action they are "doing all that is humanely possible to minimize civilian casualties and finish this campaign quickly." Unlike the last Gulf War, in which CNN dominated the narrative and General Schwarzkopf was our video-game commander, Al-Jazeera (based in Qatar) dominated the regional airwaves. Qatar was also home to General Tommy Franks, Central Command, and America's Fifth Fleet. Al-Jazeera, which was criticized by the United States and Great Britain for promoting sensationalism and acting as a mouthpiece for the Iraqi Ministry of Information, is a symbol of a new Arab region, so unaccustomed to freedom from press censorship and in search of its own ratings-driven audience. According to Mamoun Fandy, an Arab newspaper columnist, reporters and producers at Al-Jazeera knew what their viewers wanted to see: images of Arab empowerment and Muslim resistance, because of past defeats and humiliation.

The United States, by its very influence and prowess, can choose to follow the advice of the United Nations and global community at will. Under President Bush and the Bush doctrine, our international relations post-9/11 is operating under the rubric "The best defense is a good offense." Should the United States, the last remaining superpower, be apologizing for its status as the number-one nation in terms of cultural, economic, and military prowess? To some, no. To others, we can ill afford to disengage the world via methods that are more toward our own national interests. How can we take the soft power of American persuasion, influence, creativity, and culture (film, television, soda pop) and transform it into something positive? We (governments, military, civil society) must do two things: not only recognize the increasing negative perception that so many have of us in the world but, more important, work to overcome these negative perceptions through ways that are mutually beneficial. We may have to start by "walking our talk." To the world, American values of fair play, the Golden Rule, and our cherished Constitutional freedoms of religion, association, and press are held up to the world as part of a propaganda and public diplomacy campaign to win hearts and minds to American policies and national interests. These values are also seen as universal in appeal, but the rhetorical appeal of these values is not matched by America's actions in the world. In 2002, the U.S. Congress initiated the Freedom Promotion Act, to use international exchanges, sister cities programs, English-language training, international broadcasting, and so forth, to make U.S. values a reality for others. In part, this is what our own president promised to deliver post–Saddam Hussein to the people of Iraq. A promise made must be kept if we want to improve our reputation in the world.

In American-led global communications, the phone is off the hook at two primary levels. First, there exists a disconnect in the official propaganda campaign coming out of Washington between how the administration shapes its motives in the world and how others see U.S. actions in the world play out. In part, the Washington "dialogue of the deaf" is due to the reality that American values are incongruous with American interests. U.S. interests that emerge from Washington, D.C., and New York are largely about economic access and advantage and about using our global military presence to protect our economic interests. We need not wonder why the terrorists struck our economic and military heart on September 11. U.S. values are political, cultural, and social. This battle, between interests and values, is a battle between *realpolitik* (might makes right) and *soft power* (right makes might). So far, realpolitik has always won, because a sole superpower can change the rules of the game at will. The United States is so powerful that it can be inconsistent in its foreign policy and get away with it. More than any other reason, this is why America is hated today. This is in part why John Brady Kiesling, a former career diplomat with the State Department, resigned his position before the outbreak of war. He wrote in a February 27, 2003, *New York Times* op-ed:

> The policies we are now asked to advance are incompatible not only with American values but also with American interests. Our fervent pursuit of war with Iraq is driving us to squander the international legitimacy that has been America's most potent weapon of both offense and defense since the days of Woodrow Wilson. We have begun to dismantle the largest and most effective web of international relationships the world has ever known. Our current course will bring instability and danger, not security.

Two, there is a major disconnect between American news coverage as a whole and international news coverage. To an extent, the war in Iraq was not the television war of Vietnam but the Internet and Al-Jazeera War, where the United States was unable to control and manage both the messenger and the message. If you were to compare U.S. news coverage with that of international news, you would have found different wars underway—"Operation Iraqi Freedom," on FOX News Channel; "Showdown with Iraq," on CNN; and Al-Jazeera's "America's Imperial War for Domination and Occupation"—not only beaming into the living rooms of Saudi Arabia and Lebanon but also across Asia and Europe.

In true Hollywood fashion, U.S. interests and American power in the world, as packaged and manufactured by us to the world, come across as the triumph of good over evil. Any ambiguity in a truly complex world is dismissed. Instead, America's chief propagandists, such as President Bush and Secretary of Defense Rumsfeld, hand down dichotomies—"us versus them," "good versus bad," "those who are for us and those who are against." In that context, this may very well be "a clash of civilizations," as Samuel Huntington claims, or at least a clash of propagandas and perceptions, between what is perceived as "America's Imperial War" and "Operation Iraqi Freedom."

The global antiwar protests of 2002 to the present are an offspring of the antieconomic globalization protests of 1999–2001, which suggest that the world's citizens are responding in record numbers to governments that have failed them, governments that are increasingly bankrupt in moral leadership, trust, and resources. The message of many of these protesters for the commercial and government propagandists is the following: "The Empire has no clothes."

REBUILDING U.S. PUBLIC DIPLOMACY

To paraphrase Margaret Mead, governments will have to start trusting (in her words, "stop doubting") the ability of people to change the face of global society, from one of clashing civilizations and preemptive strikes to one of talking and walking together. We Americans have a large task to rebuild trust—we must better understand the world in which we wield so much awesome power. We need to see the world with honest eyes, as it is, with all of its messiness and ambiguity. We need to strive for consistency, both in our celebration of diversity and in our protection of human dignity. We need to do so even if the short-term impact suggests that hard and difficult choices have to be made. If we Americans can live with a permanent war on terrorism, we can certainly live with higher prices for oil, for example, and fewer military bases dotting the globe. We Americans need to listen better, decry arrogance, and cultivate humility—all difficult work requiring a major cultural change.

Propaganda of the American image cannot come primarily from the U.S. government or from any official source of information. We are misunderstood and increasingly resented by the world precisely because it is our president and our top government officials whose images predominate in explaining U.S. public policy. Official spin has its place, but it is always under suspicion or parsed for clues and secret codes. The primary source for America's image campaign must be drawn directly from the American people. First, it's the private citizens of the United States who are more comfortable with acknowledging with some degree of humility that the United States has made mistakes in its past. Government officials seem to have a hard time with that one. Open criticism of a country's policies tends to embarrass government leaders. Over time it can be the trump card in the deck of negotiating a peaceful (and lasting) settlement of international conflicts. The American people can better illustrate that we are a people willing to learn from our mistakes and able to redirect our dealings with other nations to mutually beneficial ends, not just purposes that serve official Washington. Second, it's the American people who can better initiate direct contact with people in other countries whose support and understanding we need on the stage of world opinion. The American public is the best ad campaign going for the world. We've got the greatest diversity in people and culture, and it shows in our receptiveness to learning, our generosity, and our creativity. We need to magnify these qualities to the world, but in the same spirit, we need to listen more, talk less.

It is also the American patriotic duty of dissent that can best illustrate to the world what a free society means. Senator J. William Fulbright wrote in *The Arrogance of Power*:

> To criticize one's country is to do it a service and to pay it a compliment. It is a service because it may spur the country to do better than it is doing; it is a compliment because it evidences a belief that the country can do better than it is doing. . . . My question is whether America can close the gap between her capacity and her performance. My hope and my belief are that she can, that she has the human resources to conduct her affairs with a maturity which few if any great nations have ever achieved: to be confident, but also tolerant, to be rich but also generous, to be willing to teach but also to learn, to be powerful but also wise.

Senator Fulbright wrote this at a time when, as chairman of the Foreign Relations Committee, he vigorously opposed President Johnson on America's involvement in Vietnam. American citizens who took to the streets to denounce U.S. policy in Vietnam heavily influenced his opposition. Now we are seeing the same spirit of dissent toward this U.S.-led war against Iraq. We need to carry this message of what a free and open society represents to all corners and not let our government leaders dictate America's brand campaign on their own.

In his 1946 essay "Politics and the English Language," George Orwell argued that language should express, not conceal, thought. However, he also observed that "in our time, political speech and writing are largely the defense of the indefensible." Political language "is designed to make lies sound truthful and murder respectable, and to give an appearance of solidity to pure wind." Orwell's classic example of language control is the slogan "War is peace." Lest we think that it's impossible to hold two opposing ideas in our minds at the same time and actually believe in them, think about the language that defines our communicating the war on terror. When our president said on September 11, 2001, "We're at war," many of us may have thought then that "war" meant something with a definite conclusion, like the pending war in Afghanistan. Yet the slogan itself, "War on Terror," is a symbol of perpetual thinking about perpetual war.

We move effortlessly from Afghanistan to Iraq, waging war for peace. Where next?

In his book *Munitions of the Mind*, Philip Taylor writes in the epilogue:

> In a nuclear age, we need peace propagandists, not war propagandists—people whose job it is to increase communication, understanding and dialogue between different peoples with different beliefs. As much of the truth as can be, must be told. A gradual process of explanation will generate greater trust and therefore a greater willingness to understand our perspective. And if this is a mutual dialogue, greater empathy and consensus will emerge. We might not always like what we see about others, but we need to recognize that fear and ignorance are the principal enemies of peace and peaceful coexistence.

If we were to accept Professor Taylor's challenge and propagandize for peace, we would need to accompany this increase in propaganda with an increase in education. Our young people and all of us who are lifelong learners need to understand how propaganda is used to promote war, how it has been used throughout modern history, and how propaganda functions to mediate information and opinions from power centers of government, corporations, and media to populations and public opinion segments of society. Two, we need to understand what the war message is and how to counter it with a just-as-powerful and just-as-persuasive message of peace. Propaganda, whether for war or peace, is about communicating something or about persuading people to do something. We need to study what is being said, how it is being said, what techniques are being used, and where education can be of the greatest service.

Increasing propaganda for peace must also be accompanied by an increase in access to information and media, upon which educated opinions can be formed. Modern forms of communication, particularly the mass media, are major instruments of propaganda. It is the monopoly concentration in media that allows the propaganda refrain "War is inevitable" to stick in our minds. It's like a song lyric you want to forget. We need to replace that lyric with something else, whether it's "Peace is a possibility" or "Peace is permanent; war is temporary." It is no longer acceptable to allow public opinion and public judgment to be bombarded with news and views from a restricted number of sources, particularly when these sources carry us from FOX's reality show *Joe Millionaire* to CNN's *Showdown with Iraq* to tomorrow's weather all in a breathless minute.

Propaganda need not remain a tool of mass persuasion in absolutist regimes, totalitarian societies, under Stalin's brutish lead or Nazi dictatorship. Who among us can doubt that Gulf War II was staged in part not only to an efficiently managed military–media relationship on the part of those who want war but also by a failure among our media institutions to challenge government leadership?

Right now, every night, as we sleep, the war propagandists, both state and stateless actors, are dominating the media landscape. This should come as no surprise, because war is viewed by many as an efficient means of carving up centralized zones of power—the power to control, the power to dominate, both through message and force.

Peace propaganda needs the same amount of diligence and hard work. If we spend too much time worrying about using propaganda for peace, we will continue to subject ourselves to governments and other interest groups who are more than willing and able to utilize propaganda methods for their own violent causes. If your cause is the cause of peace, then utilize communications responsibly, truthfully, and effectively. This is a call to arms, to arm ourselves with knowledge, content, and context generated from open and diverse channels of communication. White House news conferences, CNN, and Al-Jazeera should not be watched in a vacuum, separated from the world's people. If so, then the world will remain in the hands of the war propagandists.

3

Selling the Iraq War: The Media Management Strategies We Never Saw

Danny Schechter

Writing in 1927 in the aftermath of the First World War, sociologist Harold Lasswell explained the budding marriage of war and propaganda. He understood then what many Americans are just learning now, not quite a century later:

> A new and subtler instrument must weld thousands and thousands and even millions of human beings into one amalgamated mass of hate will and hope. A new will must burn out the canker of dissent and temper the steel of bellicose enthusiasm. The name of this new hammer and anvil of social solidarity is propaganda. Talk must take the place of drill; print must supply the dance. War dances live in literature, and at the fringes of the modern earth; war propaganda breathes and fumes in the capitals and provinces of the world.

Propaganda is not new in war. It has been a staple of every conflict, a tool that governments deploy to demonize their enemies and mobilize their nations. When you fight a war, there is a need to create and maintain ties of sentiment between soldiers and citizens. There is a need for popular mobilization and media support.

Motivating, managing, massaging, and feeding the media is a key strategic imperative to build and sustain a consensus behind any war policy—and most of the media does not need to be roped on board. Susan Carruthers, who has published a study on this very topic, *The Media at War* (2000), concluded that "following the lead of their state, mass media are frequently more willing accomplices in wartime propaganda than they care to admit, and may even play a significant part in instigating conflict."

What was new in the 2003 Iraq War was the sophisticated way in which corporate public relations techniques were adapted by the Bush administration to create the rationale for the war, orchestrate support for it, bring the media on board, and then sell it to politicians and then the public.

The techniques targeted the media through cultivation and co-optation. The techniques included message development, polling, coordinated press releases, global communications strategies, psychological warfare, and "perception" management. A number of intelligence directorates, "public diplomacy" channels, public relations firms were used, as were civilian and military agencies.

The problem was first researched and modeled. The Pentagon analyzed what had gone wrong in their media relations in earlier conflicts and thus derived appropriate lessons. They then worked to build a partnership, rather than an adversarial relationship, with journalists. This strategy was factored into the overall planning. General Tommy Franks's military doctrine divided the task into four "fronts"—political, military, intelligence, and media. The Fourth Estate thus was seen as the Fourth Front.

News management was a key component of the Iraq War "plan." If you remember the coverage of the conflict, there was constant reference by those running it and commenting upon it to the "plan," as in "We are on plan." Of course the plan was never made public or leaked to the press—perhaps because it was constantly being refined and updated.

The war itself was treated as a product to be launched and rolled out. A compliant media was constantly briefed, selectively leaked to, and fed predeveloped messages known as the "the line of the day." A proactive media strategy began to cultivate media allies and target key programs through close consultation and other services, including supplying videos, photos, and media training in war survival. Contracts were negotiated for embedment assignments.

The embed experiment grew out of experiences during the Afghan War, where there were clashes between journalists who wanted access to the story on the ground and military units who physically threatened media representatives. That war was being stage-managed, not from a tent in some outback or cave, but from the central command's military base, in Tampa, Florida. It was deliberately moved out of Washington to ensure secrecy.

As a result, Pentagon-based beat reporters, traditionally the least critical, became the media's front line. Television news showed canned video of weapons systems, and the "Rumsfeld Follies" updated the old "Five o'Clock Follies" from Vietnam, where the line was always that the light is at the end of the tunnel. At least in those days some reporters in the tunnel could see that there was no light. Today there is not even a tunnel. In all too many cases, reporting has turned into stenography, without context or analysis.

During the war in Afghanistan, journalists were also being targeted at a higher rate than soldiers, perhaps in part because of the belief that they (we) are all one-sided transmission belts for the government, which in some instances, unfortunately, is all too true.

A column in the *Dallas Morning News* by Carolyn Barta quotes Stephen Hess, a Brookings Institution scholar and author of the book *International News and Foreign Correspondents,* who notes that "American journalists are no longer considered noncombatants. At one time they were considered like the Red Cross. . . . Its part of the anti-American feeling in the world and [the feeling that] journalists are not objective professionals who are 'above country.'" According to Barta, "A few years ago, extremists might have kidnapped an American corporate executive or bombed a diplomat. Now they go after a journalist."

American news organizations understood this and thus had their own reasons for being receptive to the idea of being embedded in the far safer sanctuary of U.S. military operations. The Pentagon tried out the idea during Operation Mountain Lion and Operation Anaconda, in Afghanistan. It gave the media access to a military campaign that had kept the press at a distance and that had fueled hostility against the administration. The experiment worked. The media could become eyewitnesses to the action while the government could count on far more supportive coverage as journalists and soldiers bonded under fire.

Stratfor.com, a global intelligence consultant, says the media have been reporting the war as a great victory, while the Pentagon itself is saying that the war in Afghanistan is just the first battle and that they are planning for six more years, with consequences unknown. Here is Stratfor's take:

> Coverage of the "war on terrorism" has reversed the traditional role between the press and the military. Abandoning the hypercritical coverage of the past, the media have become cheerleaders—allowing the conflict in Afghanistan to become synonymous with the war at large and portraying that war as an unalloyed success. The reversal of roles between media and military creates public expectations that can affect the prosecution of the war.

SHAPING PUBLIC OPINION

Dealing with the media was part of a larger effort to mold public opinion. As I explain in my own study of the war, *Embedded Weapons of Mass Deception* (2003), psychological techniques that were used to divide, demoralize, and win over Iraqis were also modified for use on the home front. So explains British-based propaganda analyst Paul de Rooij in several well-sourced "assessments":

> One generally doesn't think of psychological warfare as something waged against the home population; but this is perhaps the best way to appreciate the

U.S. experience during the past few months. The objective of such a campaign was to stifle dissent, garner unquestioning support, and rally people around a common symbol. Americans, and to a lesser extent Europeans, have been subjected to a propaganda barrage in an effort to neutralize opposition to the war, and this fits directly into a psy-ops framework.

Suddenly all the networks had platoons of retired generals and prowar military experts interpreting war news. These generals in effect took on the role of reporters. U.S. television quickly resembled Chilean television after a coup. CNN's news chief Eason Jordan revealed that he had sought approval from the Pentagon for his network's key war news choices. Before the war's end, critic Michael Moore demanded the "unilateral withdrawal of the Pentagon from America's TV studios."

Pentagon media chief Tori Clarke, who had worked with big public relations firms and political campaigns before joining the administration, brought a corporate approach and politically oriented spin operation into the Pentagon. She told the *Wall Street Journal* that she was running her shop the way she used to run campaigns. This approach was coordinated throughout the administration, with orchestrated appearances by the president and members of his various teams.

Throughout, they were not just selling a message but managing the perceptions of those who received them, through polling and other feedback loops. This is ironic in light of the president's dismissal of antiwar protest sentiment, on the grounds that he doesn't make decisions based on "focus groups." There have been reports confirming that the Bush administration relies heavily on focus group data in its message development and dissemination.

At the same time the administration very carefully created and managed its own image. Nothing was left to chance. The politician playing the president was produced with unprecedented attention to detail. On May 16, 2003, the *New York Times* detailed how the Bush administration relies on media techniques to sell the president and his policies. What is significant is that media people are directing the effort.

Elisabeth Bumiller wrote:

> Officials of past Democratic and Republican administrations marvel at how the White House does not seem to miss an opportunity to showcase Mr. Bush in dramatic and perfectly lighted settings. It is all by design: the White House has stocked its communications operation with people from network television who have expertise in lighting, camera angles, and the importance of backdrops.

Television news people have been tapped in this aspect of the media war. First among equals is Scott Sforza, a former ABC producer who was hired by the Bush campaign in Austin, Texas, and who now works for Dan Bartlett, the

White House communications director. Sforza created the White House "message of the day" backdrops and helped design the $250,000 set at the United States central command forward headquarters in Doha, Qatar, during the Iraq War.

These smartly polished sales techniques worked well, and they typified the way the war itself was to be sold—and covered. It all underscores once again that we no longer live in a traditional democracy but rather a *media-ocracy,* a land in which media, the military, and politics often fuse.

New York Times columnist Paul Krugman, who has written about how media coverage shapes public opinion, makes another point about the way that television coverage distorts reality:

> The administration's anti-terror campaign makes me think of the way television studios really look. The fancy set usually sits in the middle of a shabby room, full of cardboard and duct tape. Networks take great care with what viewers see on their TV screens; they spend as little as possible on anything off camera.

No wonder we had newscasts in which images trumped information. Clearly, just as the Pentagon boasted of its war plan, there was another plan alongside it—a media marketing plan, which was even more carefully guarded lest it fall into the wrong hands. Manipulation always works best when those who are its target are unaware of its dynamics. While the political strategists led by Karl Rove directed this military, the conventional military was assigned the execution. There now is a whole branch of the military consumed with the challenges of IO, or information operations.

IO is the Pentagon's "Ministry of Truth," in the best *1984* sense of the term. There is an excellent exposé about its operations, by former Associated Press correspondent Maud S. Beelman, director of the International Consortium of Investigative Journalists, a project of the Center of Public Integrity. It appeared in *Nieman Reports*, the journal of Harvard's Nieman Fellows in Journalism. "IO groups together information functions ranging from public affairs to military deception and psychological operations or PSYOP," she writes. "What this means is that people whose job traditionally has been to talk to the media and divulge truthfully what they are able to tell, now work hand-in-glove with those whose job it is to support battlefield operations with information, not all of which may be truthful."

An August 1996 U.S. Army field manual, *100-6,* puts it point-blank: "Information is the currency of victory." To help decode this, let us turn to Maj. Gary Pounder, the chief of intelligence plans and presentations at the College of Aerospace Doctrine Research and Education at Maxwell Air Force Base. "IO practitioners," he explains, "must recognize that much of the information war will be waged in the public media." The military thus needs public affairs specialists "to become full partners in the IO planning and execution process developing the skills and expertise required to win the media war."

There you have it. The Pentagon set out to win at least three wars: the one on the battlefield of the moment, the so-called war for hearts and minds in Iraq, and "the media war." To translate further, we rely on the always blunt Richard Holbrooke, a Balkans negotiator and former UN ambassador who, true to form, doesn't mince words: "Call it public diplomacy or public affairs, or psychological warfare or . . . " he pauses, to cut through this fog, "if you really want to be blunt—propaganda."

So let's be blunt: IO is a way of obscuring and sanitizing that negative-sounding term *propaganda* so that our "information warriors" can do their thing with a minimum of public attention as they seek to engineer friendly write-ups and cumulative impact. They do so by pursing several strategies:

Overloading the Media

IO operates in some conflicts by providing too much information. During the Kosovo War, briefers at NATO's headquarters in Belgium boasted that this was the key to information control. "They would gorge the media with information," Beelman writes, quoting one as saying, "'When you make the media happy, the media will not look for the rest of the story.'" How's that for being blunt?

Offering Ideological Appeals

We saw an appeal to patriotism and to safeguarding the national interest in the fall when Condoleezza Rice and other Bush administration officials persuaded the networks to not air bin Laden videos and other Al-Jazeera work. This is nothing new. All administrations try to seduce and co-opt the media. Back in 1950, President Harry S. Truman appealed to top newspaper editors to back the Cold War with a "campaign for truth" in which "our great public information channels," as Secretary of State Dean Acheson referred to the media, would enlist. Nancy Berhard, author of *U.S. Television News and Cold War Propaganda, 1947–1960* (1999), says "None of the assembled newsmen blanched" at Truman's "enlistment to propagandize."

It is this ideological conformity and worldview that makes it relatively easy for a well-oiled and sophisticated IO propaganda machine to keep the U.S. media in line, with the avid cooperation of the corporate sector, which owns and controls most media outlets. Some of those companies, such as NBC parent General Electric, have long been a core component of that nexus of shared interests that President Eisenhower called the "military–industrial complex." Now the media is part of the complex.

Spinning Information

We see this every day at Pentagon briefings, where what's really happening is, at best, secondary. For example, the weekly *Washington Post* edition of January 14–20 tells how reporters who scoured the bombed-out ruins of the town of Qalai Niazi in Afghanistan found an estimated eighty civilians dead, yet little or no evidence of Taliban or al Qaeda forces. The villagers they interviewed insisted "there was nothing of the Taliban here." Yet most of the media minimized their own findings and instead relied on pronouncements by Pentagon officials who insisted that they were right to bomb the village to smithereens.

Withholding Information

"Sorry, I am not at liberty to explain. But do I really have to?" So says Ted Gup, who teaches journalism at Case Western Reserve University in Cleveland and writes about the secret lives of CIA operatives says: "It is easy operating behind the curtain of secrecy to conceal setbacks and pronounce progress." Underline that word—*easy*.

CO-OPTION AND COLLUSION

But why do we in the media go along with this approach time and again? We are not stupid. We are not robots. Too many of us have *died* trying to get this story (and other stories). Ask any group of journalists, and they will tell you that no one tells them what to write or what to do. Yet there is a homogenized flavor and Pentagon echo to much coverage of this war that shames our profession. Why? Because reporters buy into the ideology of the mission? Because there are few visible war critics to provide dissenting takes? Or because information management has been so effective that it disallows any other legitimate approach? An uncritical stance is part of the problem. Disseminating misinformation often adds up to an inaccurate picture of where we are in this war.

Once the "War on Terror" got underway, the Pentagon reaffirmed its commitment to these principles and then promptly forgot about them, applying an IO strategy of appearing to be open but defining the terms and framing the story whenever possible. Did our media chiefs yell bloody murder? Hell no.

No government can be depended upon to tell the truth, the whole truth, and nothing but the truth—especially not when that government makes mistakes or misjudgments in war time. Says Stanley Cloud, who ran *Time* magazine's Vietnam

reporting and was one of the post–Gulf War media negotiators; "The natural inclination then is to cover up, to hide, and the press's role, in war even more than
in peace, is to act as a watchdog and truth seeker.

We need to know more than what the government is willing to disclose. We
need hard facts about what it is doing. And this applies not just to the government! What about the industrial side of the military–industrial complex?
What are the oil companies really up to in the Middle East and Central Asia?
Tell us about interests as well as issues. Also, how about some attention to al-
ternatives to war?

Wanting the truth is not enough. It is like waiting for Godot. We have to
press for it.

4

Measuring Success: Profit and Propaganda

David J. Collison

This chapter explores the use made of propaganda to further corporate interests at the expense of other sectors of society and of whole cultures. It focuses on the Anglo-Saxon economies, particularly the United States, but the consequences go much further and have the power to destabilize cultures and destroy social cohesion across the globe. Some of these effects underlie issues addressed elsewhere in this book. How "to construct a just society and just capitalism has been given extra urgency by the emergence of international terrorism" (Hutton 2002).

Key features of Anglo-Saxon capitalism are maximization of shareholder wealth and opposition to government regulation. Nobel laureate Milton Friedman famously maintained that business meets its social responsibilities by maximizing profits (Friedman 1962/1982), but he and his right-wing adherents do not want the quid pro quo of effective government control to ensure a just and equitable society. As we shall see, he even invokes with some circularity his popular will to support his position: "Public opinion has continued to go against government. People are as suspicious as ever of government—big or small" (quoted in London 2003).

Of course corporations go to a great deal of trouble to influence what government regulation there is. For example, their funding and lobbying the "revolving door" between government and highly paid corporate positions are widely practiced and hardly a secret, though most people are perhaps unaware of just how bad things are (see Palast 2003). But this does not explain acquiescence. The relatively overt and venal steps by which corporate power secures its interests are potentially subject to democratic control—if there is

sufficient will. The point of corporate propaganda is to undermine this will—
and there is a long history for this activity:

> The clamour and sophistry of merchants and manufacturers easily persuade . . .
> that the private interest of a part, and of a subordinate part of the society is the
> general interest of the whole. (Adam Smith 1776/1880, *Wealth of Nations,* bk.
> 1, pt. II, chap. 10, 101)

This chapter can, for reasons of space, only allude to the consequences of a
world in which laissez-faire capitalism undermines more pluralistic social
market economies, such as are found in continental Europe and Japan, and
blindly uses inappropriate economic dogma to intimidate less-developed
countries, with catastrophic effects on society and the environment (see
Stiglitz 2003 for an insightful analysis of Anglo-Saxon-dominated institutions, such as the World Trade Organization and, in particular, the International Monetary Fund). The aim of this chapter is to illuminate how the informed, and the less informed, support this system, which benefits the few at
the expense of the many. Short-sighted self-interest and greed may be an adequate explanation for some behavior, but it surely does not adequately account for those who really believe.[1]

First, consider how business success is measured. Accounting is normally
presented as a dispassionate technical activity that should fairly present the
economic results and position of an entity. The characteristics that accounting
should possess include fine-sounding terms: *consistency, comparability, neutrality* (absence of bias), and *representational faithfulness.* Accountants
should, of course, abhor the kind of behavior that has notoriously gone on at
such places as Enron (and at many other corporations over many decades).
Accountants inside these corporations and their supposedly independent au-
ditors failed to meet the standards of probity or expertise expected of members of the accounting profession. But these scandals actually help to obscure
the highly contestable values that imbue accounting, even when probity and
expertise are fully respected and applied.

So what are these values that are supported by accounting? Simply put,
they are as follows—that some individuals who participate in commercial activity should, as of right, have their material rewards maximized, while others should merely receive the minimum necessary to procure their involvement. Members of the first group are called *shareholders.*[2] The slice of the
cake taken by shareholders is called *profit,* or the *bottom line,* and accountants (and all who aspire to and attain business leadership) learn that the bottom line should be maximized, which means that the other slices, typically
known as *costs* or *expenses*—for example, wages paid to employees—should
be minimized. To do so increases *efficiency.*

In the Anglo-Saxon world, maximizing shareholder value is so widely accepted and taken for granted (see Kelly 2001) that any challenge is almost unthinkable or "irrational," especially among the business educated—but why? I contend that a critical factor is a deluge of corporate propaganda: this is a topic of "incredible significance" to which little interest has been paid (see Chomsky 1996).[3]

Propaganda may be spread unwittingly by agents who are not its original instigators, and it could be argued that such a process is not true propaganda, because there is no self-interested motive. However the effect is to further the interests of the original sponsors of propaganda, and so such a process could be termed *indirect propaganda*. It was described long ago: "All the voluble men [*sic*] of the day—writers, reporters, editors, preachers, lecturers, teachers, politicians—are drawn into the service of propaganda to amplify a master voice" (Lasswell 1927/1971)

Propaganda may or may not be recognized by its audience for what it is. Much corporate propaganda is obvious, and its source is quite apparent; but it can still be pernicious. Advertising is at least visible, though it may be "steeped in subliminal psychology and imagery aimed at the subconscious" (Dowie 1995). It may also involve overwhelming exposure and a repetition of a message, thanks to the immense resources at the disposal of corporations.

But what of propaganda that cannot be recognized for what it is? One of the simplest and most powerful techniques of propaganda is concealment of its sponsors. A detailed U.S. Congress investigation into what was, and still is, one of the most influential U.S. business associations reported that

> this pretense of disinterestedness is an integral part of the propaganda campaign of the National Association of Manufacturers. . . . Deception was carried out in minute detail. . . . There can be no doubt that the . . . public was influenced by the fact that the advertisements were apparently the result of a "spontaneous movement" by independent citizens' groups. (U.S. Congress 1939, 200)

Such deceptive propaganda is by definition furtive, but evidence can be found. Nonetheless, Carey has claimed "that the success of business propaganda in persuading us, for so long, that we are free from propaganda is one of the most significant propaganda achievements of the twentieth century."

Furthermore, censorship (negative propaganda) may not be associated with commercial interests in Western democracies. Palast (1999) acknowledges the lengths to which many editors would go to resist government censorship, yet they "will slash news reports . . . or pulp entire journals based on a single note from Monsanto."

INFERRED PROPAGANDA—THE CASE OF ADAM SMITH

Adam Smith's writings and reputation are important in two respects. First, the misrepresentations of his work (Friedman refers to his "devastating comments") can be a form of "indirect propaganda"; and, second, most of the corporate propaganda cited later promotes vested interests using variations of these misrepresentations.

Adam Smith is an iconic figure whose humane and enlightened views have been misused to defend a covert partiality that underlies the way economics, finance, and accounting are presented and discussed in Anglo-Saxon culture.

Financial Times (*FT*) contributors (to take a prominent example of the increasingly international business media) are fond of words such as *ominous* to describe real wage rises; that is, such words are not used to describe profit increases. This distinction did not commend itself to Adam Smith, who was alert to double standards:

> Our merchants and master-manufacturers complain much of the bad effects of high wages in raising the price, and thereby lessening the sale of their goods both at home and abroad. They say nothing concerning the bad effects of high profits. They are silent with regard to the pernicious effects of their own gains. They complain only of those of other people. (1776/1880, *Wealth of Nations,* bk. 1, chap. 9, 76)

The central rationale for the favored treatment of shareholders is perhaps encapsulated in one of the best-known quotations from Smith's *The Wealth of Nations*:[4] "It is not from the benevolence of the butcher, the brewer, or the baker that we expect our dinner, but from their regard to their own interest." But Adam Smith's endorsement of the benefits of self-interested behavior applied to owners and employees equally, and it depends crucially on the existence of what has been called "atomistic" competition "in which no agent of the productive mechanism, on the side of labour or capital, was powerful enough to interfere with or to resist the pressures of competition" (Heilbroner 1953/1991). Challenges could come from government regulation, from organized labor, or from market concentration or other anticompetitive action taken by employers. The first two challenges have been demonized by powerful and influential forces, but enormous efforts (witting and unwitting) have gone into obscuring the third challenge.

Adam Smith was well aware that conditions did not conform to the competitive ideal, and he was not opposed to consequent regulation in pursuit of general welfare; indeed, he favored it. And he was acutely conscious of the danger of undue power in the hands of the owning class:

Whenever the legislature attempts to regulate the differences between masters and their workmen, its counsellors are always the masters. When the regulation, therefore, is in favour of the workmen, it is always just and equitable; but it is sometimes otherwise when in favour of the masters. (1776/1880, *Wealth of Nations,* bk. 1, pt. II, chap. 10, 112–13)

But, as an early example of the power of propaganda in the service of powerful interests:

By a strange injustice, the man who warned that the grasping eighteenth century industrialists "generally have an interest to deceive and even to oppress the public" came to be regarded as their economic patron saint. (Heilbroner 1953/1991, 70–71)

Smith is widely misrepresented as a champion of unbridled market forces, but this is an utterly dishonest picture. He was not against regulation in principle—he was against regulation that helped to concentrate economic power. He stated that it was to prevent the reduction of profits "by restraining that free competition which would most certainly occasion it, that all corporations, and the greater part of corporation laws, have been established" (1776/1880, *Wealth of Nations,* bk. 1, pt. II, chap. 10, 97).

Smith was against legislation that protected the strong and the privileged either by conferring monopoly powers over consumers or by worsening the already weak position of employees. Smith did not argue for the maximization of owners' wealth: his defense of self-interest did not, in principle, distinguish among any of the participants in the wealth-creation process—although he recognized that powerful interests could reduce their own exposure to competition.

Given Smith's emphasis on competition, one might expect to find propaganda dedicated to preserving this "necessary illusion" (Chomsky 1989). Galbraith has argued that a significant part of the economy (i.e., that dominated by large firms) operates without the discipline of effective competition and, crucially, that the teaching of economics obscures this reality (Galbraith and Salinger 1978). Global dominance by large corporations is widely documented (e.g., Korten 1995), and market concentration has intensified since Galbraith's first criticisms. Even in the 1930s, Berle and Means (1937) recognized that the large corporations they studied "seemed to Adam Smith not to fit into the principles which he was laying down for the conduct of economic activity." It is amusing to see the forms of words used, to justify the relaxation of "free competition" when big business is the beneficiary. An *FT* analysis of the BP–Amoco merger described the resulting market dominance as giving "a *degree of protection* from the *unfettered operation* of market pricing"; it went on to say that "modern business relies on these *slivers of elbow room* to achieve *acceptable* levels of profitability" (Martin 1998; emphasis added). It was suggested in an *FT* supplement on marketing that high-profile cases of market power abuse often serve the interests of collusive U.S. companies by confusing members of the general public, "who become convinced that covert cartels do not exist in the U.S. and that price hikes are therefore due to competitive market forces" (Parker 1998).

The misrepresentation of Adam Smith and the sustained illusion of competition are central to the teaching of economics, accounting, and finance; and the shibboleth of maximizing shareholder value. The acquiescence of those further removed from these self-serving myths is considered next.

SOME SMOKING GUNS

The insightful and prophetic eloquence of Adam Smith warned of how the rich and powerful could dishonestly identify their interests with those of general society. Smith also recognized that propaganda involved the suppression of what was inconvenient as well as the use of "clamour," stating, for example, that we rarely hear "of the combinations of masters, though frequently of those of workmen." But he warned that "whoever imagines, upon this account, that masters rarely combine, is as ignorant of the world as of the subject" (1776/1880, *Wealth of Nations,* bk. 1, chap. 8, 51–52).

These insights were echoed by Carey (1997), who described corporate propaganda as identifying "the free-enterprise system in popular consciousness with every cherished value" and "interventionist governments and strong unions (the only agencies capable of checking the complete domination of society by the corporations) with tyranny, oppression and even subversion" (18).

When utility companies were under investigation in the 1920s by the U.S. Senate, their spokesman emphasized the advantages of propaganda over conventional forms of influence: "To depend year after year on the usual political expedients for stopping hostile legislation is short sightedness. . . . Isn't it better and surer to lay a groundwork with people back home who have the votes" (Dahl 1959, 30). The potential for those with resources to use propaganda for their own ends became clear to the well informed and the prescient. The president of Harvard University reproduced the following words in a discussion of public opinion:

> Popular election . . . may work fairly well as long as those questions are not raised which cause the holders of wealth and industrial power to make full use

of their opportunities. . . . If the rich people in any modern state thought it worth their while, . . . there is so much skill to be bought . . . for production of emotion and opinion . . . that the whole condition of political contests would be changed for the future. (Lowell 1926, 43)

This was not paranoia—there was hard evidence, too. The instigator and co-ordinator of much propaganda in the United States was the National Association of Manufacturers (NAM), and the scale of its resources as well as its intentions was the subject of more than one congressional enquiry. A House committee, as early as 1913,[5] found that the NAM's plans that included a "*disguised* propaganda campaign" on "industrial, commercial, political, educational, and other lines" were "so vast and far-reaching" that the committee's members feared for the implications for democracy.

The NAM's presumption in deciding how society should be governed seems not to have abated: their current mission involves "shaping" the "legislative and regulatory environment" (NAM 2003). So not content with maximizing profits within the rules set by voters' representatives, these manufacturers also want to set the rules.

Corporate propaganda has been intensified as necessary to respond to particular threats. The depression threatened the prestige of business and the "free market" system. The climate culminated in Roosevelt's New Deal, and the NAM and others were again keen to influence events:

In 1934, concern over many of President Franklin Roosevelt's New Deal proposals and key labor issues prompted the NAM to launch a public relations campaign "*for the dissemination of sound American doctrines to the public.*" During the next 13 years, the NAM's National Industrial Information Committee spent more than $15 million on leaflets, movie shorts, radio speeches, films for schools, reprints of articles by economists, and other public relations efforts. (NAM 2003; emphasis added)

These activities could be seen from a different perspective. A U.S. Senate investigation reported that the NAM "blanketed the country with propaganda which in technique has relied upon . . . secrecy and deception" and that many "artifices of propaganda" had not "disclosed to the public their origin within the Association" (U.S. Congress 1939). The NAM propaganda program was by no means the only one, but it was, according to one of its own leaders, the most effective:

Public opinion has been shifted to the right. Now . . . I am not undertaking to tell you that the NAM program has been the only factor in the change . . . however . . . the campaign has totalled more than all other similar programs combined. . . . It has continually—day by day and week by week—expounded . . . a certain set of principles, and . . . millions of our people believe today in these principles who did not five years ago. (R. L. Lund 1938, speech to the Annual Congress of American Industry; quoted in U.S. Congress 1939, 176)

Wars tend to nurture feelings of social cohesion and interdependence, and World War II intensified government coordination of economic activity and mediation between employers and employees. Predictably, once the war was over (and in contrast to contemporary Europe), business propaganda in the United States was again put to work on a formidable scale, to roll back the trend toward a social market economy. Dominant themes continued to be symbolic, linking business free enterprise with democracy, the family, the church, and patriotism; and government regulation of business with Communism and subversion (Carey 1997, 27). The NAM and the national office of the Chamber of Commerce launched a massive postwar campaign to end price controls:

Big business in this country set out to destroy the laws that were protecting the consumer against exploitation. This drive was spearheaded by the NAM, the most powerful organisation of big business in the country. (Truman 1948, in Schnapper 1948–1949, 84–85)

President Truman also spelt out NAM's tactics, including talks, publications, and press releases—he even referred to an insider who "spilled the story." Opinion surveys before and after the campaign showed a reduction in support for the Office of Price Administration (OPA) from 85 percent to 26 percent. A cartoon exemplifies the campaign (Fones-Wolf 1994, 80): a car containing an "American Family" whose road to a gleaming city called "Prosperity" is blocked by a barricade headed "OPA Artificial Prices" with alternative directions indicated as "Inflation," "Crushing Taxes," "Dictatorship," "Hatred" "Slavery" and "Poverty."

The post–Vietnam era posed another threat to the "corporate culture" (Galambos 1975), with predictable responses. An Advertising Council campaign advocating "free enterprise," or "economic education," was described in *Fortune* magazine as a "study in gigantism saturating the media and reaching practically everyone." "Don't quote me," says the director of one economic education program, "but we're propagandising" (Weaver 1977).

Arguably, corporate propaganda in regard to certain issues—for example, the environment—has become more visible in recent years (see, e.g., Stauber and Rampton 1995; Beder 1997). A striking example is the Global Climate Coalition, whose "mendacious propaganda" (Tickell 1997) against climate change initiatives was, in comparative terms, widely reported. Nonetheless this very visibility may obscure even further the more systemic and longstanding "engineering of consent," whose effectiveness is apparent in the breathtakingly one-sided use of language in the business media.

THE BUSINESS MEDIA AND ANGLO-SAXON CORPORATE IMPERIALISM

Herman and Chomsky (1988) argued that, even in societies that appear to enjoy freedom of expression, the mass media serves the interests of a dominant elite. Writing in *FT*, Riley (1996) discussed the opportunities for American banks in continental stock markets. Noting that America's reduction in real wages (except "of course, for bosses") had led to a corporate renaissance, he discussed gains to be made in Germany if "shareholder value" were to become a key theme there. He noted that real German wages had risen relative to the United States by 35 percent over the preceding decade. The message was clear—a German society organized on U.S. lines could bring huge gains for investors at the expense of others. Goldman Sachs had a term for the prospect—"a restructuring bubble," as "share prices discount unusually high earnings growth rates." It was acknowledged that shareholder value could not "be released as aggressively"[6] in Europe as in the United States due to governments being "*overburdened* by social security commitments" (emphasis added). What is significant is that, in this remarkably frank analysis, the usual pretext is dropped—that is, "greater wealth for all" as an excuse for investor self-interest. (The social security arrangements that Riley has the presumption reject may not be unconnected with a range of social indicators. Consider some child poverty statistics: a 1995 study[7] indicated that child poverty in the United States was not only the worst among seventeen developed countries studied but 50 percent higher than the next-highest rate. It was more than three times greater than the rates in France and Germany.)

The candid tone of Riley's analysis is consistent with observations by Chomsky about the "elite" and the media that serves it. Riley explicitly refers to the euphemism of "America's famous labour market flexibility" and then bluntly translates it into operational terms, namely, reducing real wages. He notes that the educational system for the elite, unlike that for the general population, has to allow creativity and independence; "otherwise they won't be able to do their job of making money." The same phenomenon can be found in the press: "That's why I read the *Wall Street Journal* and the *Financial Times* and *Business Week*. They just have to tell the truth" (Chomsky 1996). This does not, of course, preclude extreme partisanship.

Plender (1997) wrote in *FT* of deregulation of European labor markets continuing at "snail's pace," as "treasured social cohesion" impeded "a more robust, Anglo-Saxon style of capitalism." An *FT* feature on the Japanese economy described in mocking terms Japan's "cherished social contract" and called for "a more flexible labour market" (Nakamoto 1997). Nakamoto (1999) notes in *FT* that Western accounting techniques will help to change attitudes.

The lead in an *FT* supplement on Japan notes disapprovingly that "conversion of executives to shareholder value is not always entirely wholehearted"; that investment bankers lament executives' attachment to the interests of employees; that "Japan Inc will no longer be able to afford lifetime employment"; and that although "the social dislocation could be huge," these are the "consequences of a greater emphasis on the cost and return of capital" (Abrahams 1999). This is grotesque and irresponsible self-interest made respectable. The changes to be foisted on Japan may have been slow in coming, as "foreign investors first drooled about the potential for re-engineering back in 1993" (Riley 1999); but now, according to a senior figure, "we are at an historic moment . . . seeing the unravelling of 50 years of history" (Abrahams 1999). The values that are implicit in all this language are, of course, those of accounting in which only one group of stakeholders does not have its share of the cake counted as a cost.

An *FT* article (Tett 2000) reports a sharp rise in the crime rate in Japan, "one of the world's safest countries," and notes concerns over growing income inequality and unemployment. Tett blames an economic downturn—there is no mention of sacrificing social cohesion on the altar of Anglo-Saxon capitalism in this piece.

If sophisticated industrialized countries risk having their social fabric ripped apart by Anglo-Saxon corporate interests, what chance have less-developed countries? Popular leaderships with the understanding and inclination to promote social interests (and national self-respect) over those of foreign investors do exist (see Stiglitz 2003), but they are rare. And, of course, they may be removed, since, notwithstanding current rhetoric, democratic government (like social cohesion) has often been shown to be expendable if it is not seen to be in the interests of foreign investors.[8]

Healthy and productive businesses should not, and need not, be bought at the expense of social (or environmental) justice and responsibility. Business success is a means to an end, not an end in itself and should not be synonymous with the interests of a dominant elite. That is the source of systemic injustice and disharmony with ultimately catastrophic consequences for individuals and society. We should be aware of "clamour and sophistry" that identify the interests of the few as the interests of the many.

NOTES

1. For example, Tony Blair as reported by Palast (2003, 315).

2. For a clever and insightful critique of this system of privilege, the tellingly entitled *Divine Right of Capital* (Kelly 2001) is warmly recommended. And for an examination of the behavior that it can induce in organizations, try *Tyranny of the Bottom Line: Why Corporations Make Good People Do Bad Things* (Estes 1996).

3. There are notable exceptions to this lack of interest: Chomsky (1996) has cited, in particular, the work of Carey (1997) and also that of Fones-Wolf (1994). Carey and Chomsky have been major influences on the ideas in this chapter and also on Collison (2003), on whom part of this chapter draws.

4. Other rationales for a privileged position for shareholders may be put forward—such as their being "residual risk takers." This, too, is spurious—finance theory makes clear that owners can readily diversify their risk, unlike employees. Rights of ownership may also be invoked—a circular argument begging the question of what such rights should be. It should be noted that a reasonable return to shareholders is not being questioned—nor is the importance of financial viability or accounting itself—the issue is the *maximization* of shareholder value. For a rebuttal of the argument that, in any case, "we are all shareholders now," see Kelly (2001). Anglo-Saxon capitalism may also be "justified" on productivity grounds. Even if the productivity claim were shown to be true, it would hardly excuse the grotesque inequalities that laissez-faire policies promote; but it is *not* true, as powerfully demonstrated by Hutton (2002).

5. Quoted in Lane (1950, 18; 63rd Cong., 1st sess., House report 113, *Congressional Record* 51:565–84).

6. The overtones of the word *released* in this example are worth consideration—would *acquired* have quite the same ring of barely perceptible self-justification?

7. Rainwater and Smeeding (1995), cited in Annie E. Casey Foundation (2000).

8. Ironically, it was a Middle East country that set the pattern for such events. See Kinzer (2003) for a description of how the United States, at the behest of the United Kingdom, removed Iran's fledgling democracy in 1953, when it proved injurious to business interests.

REFERENCES

Abrahams, Paul. 1999. "Dressing a New Economic Model." *Financial Times* survey, *Japan: Corporate Fund-Raising.* December 17, 1–2.

Annie E. Casey Foundation. 2000. *2000 Kids Count Online,* at www.aecf.org/kidscount/kc2000/sum_11.htm.

Beder, Sharon. 1997. *Global Spin: The Corporate Assault on Environmentalism.* Totnes, U.K.: Green Books.

Berle, A. A., and G. C. Means. 1937. *The Modern Corporation and Private Property.* New York: Macmillan.

Carey, A. 1997. *Taking the Risk Out of Democracy: Corporate Propaganda versus Freedom and Liberty*. Champaign: University of Illinois Press.

Chomsky, N. 1989. *Necessary Illusions: Thought Control in Democratic Societies*. London: Pluto Press.

———. 1996. *Class Warfare: Interviews with David Barsamian*. London: Pluto Press.

Collison, D. J. 2003. "Corporate Propaganda: Its Implications for Accounting and Accountability." *Accounting, Auditing and Accountability Journal* 16, no. 5: 853–86.

Dahl, R. A. 1959. "Business and Politics: A Critical Appraisal of Political Science." In *Social Science Research on Business: Product and Potential*, edited by R. A. Dahl, M. Haire, and P. F. Lazarsfeld. New York: Columbia University Press.

Dowie, M. 1995. "Torches of Liberty." Introduction to *Toxic Sludge Is Good for You*, by J. Stauber and S. Rampton. Monroe, Maine: Common Courage Press.

Estes, Ralph. 1996. *Tyranny of the Bottom Line: Why Corporations Make Good People Do Bad Things*. San Francisco: Berrett-Koehler.

Fones-Wolf, Elizabeth A. 1994. *Selling Free Enterprise: The Business Assault on Labor and Liberalism, 1945–1960*. Champaign: University of Illinois Press.

Friedman, M. 1962/1982. *Capitalism and Freedom*. Chicago: University of Chicago Press.

Galambos, L. 1975. *The Public Image of Big Business in America, 1880–1940: A Quantitative Study in Social Change*. Baltimore: Johns Hopkins University Press.

Galbraith, J. K., and N. Salinger. 1978. *Almost Everyone's Guide to Economics*. Boston: Houghton Mifflin.

Heilbroner, R. 1953/1991. *The Worldly Philosophers*. New York: Simon & Schuster (orig. ed.); New York: Penguin (new ed.).

Herman, E. S., and N. Chomsky. 1988. *Manufacturing Consent: The Political Economy of the Mass Media*. New York: Pantheon Books.

Hutton, W. 2002. *The World We're In*. London: Little & Bown.

Kelly, Marjorie. 2001. *The Divine Right of Capital: Dethroning the Corporate Aristocracy*. San Francisco: Berrett-Koehler.

Kinzer, Stephen. 2003. *All the Shah's Men: An American Coup and the Roots of Middle East Terror*. New York: Wiley.

Korten, David C. 1995. *When Corporations Rule the World*. San Francisco: Berrett-Koehler Publishers; Bloomfield, Conn.: Kumarian Press.

Lane, E. 1950. "Some Lessons from Past Congressional Investigations of Lobbying." *Public Opinion Quarterly* 14.

Lasswell, H. D. 1927/1971. *Propaganda Technique in World War I*. Cambridge, Mass.: MIT Press.

London, Simon. 2003. "Lunch with the FT." *Financial Times*, June 7, 12–13.

Lowell, A. L. 1926. *Public Opinion and Popular Government*. New York: Longmans, Green & Co.

Martin, Peter. 1998. "Big Oil, Big Bucks." *Financial Times*, August 18, 14.

National Association of Manufacturers (NAM). 2003. Retrieved from www.nam.org (accessed August 5, 2003).

Nakamoto, Michiyo. 1997. "Revolution Coming, Ready or Not." *Financial Times*, October 24, 18.

———. 1999. "No Longer Taboo." *Financial Times,* August 25, 1999.

Palast, G. 1999. "Dreaming in Monsanto." *Index on Censorship,* March, 62–66.

———. 2003. *The Best Democracy Money Can Buy.* London: Robinson.

Parker, Philip. 1998. "How Do Companies Collude." *Financial Times,* Mastering Marketing 3, September 28, 10–11.

Plender, J. 1997. "When Capital Collides with Labour." *Financial Times,* October 24, 1997, 18.

Rainwater, L., and T. M. Smeeding. 1995. "Doing Poorly: The Real Income of American Children in a Comparative Perspective." Working Paper 127, Luxembourg Income Study, Maxwell School of Citizenship and Public Affairs, Syracuse University, New York.

Riley, Barry. 1996. "Shareholder Value Revives in Germany's Graveyard." *Financial Times,* November 21, 21.

———. 1999. "Time for a Tokyo Play." *Financial Times,* March 17, 19.

Schnapper, M. B., ed. 1948–1949. *The Truman Program: Addresses and Messages by President Harry S. Truman.* Washington, D.C.: Public Affairs Press.

Smith, A. 1776/1880. *An Inquiry into the Nature and Causes of the Wealth of Nations; or, The Wealth of Nations.* New York: Routledge.

Stauber, J., and S. Rampton. 1995. *Toxic Sludge Is Good for You.* Monroe, Maine: Common Courage Press.

Stiglitz, J. E. 2003. *Globalisation and Its Discontents.* London: Norton.

Tett, Gillian. 2000. "Crime Wave Raises Fears for Japanese Social Stability." *Financial Times,* February 29, 18.

Tickell, C. 1997. BBC Radio 4 interview on *Today* program. October.

U.S. Congress. La Follette Committee. 1939. *Violations of Free Speech and Rights of Labour: Report of the Committee on Education and Labour.* Washington, D.C.: GPO.

Weaver, P. 1977. "Corporations Are Defending Themselves with the Wrong Weapons." *Fortune,* June, 186–96.

5

Spinning War and Blotting Out Memory

Norman Solomon

Without a hint of intended irony, the *NewsHour* on PBS concluded its program on September 9, 2003, with a warm interview of Henry Kissinger and then a segment about a renowned propagandist for the Nazi war machine. Kissinger talked about his latest book. Then a professor of German history talked about Leni Riefenstahl, the pathbreaking documentary filmmaker who just died, at age 101.

The conversation was cozy with Kissinger, the man who served as the preeminent architect of U.S. policy during the last half-dozen years of the Vietnam War. Tossed his way by host Jim Lehrer, the questions ranged from softball to beach ball. And when the obsequious session ended, Lehrer went beyond politeness: "Dr. Kissinger, good to see you. Thank you for being with us. Good luck on your book."

After focusing on Kissinger's efforts during the 1973 Arab–Israeli war, the *NewsHour* interview discussed his role in the April 1975 final withdrawal of U.S. troops from Vietnam. Previously, Kissinger had been the Nixon administration's main foreign-policy man while more than twenty-five thousand American soldiers and upward of five hundred thousand Vietnamese people—most of them civilians—were killed. The Nixon–Kissinger policies in Southeast Asia also included the illegal and deadly bombing of Cambodia, where the Pentagon flew 3,630 raids over a period of fourteen months from 1969 to 1970. (Cambodia's neutrality in the Cold War and the Vietnam War had infuriated Washington.) Military records were falsified to hide the bombing from Congress. Massive carnage among civilians also resulted from U.S. air strikes on Laos.

But in September 2003, the man who largely oversaw those activities sat under bright television lights and basked in yet more media deference. This has been routine for Kissinger. But once in a great while, a mainstream news outlet has summoned the gumption necessary to explore grim truth about those in our midst who have exercised bloody power. That's what happened in February 2001, when *NewsHour* correspondent Elizabeth Farnsworth interviewed Kissinger about his direct contact with Gen. Augusto Pinochet, the Chilean dictator who came to power in a coup on September 11, 1973. Kissinger was President Nixon's national security advisor at the time.

Nearly three years after the coup—which overthrew the elected socialist president Salvador Allende—Kissinger huddled with Gen. Pinochet in Chile. By then, Kissinger was in his third year as secretary of state; by then, thousands of political prisoners had died, and many more had been tortured at the hands of the Pinochet regime. At the 1976 meeting, a declassified memo says that Kissinger told Pinochet: "We are sympathetic with what you are trying to do here."

Farnsworth confronted Kissinger about the memo's contents during the 2001 interview. She asked him point-blank about the discussion with Pinochet: "Why did you not say to him, 'You're violating human rights. You're killing people. Stop it'?"

Kissinger replied: "First of all, human rights were not an international issue at the time, the way they have become since. That was not what diplomats and secretaries of state and presidents were saying generally to anybody in those days." He added that at the June 1976 meeting with Pinochet, "I spent half my time telling him that he should improve his human rights performance in any number of ways." But the American envoy's concern was tactical. As Farnsworth noted in her reporting: "Kissinger did bring up human rights violations, saying they were making it difficult for him to get aid for Chile from Congress."

During the past quarter of a century, Kissinger has become a multimillionaire as a wheeler-dealer international consultant and a member of numerous boards at huge corporations, including media firms. Along the way, he has accumulated many friends in high media places. When *Washington Post* owner Katharine Graham wrote her autobiography, she praised Kissinger as a dear friend and all-around wonderful person.

As it happened, the *NewsHour* interview with Kissinger on September 9, 2003, came just two days before the thirtieth anniversary of the coup in Chile. Although declassified documents show that Kissinger was deeply involved in making that coup possible, Lehrer's hospitality was such that the anchor did not mention it.

Minutes later, during another *NewsHour* interview, historian Claudia Koonz was aptly pointing out that Riefenstahl "saw herself as a documentary maker, not as a propagandist. But what she understood so much before anyone else is that the best propaganda is invisible. It looks like a documentary. Then you realize all you're seeing is glory, beauty and triumph, and you don't see the darker side."

The millions of people who have mourned the victims of the U.S. war in Southeast Asia might feel that such words describe the standard U.S. media coverage of Henry Kissinger.

Quagmire is a word made famous during the Vietnam War. The 2003 war on Iraq and the subsequent occupation came out of a very different history, but there were some chilling parallels. One of them was that the editorial positions of major U.S. newspapers had an echo like a dirge.

Of course, the nation's mainstream press does not speak with a monolithic editorial voice. And so, at one end of the limited spectrum, the strident and influential *Wall Street Journal* could not abide any doubts. Its editorials explained, tirelessly, that the war was Good and the occupation was Good—and those who doubted were fools and knaves. (LBJ called such dissenters "Nervous Nellies.") The *Journal*'s editorial writers fervently promoted what used to be called the "domino theory." The day after the UN headquarters in Baghdad blew up in August 2003, the paper closed its gung-ho editorial by touting a quote from Centcom commander Gen. John Abizaid: "If we can't be successful here, then we won't be successful in the global war on terror. It is going to be hard. It is going to be long and sometimes bloody, but we just have to stick with it."

As the summer of 2003 came to an end, most newspaper editorials were decidedly less complacent about the occupation of Iraq. Some lambasted the Bush administration for deceptive spin, poor planning, and go-it-alone arrogance. A big worry was that the U.S. government faced a quagmire.

During the late 1960s, that kind of concern grew at powerful media institutions. After several years of assurances from the Johnson administration about the Vietnam War, rosy scenarios for military success were in disrepute. But here's a revealing fact: In early 1968, the *Boston Globe* conducted a survey of thirty-nine major U.S. daily newspapers and found that not a single one had editorialized in favor of U.S. withdrawal from Vietnam. While millions of Americans were demanding an immediate pullout, such a concept was still viewed as extremely unrealistic by the editorial boards of big daily papers—including the liberal *New York Times* and *Washington Post*. Yes, some editorials fretted about a quagmire. But the emphasis was on developing a winnable strategy—not ending the war. Pull out the U.S. troops? The idea was unthinkable.

And so it was thirty-five years later. Consider the lead editorial that appeared in the *New York Times* on the same day that the *Wall Street Journal* was giving General Abizaid the last word. "The Bush administration has to commit sufficient additional resources, and, if necessary, additional troops," the *Times* editorialized. The newspaper went on to describe efforts in Iraq as "now the most important American foreign policy endeavor." In other words, the occupation that resulted from an entirely illegitimate war should be seen as entirely legitimate.

A week later, the *Times* followed up with a similar tone—reminiscent of the can't-back-down resolve that propelled countless entreaties for more effective "pacification" during the Vietnam War. Articulating what passes for dissent among elite U.S. media, the August 27, 2003, editorial cautioned that "the United States will pay a high price in blood and treasure if the Bush administration persists in its misguided effort to pacify and rebuild Iraq without extensive international support."

Troops from other nations were being imported. But that did little to make the occupation of Iraq less of a U.S. operation. The Vietnam War had its multilateral fig leaves, too; the war was supposedly an "allied" effort because it included participation from Filipino, Australian, and South Korean troops.

When the Bush administration was striving to use the United Nations in autumn 2002, *New York Times* columnist Thomas Friedman had applauded the attempt to manipulate the world body. For a while, in November of that year, he was happy: "The Bush team discovered that the best way to legitimize its overwhelming might—in a war of choice—was not by simply imposing it, but by channeling it through the UN."

But in late 2003, the U.S. media appeals for multilateral policies rarely went beyond nostrums, such as giving the handpicked Iraqi leaders more prominent roles, recruiting compliant natives and foreigners for security functions, and getting the United Nations more involved. Whatever the UN's role in Iraq was to be, the U.S. government still insisted on remaining in charge. Despite the offered compromises, that was the bottom line. The Bush administration would not let go of a country with so many attractive features to offer—including a central geopolitical foothold in the Middle East, access to extensive military bases for the Pentagon, and . . . oh yes . . . about 112 billion barrels of known oil reserves under the sand.

The Bush administration never hesitated to exploit the general public's anxieties that arose after the traumatic events of September 11, 2001.

Testifying on Capitol Hill exactly fifty-three weeks later, Donald Rumsfeld did not miss a beat when a member of the Senate Armed Services Committee questioned the need for the United States to attack Iraq.

> SENATOR MARK DAYTON: "What is it compelling us now to make a precipitous decision and take precipitous actions?"
> DEFENSE SECRETARY RUMSFELD: "What's different? What's different is 3,000 people were killed."

As a practical matter, it was almost beside the point that allegations linking Baghdad with the September 11 attacks lacked credible evidence. The key factor was political manipulation, not real documentation.

Former CIA analyst Kenneth Pollack got enormous media exposure in late 2002 for his book *The Threatening Storm: The Case for Invading Iraq*. Pollack's book-promotion tour often seemed more like a war-promotion tour. During a typical CNN appearance, Pollack explained why he had come to see a "massive invasion" of Iraq as both desirable and practical: "The real difference was the change from September 11th. The sense that after September 11th, the American people were now willing to make sacrifices to prevent threats from abroad from coming home to visit us here made it possible to think about a big invasion force."

Middle East correspondent Robert Fisk, with the London-based *Independent* newspaper, was on the mark when he wrote: "Iraq had absolutely nothing to do with 11 September. If the United States invades Iraq, we should remember that."

But at psychological levels, the Bush team was able to manipulate post-9/11 emotions well beyond the phantom of Iraqi involvement in that crime against humanity. The dramatic changes in political climate after 9/11 included a drastic upward spike in an attitude — fervently stoked by the likes of Rumsfeld, Dick Cheney, and the president — that our military should be willing to attack potential enemies before they might try to attack us. Few politicians or pundits were willing to confront the reality that this was a formula for perpetual war and for the creation of vast numbers of new foes who would see a reciprocal logic in embracing such a credo themselves.

One of the great media clichés has been that 9/11 "changed everything." The portentous idea soon became a truism for news outlets nationwide. But the shock of September 11 could not endure. And the events of that horrific day — while abruptly tilting the political landscape and media discourse — did not transform the lives of most Americans. Despite all the genuine anguish and the overwhelming news coverage, daily life gradually went back to an approximation of normal.

Some changes are obvious. Worries about terrorism have become routine. Out of necessity, stepped-up security measures are in effect at airports. Unnecessarily, and ominously, the Patriot Act is chipping away at civil liberties. Yet the basic, pre–September 11 concerns remain with us today.

The nation's economic picture includes the familiar scourges of unemployment, job insecurity, eroding pension benefits, and a wildly exorbitant health-care system that endangers huge numbers of people who are uninsured or underinsured. After 9/11, the power of money is undiminished — notwithstanding every platitude that bounced around the media echo chamber in the wake of September 11.

During the last months of 2001, many media powerhouses heralded the arrival of humanistic values for the country. Typically, the December issue of *O* — the "Oprah Magazine" — was largely devoted to the cover story "We Are Family." In the leadoff essay, Oprah Winfrey served up a heaping portion of sweet pabulum. "Our vision of family has been expanded," she wrote. "From the ashes of the World Trade Center, the Pentagon, and that field in Pennsylvania arose a new spirit of unity. We realize that we are all part of the family of America." Later in the glossy, ad-filled magazine, the "We Are Family" headline reappeared under Old Glory and over another message from Oprah, who declared: "America is a vast and complicated family, but—as the smoke clears and the dust settles—a family nonetheless."

From the vantage point of the present day, the late-2001 claims about a new national altruism invite disbelief, if not derision. No amount of media spin about "the family of America" can negate the fact that gaps between wealth and poverty have never been wider. What kind of affluent family would leave so many of its members in desperate need?

News about Halliburton's and Bechtel's cashing in on the occupation of Iraq was a counterpoint to revelations that the White House strongly pressured the Environmental Protection Agency in the days after 9/11 to mislead the public about dangers of airborne toxic particles from World Trade Center debris. The EPA's Office of the Inspector General reported in August 2003 that "the desire to reopen Wall Street" was a major factor in the Bush administration's misleading assurances. Although the public was told that everything had changed, powerful elites gave the highest priority to resuming business as usual.

After September 11, while many thousands of people grieved the sudden loss of their loved ones, a steady downpour of politically driven sentimentality kept blurring the U.S. media's window on the world. Politicians in high office, from President Bush on down, rushed to identify themselves with the dead and their relatives. Cataclysmic individual losses were swiftly expropriated for mass dissemination.

In a cauldron of media alchemy, the human suffering of 9/11 became propaganda gold. Sorrow turned into political capital.

The human process of mourning is intimate and often at a loss for words; journalists and politicians tend to be neither. Grief borders on the ineffable. News coverage gravitates toward clichés and facile images.

In tandem with the message that September 11 "changed everything" came an emboldened insistence on the U.S. prerogative to attack other countries at will. In a bait-and-switch operation that took hold in autumn 2001, emblems of 9/11 soon underwent double exposure with prevailing political agendas.

Displayed by many as an expression of sorrow and solidarity with the September 11 victims, the American flag was promptly overlaid on the missiles bound for Afghanistan. In television studios, like angelic symbols dancing on the heads of pins, the Stars and Stripes got stuck on the lapels of many newscasters.

Network correspondents routinely joined in upbeat assessments of the U.S.-led assault on Afghanistan that took the lives of at least as many blameless civilians as 9/11 did. Later, the U.S.-led invasion of Iraq, which overthrew a regime in Baghdad with no links to the September 11 hijackings or al

Qaeda, took more civilian lives than 9/11 did. For the United States, moral reflection could not hold a candle to the righteous adrenaline of war.

In the early autumn of 2001, W. H. Auden's mournful poem "September 1, 1939" suddenly drew wide media attention. Set amid the "blind skyscrapers" of Manhattan, where "buildings grope the sky," the poem seemed to eerily echo the World Trade Center calamity with the words that closed the first stanza: "The unmentionable odor of death / Offends the September night."

The concluding lines of the next verse received less notice: "Those to whom evil is done / Do evil in return."

During the summer of 2003, many journalists seemed to be in hot pursuit of the Bush administration. But they had an enormous amount of ground to cover. After routinely lagging behind and detouring around key information, major American news outlets were playing catch-up.

The default position of U.S. media coverage gave the White House the benefit of doubts. In stark contrast, the British press had been far more vigorous in exposing deceptions about Iraq. For example, BBC News broke crucial stories to boost public knowledge of governmental duplicities; the same could hardly be said for NPR News in the United States.

One of the main problems with American reporting has been reflexive deference—and, in the wake of 9/11, for a long time even reverence—toward pivotal administration players, such as Donald Rumsfeld, Colin Powell, and Condoleezza Rice. Journalists habitually failed to scrutinize contradictions, false statements, and leaps of illogic.

Powell's watershed speech to the UN Security Council in early February 2003 was so effective at home because journalists swooned rather than draw on basic debunking information that was readily available at the time. To a great extent, reporters on the American side of the Atlantic provided stenography for top U.S. officials, while editorial writers and pundits lavished praise.

The most deferential coverage was devoted to the president himself, with news outlets treating countless potential firestorms as minor sparks or one-day brushfires. Even later, after numerous deceptions came to light in some U.S. media reports, George W. Bush benefited from media presumptions of best intentions and essential honesty, an updated "teflonization" of the man in the Oval Office.

Midway through July 2003—even while *Time*'s latest cover was asking "Untruth & Consequences: How Flawed Was the Case for Going to War against Saddam?"—the president told reporters: "The fundamental question is, did Saddam Hussein have a weapons program? And the answer is, absolutely. And we gave him a chance to allow the inspectors in, and he wouldn't let them in. And, therefore, after a reasonable request, we decided to remove him from power."

Bush's assertion about Hussein and the inspectors—that he "wouldn't let them in"—was out of touch with historic reality. Some journalists gingerly noted that the statement was false. But the media response was mild. The president's openly uttering significant falsehoods was no big deal.

Meanwhile, reporting on the deaths of U.S. troops in Iraq was understated. *Editor & Publisher* online pointed out that while press accounts were saying thirty-three American soldiers had died between the start of May and July 17 in 2003, "actually the numbers are much worse—and rarely reported by the media." During that period, according to official military records, eighty-five U.S. soldiers died in Iraq. "This includes a staggering number of non-combat deaths. . . . Nearly all of these people would still be alive if they were back in the States." In a follow-up a week later, editor Greg Mitchell reported that his news analysis had caused "the heaviest e-mail response of any article from *E&P* in the nearly four years I have worked for the magazine." He added: "These weren't the usual media junkies or political activists, but an apparent cross-section of backgrounds and beliefs."

News coverage often involves plenty of absurdity. That's the case with routine U.S. media spin about the Israeli–Palestinian conflict.

So, on the July 29, 2003, edition of NPR's *All Things Considered* program, host Robert Siegel and correspondent Vicky O'Hara each recited scripts referring to a "security barrier" that Israel's government is building in the West Bank. The next day, many news outlets—including the *Los Angeles Times, Baltimore Sun, New York Times, Chicago Tribune,* and the Associated Press—also used the "security barrier" phrase without quotation marks, treating it as an objective description rather than the Israeli government's preferred characterization. Meanwhile, in contrast, a *Washington Post* article managed to be more evenhanded. When the phrase *security fence* appeared, it was inside a quotation from Israeli prime minister Ariel Sharon. And the *Post* story explained that part of the barrier "divides farmers from their fields, or other Palestinians from their neighbors." It took varied form as a twenty-foot-tall concrete wall and fortified stretches of razor wire, trenches, and electronic fencing.

Overall, U.S. news media do not talk straight about the fundamental injustice of Israel's occupation of the West Bank and Gaza. Illegal and morally indefensible, the occupation will fuel more killings on both sides until it ends completely.

From a media standpoint, the war on Iraq presented the administration with much bigger problems. During the summer of 2003, the Bush team felt appreciable heat because of sixteen words in the president's State of the Union speech: "The British government has learned that Saddam Hussein recently sought significant quantities of uranium from Africa." While journalists highlighted the fact that Bush's statement was false, deeper and broader questions were scarce.

"Do you take personal responsibility for that inaccuracy?" That was a question that a reporter asked at Bush's news conference on July 30, 2003. "I take personal responsibility for everything I say, of course. Absolutely," Bush replied—and immediately launched into boilerplate rhetoric to justify the war. It was a classic politician's nonresponse. And, in the absence of strong media follow-up, the meaningless answer rendered the question ineffectual (a few decades earlier, the French leader Charles de Gaulle wryly alluded to such dynamics when he began a press conference this way: "Gentlemen, I am ready for the questions to my answers").

A whole lot more than sixteen words deserved to be under scrutiny. For instance, eight days after the later-to-become-infamous State of the Union address, when Colin Powell spoke to the UN Security Council in early February 2003, he fudged, exaggerated, and concocted. Powell played fast and loose with translations of phone intercepts, to make them seem more incriminating. And, as researchers at the media watch group Fairness and Accuracy in Reporting (FAIR; where I'm an associate) have pointed out, "Powell relied heavily on the disclosure of Iraq's pre-war unconventional weapons programs by defector Hussein Kamel, without noting that Kamel had also said that all those weapons had been destroyed." But the secretary of state wowed U.S. journalists.

Many liberals were among the swooning pundits. In her *Washington Post* column the morning after Powell spoke, Mary McGrory proclaimed that "he persuaded me." She wrote: "The cumulative effect was stunning." And McGrory, a seasoned and dovish political observer, concluded: "I'm not ready for war yet. But Colin Powell has convinced me that it might be the only way to stop a fiend, and that if we do go, there is reason."

Also smitten was the editorial board of the most influential U.S. newspaper leaning against the war. Hours after Powell finished his UN snow job, the *New York Times* published an editorial with a mollified tone—declaring that he "presented the United Nations and a global television audience yesterday with the most powerful case to date that Saddam Hussein stands in defiance of Security Council resolutions and has no intention of revealing or surrendering whatever unconventional weapons he may have."

By sending Powell to address the Security Council, the *Times* claimed, President Bush "showed a wise concern for international opinion." And the paper rejoiced that "Mr. Powell's presentation was all the more convincing because he dispensed with apocalyptic invocations of a struggle of good and evil and focused on shaping a sober, factual case against Mr. Hussein's regime."

The prevailing media standards of sobriety and accuracy remained dangerously low.

The superstar columnist George Will has an impressive vocabulary. Too bad it doesn't include the words "I'm sorry."

In the early autumn of 2002, Will led the media charge when a member of Congress dared to say that President Bush would try to deceive the public about Iraq. By the next summer, strong evidence had piled up that Bush tried and succeeded. But back in late September 2002, when media frenzy erupted about Representative Jim McDermott's live appearance from Baghdad on ABC's *This Week* program, what riled the punditocracy as much as anything else was McDermott's last statement during the interview: "I think the president would mislead the American people."

First to wave a media dagger at the miscreant was Will, a regular on the ABC television show. Within minutes, on the air, he denounced "the most disgraceful performance abroad by an American official in my lifetime." But the syndicated columnist was just getting started. Back at his computer, Will churned out a piece that appeared in the *Washington Post* two days later, ripping into McDermott and a colleague on the trip, Representative David Bonior. "Saddam Hussein finds American collaborators among senior congressional Democrats," Will wrote. There was special venom for McDermott in the column. Will could not abide the spectacle of a congressperson's casting doubt on George W. Bush's utter veracity: "McDermott's accusation that the president—presumably with Cheney, Powell, Rumsfeld, Rice and others as accomplices—would use deceit to satisfy his craving to send young Americans into an unnecessary war is a slander."

During early October 2002, the national media echo chamber kept rocking with countless reprises of Will's bugle call. One of the main reasons for the furor was widespread media denial that "the president would mislead the American people." An editorial in the *Rocky Mountain News* fumed that "some of McDermott's words, delivered via TV, were nothing short of outrageous." In Georgia, the *Augusta Chronicle* declared: "For a U.S. congressman to virtually accuse the president of lying while standing on foreign soil—especially the soil of a nation that seeks to destroy his nation and even tried to assassinate a former U.S. president—is an appallingly unpatriotic act."

Nationally, on the FOX News Channel, the one-man bombast factory Bill O'Reilly accused McDermott of "giving aid and comfort to Saddam while he was in Baghdad." O'Reilly said that thousands of his viewers "want to know why McDermott would give propaganda material to a killer and accuse President Bush of being a liar in the capital city of the enemy." A syndicated column by hypermoralist Cal Thomas followed with similar indignation: "We have seen Reps. Jim McDermott of Washington and David Bonior of Michigan—the Bozos of Baghdad—accuse President Bush of lying for political gain about Iraq's threat to civilization."

But such attacks did not come only from right-wing media stalwarts. Plenty of middle-road journalists were happy to go the way of the blowing wind. During one of her routine appearances on FOX television, National Public Radio political correspondent Mara Liasson commented on McDermott and Bonior: "These guys are a disgrace. Look, everybody knows its 101, politics 101, that you don't go to an adversary country, an enemy country, and badmouth the United States, its policies and the president of the United States. I mean, these guys ought to, I don't know, resign."

Yet the president of the United States not only "would" mislead the American people but actually did—with the result of a horrendous war. However, when the evidence became incontrovertible, the pundits who had gone after McDermott with a vengeance did not publicly concede that he'd made a valid and crucial point.

To use George Will's inadvertently apt words, it was prescient to foresee that "the president—presumably with Cheney, Powell, Rumsfeld, Rice and others as accomplices—would use deceit to satisfy his craving to send young Americans into an unnecessary war."

Much more important, if a mainstream political journalist such as Mara Liasson was so quick to suggest that McDermott resign for inopportunely seeking to prevent a war, why didn't she later advocate that the president resign for dishonestly promoting a war—or, failing resignation, face impeachment?

Mainstream U.S. media coverage of the war on Iraq in spring 2003 was quite biased. The media watch group FAIR conducted a study of the 1,617 on-camera sources who appeared on the evening newscasts of six U.S. television networks during the three weeks beginning with the start of the war, on March 20: "Nearly two-thirds of all sources, 64 percent, were pro-war, while 71 percent of U.S. guests favored the war. Anti-war voices were 10 percent of all sources, but just 6 percent of non-Iraqi sources and only 3 percent of U.S. sources. Thus viewers were more than six times as likely to see a pro-war source as one who was anti-war; counting only U.S. guests, the ratio increases to 25 to 1."

Less than 1 percent of the U.S. sources were antiwar on Dan Rather's flagship program, the *CBS Evening News*, during the war's first three weeks. Meanwhile, public television's PBS *NewsHour* program, hosted by Jim Lehrer, "also had a relatively low percentage of U.S. anti-war voices—perhaps because the show less frequently features on-the-street interviews, to which critics of the war were usually relegated." Once the war began, the major network studios were virtually off-limits to vehement American opponents of the war.

For the most part, major U.S. networks sanitized their war coverage, which was wall-to-wall on cable. As always, the enthusiasm for war was rabid on FOX News Channel. After a prewar makeover, the fashion was the same for MSNBC. At the other end of the narrow cable-news spectrum, CNN cranked up its own militaristic fervor.

There were instances of exceptional journalism in the mainstream U.S. press. Some news magazines provided a number of grisly pictures. A few reporters, notably Anthony Shadid of the *Washington Post* and Ian Fisher of the *New York Times,* wrote vivid accounts of what the Pentagon's firepower did to Iraqi people on the ground; only a closed heart could be unmoved by those stories. But our country remained largely numb.

Media depictions of human tragedies may have momentary impact, but the nation's anesthetic flood of nonstop media encourages us to sense that we're somehow above or beyond the human fray: Some lives, including ours of course, matter a great deal; others, while perhaps touching, are decidedly secondary. The official directives needn't be explicit to be well understood: Do not let too much empathy move in unauthorized directions.

In wartime, mainstream news outlets were more eager than ever to limit the range of discourse. Here's a small example: When U.S. forces took former Iraqi deputy prime minister Tariq Aziz into custody, the *Houston Chronicle* quoted two sentences from me in an April 27 editorial: "Aziz epitomized the urbanity of evil. He was articulate and deft at rationalizing government actions that caused enormous suffering." But the daily newspaper's editorial did not quote the next sentence of my statement, which had appeared in a news release from the Institute for Public Accuracy: "His similarities to top U.S. officials are much greater than we're comfortable acknowledging."

That sort of point was pretty much taboo in U.S. mass media coverage, which sometimes included vehement tactical arguments about the Bush administration's war—but not about the prerogatives of Washington to intervene militarily around the world. A basic media assumption was that leaders in the United States are cut from entirely different cloth than the likes of Tariq Aziz. But in some respects, the terrible compromises made by Aziz are more explainable than the ones that are routine in U.S. politics. Aziz had good reason to fear for his life—and the lives of loved ones—if he ran afoul of Saddam Hussein. In contrast, many politicians and appointed officials in Washington went along with lethal policies merely because of fear that dissent might cost them reelection, prestige, or power.

6

Weapons of Mass Distraction: World Security and Personal Politics

Naren Chitty

I have been invited to provide a view from a diverse multicultural society with an Anglo-Celtic political inheritance—Australia. Two broad streams are represented by front-running Australian political forces: the Liberal-National (conservatives, led by John Howard) and the Labor Party (liberals, led by Simon Crean). Culturally, there are some attitudes that are typically Australian, a healthy skepticism being one that will color this piece. Historically, Australians have not viewed the rough-and-tumble of domestic politics as the natural habitat of truth hounds. Politics was seen as a terrain dotted with half-truths, broken promises, and white lies. Ironically, the more distant and forbidding terrain of world politics presented a different picture. The game of "strategic confrontation," extant from the mid-twentieth century to the twenty-first, had been an area where Australia could note that promises had indeed been kept through the logic of nuclear deterrence. "Collective security," despite and because of the face-off of weapons of mass destruction (WMD), had grown on us like a protective fleece in the climate of the Cold War. Reagan's "Star Wars" policy of "strategic ambiguity" is said to have precipitated the thaw in the Cold War. His *laissez-faire* (leave alone) politics and economics have spread across the world in outbursts of democracy and deregulation. An unhappy by-product has been a hot blast of terrorist-generated "collective insecurity," reaching Australia's neighborhood with the Bali bombing of 2002.

The new "Hot Peace" has come at a time of media's format-driven elastic interest in keeping tabs on the promises and pronouncements of politicians. Bill O'Reilly of FOX News is an example of an effective tab keeper. While Machiavellian expediency continues to shape political behavior, community and media-driven Weberian accountability has waxed important. An effect on the affluent, of today's dangerous peace, is a shift to center-right. In the prioritization of homeland security, natural dissonances emerge in the quartet consisting of political expediency, accountability, freedom, and security. Emerging also are clear limits to the practice of the Machiavellian art. In this chapter I want to remark on the sometimes contradictory imperatives of expedience and accountability, namely, by looking at political ambiguity and strategic ambiguity.

POLITICAL AMBIGUITY

Detaching political theory from ethics, Machiavelli saw a need for rulers to deceive subjects for reasons of state (*raison d'etat*).[1] He has inspired political behavior ever since the sixteenth century, exhorting the ruler to exercise fox-like cunning and leonine strength: "The fox represents a person knowing when he should keep the promises, and how to break his promises when it is necessary to do so. The lion is the symbol of physical power.[2] Nowhere are the strengths of the lion and the fox more crucial than in war. Samuel Johnson wrote that "among the calamities of war may be jointly numbered the diminution of the love of truth, by the falsehoods which interest dictates and credulity encourages" (in *The Idler,* 1758).[3] With the invasion of Iraq only days away, the Melbourne-based *Age* (March 12, 2003) carried a story, at odds with the Johnsonian insight, entitled "Truth Mustn't Be a Casualty." Coalition forces invaded Iraq, offering many justifications: Saddam Hussein was said to have the will and capacity to deploy WMD within forty-five minutes; he was in noncompliance with UN resolutions; and he was an oppressor of his countrymen and countrywomen. Tony Blair, in his opening statement on the Iraq debate (March 18, 2003), said that the weapons inspectors' "final report is a withering indictment of Saddam's lies, deception and obstruction, with large quantities of WMD remained unaccounted for."[4] There were demonstrations for and against the proposed war. Many journalists promoted the invasion, in a spirit of adventurous patriotism, without seeking verification as they might in times of peace. Now that coalition troops are deeply embedded in Iraq, questions are being asked about the veracity of the claims made by coalition leaders. William Kristol, editor of *Weekly Standard*, believes that the president of the United States and the secretary of state might have made misstatements, wanting "to convey the urgency about removing Saddam"; thus, debates and inquiries rage on about "what the public in three countries — the U.S., Britain and Australia — were actually told by their leaders before the war" (*Lateline,* July 17, 2003).

The article in the *Age*, cited earlier, refers to the pre-9/11 (by a matter of weeks) *Tampa,* Afghan-refugee incident, when photographs (allegedly of refugees throwing their children overboard) figured in an Australian election campaign. John Howard is said to have "averted his gaze from the truth that children had not been thrown overboard . . . tapped into emotions of fear."[5] The *Age* noted that Howard had assured Australians that "the truth is that I was never told by my department, by any of my colleagues, or by any other officials, that the original advice that children had been thrown overboard was wrong."[6] Internal misinformation, personal belief, and naïveté are only a few of several credible defenses. In the topsy-turvy world of Machiavelli, truth matters less than credibility. Machiavelli did not view "politics as a matter of uttering the truth, but rather a question of being believed" (Gane and Chan 1997, 69). Another credible defense is the a posteriori prioritization of promises. Howard is brilliant at a posteriori highlighting and deleting of campaign promises. When a policy "violated or appeared to violate many of the pre-election pledges he had made" and "the press accused him of having lied, he stated that some of these had been 'core' promises. 'Non-core' promises would not necessarily be honoured immediately (or at all)."[7] On occasion similar reprioritizations have upset conservative supporters of Howard, such as Reverend Fred Nile (the Australian Jerry Falwell), who knew him as "honest John."[8] President Clinton sought refuge in definitional briar patches.[9] Tony Abbot, an Australian member of Parliament, makes a distinction between deception of media and government: "misleading the ABC is not quite the same as misleading the Parliament as a political crime."[10] American presidents are not princes who inherit or usurp thrones. The folklore of American presidency insists that presidents should be paradigms of honesty. The story of the six-year-old George Washington admitting to hacking his father's prized cherry-tree is well known. When the young George confesses, his father (here read "the American people") applauds his honesty and forgives him.[11] Abraham Lincoln, beloved of Americans and the world, is said to have "brought a new honesty and integrity to the White House. He would always be remembered as 'honest Abe.'"[12] He said "if you once forfeit the confidence of your fellow citizens, you can never regain their respect and esteem."[13] Had Machiavelli said so, rather than Honest Abe, the advice would be viewed as Machiavellian. Contemporary American presidents, more than any other rulers, have a difficult time in taking Machiavelli's counsel.

There are various shades between absolute truth and diabolical lies. Consider the arsenal of terms for expressing that which is not correct, from *misinform, misspeak, misstate,* and *misrepresent* to *doctor, distort, disinform, engage in subterfuge, mislead, package, gild the lily, dissemble, dissimulate, prevaricate, be disingenuous, be duplicitous, fabricate, falsify,* and *deceive,* to name a few. Distraction, opacity, and even transparency can be useful weapons. The strategic game played by Iraq and the United States did not involve equal capabilities or transparencies. U.S. transparency is a double-edged sword in dealing with an opaque opponent such as Saddam Hussein. The much-vaunted "shock and awe" campaign battered Iraqi resolve, and its delivery crippled the regime. At the same time Iraq was able to anticipate American actions and steal a sorry measure of victory out of defeat: Saddam's foxiness kept him and dissent alive months after the official end of the war in Iraq.

Can we, today, do without international dissembling in the national interest? When asked the question of whether Israel's nuclear ambiguity is an acceptable deception, Shimon Peres pointed out in a BBC documentary entitled *Secret Weapons* (2003) that "if someone is trying to kill you, and you use deception—it's not immoral" (ABC, August 21 2003). This is a fundamentally realist argument, a matter of self- or national interest. Peres hastened to point out that there was no moral equivalence between Saddam and Israel. As perceptions of national interest are partially colored by party and self-interest, how do we balance the public cry for accountability with the state's need for acting expediently? At the level of domestic politics in Australia, Britain, and the United States, the electorate knows and accepts that party platforms are riddled with noncore promises. However, utterances in office are scrutinized more carefully by media and therefore by the public. Four reasons for this are offered in the conclusion.

STRATEGIC AMBIGUITY

The philosopher Nietzsche had little time for either liberals or conservatives, regarding liberalism as only a symptom of the timidity of affluent classes; he did not think much of the honesty of conservatives (Gane and Chan 1997, 66). Modern history in Western societies has been shaped by a struggle between conservative and liberal values. The postwar (1939–1945) ecology favored the burgeoning of liberal values in the United States as well as in other Western societies. Interestingly, the mature Cold War provided a hospitable climate for laissez-faire societies, such as Anglo-Celtic countries. Experiencing rising prosperity, Anglo-Celtic societies progressed self-assuredly toward being havens of affluence, multiculturalism, and political correctness. Conservative backlashes under Thatcher and Reagan rode the waves of rising blue-collar conservatism. Liberal incursions into laissez-faire economic territory, in democratic capitalist societies, pushed back conservatives into a traditional heartland of security issues. These were led in the Australian Labor

Party by Hawke and Keating, in the U.S. Democratic Party by Clinton, and in the British Labour Party by Blair. The remaining badges of differentiation, for conservatives, were the issues of national security ("axes of evil") and fiscal conservatism ("taxes of evil"), the latter being germane to the issue of social security.

In the United States, national security issues are tied up with the core value of "defense of liberty" arising from the American War of Independence, when liberty was juxtaposed with tyranny (Chitty 2003, xiv). Barry Goldwater justified disproportionate means to achieve just ends, when the just end is the defense of a core value, when he said, famously, "I would remind you that extremism in the defense of liberty is no vice! And let me remind you also that moderation in the pursuit of justice is no virtue!"[14] A split in public attitudes may be seen in the United States in relation to tolerance or to intolerance of extremism in the defense of core values.

"Strategic ambiguity" related to "Star Wars" expenditure by the Reagan administration prompted reciprocal behavior in the Soviet Union and consequent collapse of that failing empire. The subsequent rise of American-led unipolarity unleashed unparalleled forces of globalization (political and economic modernization within a liberal framework), prompting disquiet in the Islamic world. As we well know, disenchanted traditionalists, particularly extremist Islamists, have resorted to violence. Two new antiglobalization forces stood out among noteworthy dissenters—Islamists and terrorists. Muslims who could not reconcile their faith with the brave new world of globalization were dealt with famously by Huntington in his article "The Clash of Civilisations?" (Huntington 1993). The end of the Cold War appeared to provide geopolitical windows of opportunity. In a liminal moment in world politics, Saddam Hussein, mounted on his steed and firing a gun into the air, emerged as a challenger of established order. In hindsight his invasion of Kuwait was a clear miscalculation. It led to his containment by the first Bush administration. Osama bin Laden also emerged as a challenger. Coalition governments believe that both possess WMD. In a world of mediated politics, WMD become in effect weapons of mass distraction in the struggle between the United States (upholding world security) and international terrorists (spreading world insecurity). For Saddam Hussein, following the path of "strategic ambiguity" (vis-à-vis the United States, his neighbors, and the Kurds and Shiites), WMD were indeed weapons of mass distraction but ones that would incur a heavy price. Just war theory requires there to be a "just cause" for a war:

> The principles of the justice of war are commonly held to be: having just cause, being declared by a proper authority, possessing right intention, having a reasonable chance of success, and the end being proportional to the means used.[15]

WMD, perhaps nonexistent, became this just cause. Was it a case of Saddam crying wolf, about himself, one time too many? The "just cause" that was publicized by the Bush administration was also, reportedly, a banner for rallying individuals with disparate views, a sophisticated exercise in discourse management. "For bureaucratic reasons we settled on one issue, weapons of mass destruction, because it was the one reason everyone could agree on," explained Paul Wolfowitz in the July 2003 issue of *Vanity Fair*.[16] Discourse management is made difficult because of the insistence by the media on truth, and it is made easier because "the organisation of the community for war takes advantage of the concentrated aggressiveness which accumulates in any crisis" (Lasswell 1950, 39). Viewed also by the enemy, media become willing or unwitting extensions of strategic ambiguity. They can also become allies: In the lead-up to the invasion of Iraq, several media in the United States chose not to ask probing questions about WMD claims. Discourse management is also made easier by the fact that "during crises elites value obedience rather than originality" (Lasswell 1950, 120), so the political elite are likely to be supportive of the commander in chief.

While all media today are great distractions, cable television is particularly so because of its appetite for news and its predilection for entertainment, a combination that is seen in its most successful form in FOX News. FOX News is of particular interest as it takes further the rightward-ho gains of Nixon, Reagan, and Gingrich. Nixon conceived of a Republican-voting majority that Reagan and Gingrich later helped forge. Gingrich also made it politically correct to problematize political correctness. FOX News gave neoconservatives an attractive forum for their views, within and outside the Bush administration, in a multiview package during the wars in Afghanistan and Iraq. Rupert Murdoch showed sagacity in selecting Roger Ailes as the founder president of FOX News:

> Fox's founder and president, Roger Ailes, was for decades one of the savviest and most pugnacious Republican political operatives in Washington, a veteran of the Nixon and Reagan campaigns. Ailes is most famous for his role in crafting the elder Bush's media strategy in the bruising 1988 presidential race.[17]

Ailes was able to bring to the Murdoch enterprise the entire constellation of Republican heavyweights from the Reagan–Bush era as FOX News consultants or regular guests. These consultants and guests included Henry Kissinger, Newt Gingrich, George Schultz, and Pat Buchanan. In "The Most Biased Name in News: FOX News Channel's Extraordinary Right-Wing Tilt," Seth Ackerman writes in *FAIR* August 2003,[18] of Sean Hannity of *Hannity & Colmes,* that "co-host Sean Hannity is an effective and telegenic ideologue, a protégé of Newt Gingrich and a rising star of conservative talk radio who is perhaps more plugged into the GOP leadership than any media figure besides Rush Limbaugh."[19] Not surprisingly, the American Right applauds FOX News Channel's "Fair and Balanced" reporting, and the Left views the reporting as partisan. It would appear that each side has a different system of evaluating what is true and that each side has fundamental disagreements about the other side's methods. "Clearly truth and falsehood only makes sense in an agreed system for evaluating what is true."[20] While there are differences within and between our Western polities, there can be greater differences between the West and other societies.

In terms of raison d'etre for joining the coalition, the British, Australian, Spanish, and Italian prime ministers believed that the Saddam Hussein regime posed a clear and present danger that required action forthwith. France, Germany, Russia, and China wanted more UN-led inspections. FOX News star Bill O'Reilly's critique of the French president is a theorization about why some major European powers were unwilling to join the coalition: "'Talking Points' believes President Chirac is a man who does not care about the American people at all, a man who's jealous of U.S. power and who has placed his country's economic interests above the security of Americans."[21] O'Reilly explains his hard-hitting position in a March 23, 2003, article in *Jewish World Review*, suggesting that his behavior comes from his not being an internationalist.

> There are major problems with covering the American war on terror from an internationalist point of view. As a journalist I want to be fair, but I also want President Bush to put the protection of Americans above the economic and political concerns of other countries. . . . So if some egomaniacal leader like Jacques Chirac is going to protect Saddam Hussein because he doesn't like Bush's style, I am going to knock Chirac. Hard.[22]

Even critiques of FOX News can find it compelling, and Jamie Mentis warns "that you are watching because it's entertaining, simple to understand and helps you to relax from a stressful day. FOX allows you to doze off with little mental worry and is cheaper than a prescription for sleeping pills."[23] Conservative voices are less at home on CNN than on FOX News. I have focused here on FOX News because it is so charmingly distracting—Barnes, Cavuto, Colme, Doucey, Kondrache, Hannity, Hill, Hume, Gabler, Kilmeade, Mancow, O'Reilly, Pinkerton, and Thomas are endearing personalities. But other news-only media are also weapons of mass distraction. Can you recall the conditions of news distraction immediately prior to 9/11?

Noam Chomsky would be an unlikely guest on both FOX News and CNN. But he actually debated William Bennett on CNN on May 30, 2002. "Noam Chomsky Unlikely Superstar: How a Left-Wing Anarchy-Libertarian Linguist

Became an International Cult Figure, Thanks to George W. Bush" is the cover headline of *Good Weekend—The Sydney Morning Herald* Magazine (June 24, 2003). In fact Noam Chomsky has been a cult figure of many academics all over the world who have disagreed with American foreign policy, ever since his opposition to the war in Vietnam. But the recent headline is particularly interesting because of Noam Chomsky's critical role in relation to the responses to 9/11 and Saddam Hussein by the Bush–Cheney administration. Writing in the *Sydney Morning Herald*, MacFarquhar writes:

> As Chomsky has become increasingly distanced from the mainstream, though, his role in the American political debate has grown more important, not less. In the '60s, he was one of many protesting against the war; now when he opposes bombing in Afghanistan, he is almost alone. For those who doubt the consensus of the '90s and the war on terrorism, Chomsky is almost the only voice there is. (MacFarquhar 2003, 21)

Like Chomsky, John Pilger may be an unwitting weapon of mass distraction, distracting from policy juggernauts of Washington, London, and Canberra. Are Pilger and Chomsky but annoying distractions for the powers, lightning rods for dissent that do not in fact impede the progress of policy? Pilger appears to be of that view, in terms of short-term effects. In a speech delivered at the antiwar rally in Sydney on February 16, 2003, attended by five hundred thousand people, he recognized that it may not be possible to stop the "Bush gang" immediately. He emphasized however that

> Howard fears public opinion. Blair fears it. Bush fears it. They fear the best of Australia. They fear the best of Britain. They fear the best of America. That's why their propaganda is so virulent and their apologists so shrill. They prefer the old lie that people are apathetic.[24]

If we are to believe the reports of Iraqi information minister Mohammed Saeed al-Sahaf's claims that he had been taken into custody and released (*Sydney Morning Herald* June 28–29, 2003, 19) the temptation might be to surmise that coalition authorities did not view al-Sahaf's fabrications in support of Saddam Hussein as being worthy of punishment. The minister was only managing discourse, exercising in mass distraction; he was not hiding WMD.

CONCLUSION

Fabricating WMD, with real metals and chemicals, is outside the realm of what is ethically permissible, at present, in the defense of liberty. The coalition lions have had every opportunity to plant WMD in Iraq but have not done so. Machiavelli would have frowned at this lapse, but members of coalition countries must applaud our forces and government for not tampering with material evidence. The question of accountability of politicians is one that electorates, civic organizations, and parties need address over a period of time. There can be regimes of both political and economic accountability within laissez-faire societies. There can be a regime of accountability at the international level as well, if the international community, led by the United States, has the will to pursue this. The selective problematization of countries with WMD programs is but a beginning. There also are other issue areas and countries.

I offer four reasons why there is so much attention to truth in politics, in news-only media, today. First, contemporary news-only media have a capacity to record and replay speeches ad nauseam; second, news-only media have an unassuageable appetite for news as entertainment; third, the weapon of accountability is one that ordinary people today like to hold to the heads of politicians and business folk. This may be the lesson of the jailing of One Nation Party founders Pauline Hanson and David Ettridge for three years: A jury convicted them for fraudulently registering One Nation Party in 1997 and "dishonestly obtaining almost $500,000 in electoral reimbursements after One Nation's 11-seat sweep at the 1998 state election."[25] However, many ordinary Australians as well as Howard believe that the punishment does not fit the crime. "Like many other Australians, on the face of it, it does seem a very long unconditional sentence for what she's alleged to have done," he said. "You're dealing here with a breach of the law which is not naturally a crime"—natural crimes being assault, murder, rape, robbery and theft.[26]

The fourth reason came to mind after listening to Neil Gabler and John Pinkerton on *FOX News Watch* on August 24, 2003. They agreed that contemporary journalists seek to hitch their wagons to political stars, as quick routes to personal celebrity, rather than cut their teeth on local social issues. They also seek to hitch their wagons to the cavalry as it charges forward to defend freedom. Less attention is paid to truth in war (as watch dogs), an outcome of which, in the case of Iraq, may very well be that Saddam's WMD plot may has been turned into a shaggy-dog story.

NOTES

1. Retrieved from www.wsu.edu:8080/~dee/REN/MACHIAV.HTM.

2. Retrieved from www.geocities.com/thuyms/essay1.htm.

3. Retrieved from www.guardian.co.uk/notesandqueries/query/0,5753,-21510,00.html.

4. Retrieved from www.number-10.gov.uk/output/Page3294.asp.
5. Retrieved from www.theage.com.au/articles/2003/03/11/1047144969158.html.
6. Retrieved from www.abc.net.au/7.30/s481879.htm.
7. Retrieved from www.wikipedia.org/wiki/John_Howard.
8. Retrieved from www.pastornet.net.au/fwn/1997/may/art08.htm.
9. Retrieved from www.nationalreview.com/goldberg/goldberg092498.html.
10. Retrieved from www.abc.net.au/am/content/2003/s932792.htm.
11. Retrieved from http://gwpapers.virginia.edu/documents/weems/.
12. Retrieved from www.usemb.ee/lincoln.php3.
13. Retrieved from www.panettainstitute.org/Commentaries/031801.htm.
14. Retrieved from http://capmag.com/article.asp?ID=183.
15. Retrieved from www.utm.edu/research/iep/j/justwar.htm.
16. Retrieved from www.blink.org.uk/pdescription.asp?key=2141&grp=2.
17. Retrieved from www.fair.org/extra/0108/fox-main.html.
18. Retrieved from www.fair.org/extra/0108/fox-main.html.
19. Retrieved from www.fair.org/extra/0108/fox-main.html.
20. Retrieved from www.brow.on.ca/Articles/Truth.htm.
21. Retrieved from www.foxnews.com/story/0,2933,80999,00.html.
22. Retrieved from www.jewishworldreview.com/cols/oreilly032403.asp.
23. Retrieved from www.g21.net/amdream59.html.
24. Retrieved from www.greenleft.org.au/back/2003/527/527p28.htm.
25. Retrieved from www.theage.com.au/articles/2003/08/22/1061507084422.html.
26. Retrieved from http://asia.news.yahoo.com/030822/afp/030822072633int.html.

REFERENCES

Chitty, Naren. 2003. "Subject(s) of Terrorism and Media." In *Studies in Terrorism: Media Scholarship and the Enigma of Terror,* edited by Naren Chitty, Ramona R. Rush, and Mehdi Semati. Penang: Southbound.

Gane, Laurence, and Kitty Chan. 1997. *Introducing Nietzsche.* Duxford: Icon Books.

Hammond, Andrew. 2003. "Comical Ali Surfaces with Another Fine Story." *Sydney Morning Herald,* June 28–29, 19.

Huntington, Samuel P. 1993. "The Clash of Civilizations?" *Foreign Affairs,* summer.

Lasswell, Harold. 1950. *Politics: Who Gets What, When, How?* New York: Peter Smith.

MacFarquhar, Larissa. 2003. "Life in the Left Lane." *Good Weekend: The Sydney Morning Herald Magazine*, June 21, 21.

7

Spectacle and Media Propaganda in the War on Iraq: A Critique of U.S. Broadcasting Networks

Douglas Kellner

The 2003 Iraq War was a major global media event constructed very differently by varying broadcasting networks in different parts of the world. While the U.S. networks framed the event as "Operation Iraqi Freedom" (the Pentagon concept) or "War in Iraq," the Canadian CBC used the logo "War on Iraq," and various Arab networks presented it as an "invasion" and "occupation." In this chapter, I provide critique of the U.S. broadcasting network construction of the war, which I interpret as providing a conduit for Bush administration and Pentagon propaganda.[1]

As 2002 unfolded, the Bush administration intensified its ideological war against Iraq, advanced its doctrine of preemptive strikes, and provided military buildup for what now looks like an inevitable war. Whereas the explicit war aims were to shut down Iraq's "weapons of mass destruction" and thus enforce UN resolutions that mandated that Iraq eliminate its offensive weapons, the Bush administration hid many agendas in its offensive against Iraq. To be reelected, Bush needed a major victory and a symbolic triumph over terrorism to deflect from the failings of his regime both domestically and in the realm of foreign policy.

Moreover, ideologues within the Bush administration wanted to legitimate a policy of preemptive strikes, and a successful attack on Iraq could inaugurate and normalize this policy. Some of the same militarist unilateralists in the Bush administration envisage U.S. world hegemony, the elder Bush's "New World Order," with the United States as the reigning military power and world's policeman (Kellner 2003b). Increased control of the world's oil supplies provided a tempting prize for the former oil executives who maintain key roles in the Bush administration. And, finally, one might note the Oedipus Tex drama, where George W. Bush's desires to conclude his father's unfinished business and simultaneously defeat Evil to constitute himself as Good helped drive Bush to war against Iraq with the fervor of a religious crusade.

With all these agendas in play, a war on Iraq appears to have been inevitable. Bush's March 6, 2003, press conference made it evident that he was ready to go to war against Iraq. His handlers told him to speak slowly and keep his big stick and Texas macho out of view, but he constantly threatened Iraq and evoked the rhetoric of good and evil that he used to justify his crusade against bin Laden and al Qaeda. Bush repeated the words "Saddam Hussein" and "terrorism" incessantly, mentioning Iraq as a "threat" at least sixteen times, which he attempted to link with the September 11 attacks and terrorism. He used the word "I" as in "I believe" countless times, and he talked of "my government" as if he owned it, depicting a man lost in words and self-importance, positioning himself against the "evil" that he was preparing to wage war against. Unable to make an intelligent and objective case for a war against Iraq, Bush could only invoke fear and a moralistic rhetoric, attempting to present himself as a strong nationalist leader.

Bush's rhetoric, like that of fascism, deploys a mistrust and hatred of language, reducing it to manipulative speechifying, speaking in codes, repeating the same phrases over and over. This is grounded in anti-intellectualism and hatred of democracy and intellectuals. It is clearly evident in Bush's press conferences and snitty responses to questions and general contempt for the whole procedure. It plays to anti-intellectual proclivities and tendencies in the extreme conservative and fundamentalist Christian constituencies who support him. It appears that Bush's press conference was orchestrated to shore up his base and prepare his supporters for a major political struggle rather than to marshal arguments to convince those opposed to go to war with Iraq that it was a good idea to do so. He displayed, against his will, the complete poverty of his case to go to war against Iraq; he had no convincing arguments, nothing new to communicate, and just repeated the same tired clichés over and over.

Bush's discourse also displayed Orwellian features of doublespeak, where war against Iraq is for peace, the occupation of Iraq is its liberation, destroying its food and water supplies enables "humanitarian" action, and where the murder of countless Iraqis and destruction of the country will produce "freedom" and "democracy." In a prewar summit with Tony Blair in the Azores and in his first talk after the bombing began, Bush went on and on about the "coalition of the willing" and about how many countries were supporting and participating in the "allied" effort. In fact, however, it was a "Coalition of Two," with the United States and the United Kingdom doing most of the fighting and with many of the countries that Bush claimed supported his war quickly backtracking and expressing reservations about the highly unpopular assault that was strongly opposed by most people and countries in the world.

On March 19, the media spectacle of the war against Iraq unfolded with a dramatic attempt to "decapitate" the Iraqi regime. Large numbers of missiles were aimed at targets in Baghdad where Saddam Hussein and the Iraqi leadership were believed to be staying, and the tens of thousands of ground troops on the Kuwait–Iraq border poised for invasion entered Iraq in a blitzkrieg toward Baghdad.[2] The media followed the Bush administration and Pentagon slogan of "shock and awe" and presented the war against Iraq as a great military spectacle, while triumphalism marked the opening days of the U.S. bombing of Iraq and invasion.

The Al-Jazeera network's live coverage of the bombing of a palace belonging to the Hussein family was indeed shocking, as loud explosions and blasts jolted viewers throughout the world. Whereas some Western audiences experienced this bombing positively as a powerful assault on "evil," for Arab audiences it was experienced as an attack on the body of the Arab and Muslim people, just as the September 11 terror attacks were experienced by Americans as assaults on the very body and symbols of the United States. During Gulf War I, CNN was the only network live in Baghdad, and throughout the war it framed the images, discourses, and spectacle. For the 2003 Iraq War, there were over twenty broadcasting networks in Baghdad, including several Arab networks, and the different television companies presented the war quite diversely.

Al-Jazeera and other Arab networks, as well as some European networks, talked of an "invasion" and of an illegal U.S. and British assault on Iraq. While Donald Rumsfeld bragged that the bombings were the most precise in history and were aimed at military and not civilian targets, Arab and various global broadcasting networks focused on civilian casualties and presented painful spectacles of Iraqis' suffering. Moreover, to the surprise of many, after a triumphant march across the Kuwaiti border and rush to Baghdad, the U.S. and British forces began to take casualties, and during the weekend of March 22–23, images of POWs and soldiers' dead bodies were shown throughout the world. Moreover, the Iraqis began fiercely resisting, and rather than cheer for British and U.S. forces to enter the southern city of Basra, the Iraqis demonstrated fierce resistance throughout southern Iraq.

Soon after, an immense sandstorm slowed the march to Baghdad, and creating a tremendously dramatic story were the now available images of Iraqi civilians maimed or killed by U.S. and British bombing, accounts of mishaps, stalled and overextended supply lines, and unexpected dangers to the invading forces. The intensity and immediacy of the spectacle was multiplied by "embedded reporters" who were accompanying the U.S. and British forces and who beamed back live pictures, first of the triumphant blitzkrieg through Iraq and then of the invading forces stalling and becoming subject to perilous counterattack.

A great debate emerged around the embedded reporters' ability to be objective when such journalists depended on the protection of the U.S. and British military, lived with the troops, and signed papers agreeing to a rigorous set of restrictions on their reporting. From the beginning, it was clear that the embedded reporters were indeed "in bed with" their military escorts, and as the U.S. and Britain stormed into Iraq, the reporters presented exultant and triumphant accounts that trumped any paid propagandist. The embedded U.S. network television reporters were gung-ho cheerleaders and spinners for the U.S. and U.K. military and lost any veneer of objectivity. But the blitzkrieg stalled, as a sandstorm hit, and U.S. and British forces soon came under attack. It was during this time that the embedded reporters reflected genuine fear, helped capture the chaos of war, provided often vivid accounts of the fighting, and occasionally deflated propaganda lies of the U.S. or U.K. military (more on this later).

Indeed, U.S. and British military discourse was exceptionally mendacious, as happens so often in recent wars that are as much for public opinion and political agendas as they are for military goals. British and U.S. sources claimed that during the first days into Iraq the border port of Umm Qasar and the major southern city of Basra were under coalition control, whereas television images showed quite the opposite. When things went very badly for U.S. and British forces on March 23, a story originated from an embedded reporter with the *Jerusalem Post* that a "huge" chemical weapons production facility was found, a story allegedly confirmed by a Pentagon source to the FOX television military correspondent who quickly spread it through the U.S. media (BBC was skeptical from the beginning).[3]

When U.S. officials denied that they were responsible for major civilian atrocities in two Baghdad bombings during the week of March 24, reporters on the scene described witnesses who saw planes flying overhead; and in one case, journalists found pieces of a missile with U.S. markings and numbers on it. And after a suicide bombing killed four U.S. troops at a checkpoint in late March, U.S. soldiers killed seven civilians by firing on a vehicle that ran a checkpoint. The U.S. military claimed that it had fired a warning shot, but a *Washington Post* reporter on the scene reported that a senior U.S. military official had shouted to a younger soldier to fire a warning shot first; but when the young soldier failed to do so, the official yelled, "You [expletive] killed them." Embedded newspaper reporters also often provided more-vivid accounts of "friendly fire" and other mishaps, getting their information from troops on the ground and on the site, instead of from military spinners, who tended to be propagandists.[4]

Hence, the embedded reporters and other on-site journalists provided documentation of the more raw and brutal aspects of war and likewise gave telling accounts that often put into question official versions of the events, namely, bringing to light propaganda and military spin. But since their every posting and broadcast was censored by the U.S. military, it was the independent, "unilateral" journalists who provided the most accurate account of the horrors of the war and of the Coalition of Two military mishaps. Thus, on the whole, the embedded journalists were largely propagandists who often outdid the Pentagon and the Bush administration in spinning the message of the moment.

Moreover, the U.S. broadcast networks, on the whole, tended to be more embedded in the Pentagon and in the Bush administration than were the reporters in the field and print journalists. The military commentators on all networks provided little more than the Pentagon spin of the moment and often repeated gross lies and propaganda, as in the examples mentioned here concerning the U.S. bombing of civilians or the checkpoint shooting of innocents. Entire networks, such as the FOX and NBC cable networks, provided little but propaganda and one-sided patriotism, as did, for the most part, CNN. All these twenty-four/seven cable networks, as well as the big three U.S. broadcasting networks, tended to provide highly sanitized views of the war, rarely showing Iraqi casualties, thus producing a view of the war totally different from that shown in other parts of the world.

The dramatic story of "Saving Private Lynch" was one of the more spectacular human-interest stories of the war that revealed the constructed and spectacle nature of the event and the ways that the Pentagon constructed mythologies to be replicated by the television networks. Private Jessica Lynch was one of the first American POWs shown on Iraqi television, and since she was young, female, and attractive, her fate became a topic of intense interest. Stories circulated that she was shot and stabbed and then tortured by Iraqis holding her in captivity.[5] Eight days after her capture, the U.S. media broadcast footage of her dramatic rescue, obviously staged like a spectacle on reality television. Soldiers stormed the hospital, found Lynch, and claimed a dramatic rescue under fire from Iraqis. In fact, several media institutions interviewed the doctors in the hospital, who claimed that Iraqi troops had left the hospital two days before; that the hospital staff had tried to take Jessica to the Americans but that they fired on them; and that in the "rescue" the U.S. troops shot through the doors, terrorized doctors and patients, and created a dangerous scene that could have resulted in deaths, simply to get some dramatic rescue footage for television audiences.[6]

The FOX network was especially gung-ho, militarist, and aggressive, yet the FOX footage shown on April 5–6 of the daring U.S. incursion into Baghdad displayed a road strewn with destroyed Iraqi vehicles, burning buildings, and Iraqi corpses. This live footage, replayed for days, caught something of the carnage of the hi-tech slaughter and destruction of Iraq that the U.S. networks tended to neglect. And an Oliver North commentary to footage of a U.S. warplane blasting away one Iraqi tank and armored vehicle after another put on display the hi-tech massacre of a completely asymmetrical war in which the Iraqi military had no chance whatsoever against the U.S. war machine.

U.S. military commanders claimed that in the initial foray into Baghdad two thousand to three thousand Iraqis were killed, suggesting that the broadcasting networks were not really showing the brutality and carnage of the war. Indeed, most of the bombing of Iraqi military forces was invisible, and dead Iraqis were rarely shown. An embedded CNN reporter, Walter Rogers, later recounted that during the one time his report showed a dead Iraqi, the CNN switchboard "lit up like a Christmas tree," with angry viewers demanding that CNN not show any dead bodies, as if the U.S. audience wanted to be in denial concerning the human costs of the war.[7]

An April 6 interview on FOX with *Forbes* magazine publisher and former presidential candidate Steve Forbes made it clear that the United States intended to get all the contracts on rebuilding Iraq for American firms, that Iraqi debts held by French and Russians should be canceled, and that to the victors would go all the spoils of war. Such discourse put on display the arrogance and greed that drove the U.S. effort and subverted all idealistic rhetoric about democracy and freedom for the Iraqis. The very brutality of FOX war pornography graphically displayed the horrors of war and the militarist, gloating, and barbaric discourse that accompanied the slaughter of Iraqis, and the graphic destruction of the country showed the new barbarism that characterized the Bush era.[8]

Comparing American broadcasting networks with the BBC, Canadian, and other outlets (as I did during the opening weeks of the U.S. war against Iraq) showed two different wars being presented. The U.S. networks tended to ignore Iraqi casualties, Arab outrage about the war, global antiwar and anti-U.S. protests, and the negative features of the war; however, the BBC and the CBC often featured these more critical themes. As noted, the war was framed quite differently by various countries and networks, while analysts noted that in Arab countries the war was presented as an invasion of Iraq, a slaughter of its peoples, and a destruction of the country.

On the whole, U.S. broadcasting networks tended to present a sanitized view of the war while Arab, Canadian, British, and other European broadcasters presented copious images of civilian casualties and the horrors of war. U.S. television coverage tended toward promilitary patriotism, propaganda, and technological fetishism, celebrating the weapons of war and military humanism, highlighting the achievements and heroism of the U.S. troops. However, other global broadcasting networks were highly critical of the U.S. and U.K. militaries and often presented highly negative spectacles of the assault on Iraq and the hi-tech, shock-and-awe-type massacre.

In a sense, the U.S. and U.K. war on Iraq found itself in a double bind. The more thoroughly they annihilated Iraqi troops and conquered the country, the more aggressive, bullying, and imperialist they would appear to the rest of the world. Yet the dramatic pictures of civilian casualties and harrowing images of U.S. bombing and destruction of Iraq made it imperative to end the war as soon as possible. Producing an extremely negative media spectacle of the war on Iraq were an apparently failed attempt to kill Saddam Hussein and the Iraqi leadership on April 7, which destroyed a civilian area and killed a number of people, and the U.S. military's inadvertent killing of journalists in two separate episodes on April 8. But the apparent collapse of the Iraqi regime on April 9, where for the first time there were significant images of Iraqis' celebrating the demise of Hussein, provided the material for a spectacle of victory.

Indeed, the destruction of a statue of Saddam Hussein on live global television provided precisely the images desired by the Pentagon and the Bush administration. Closer analysis of this spectacle revealed, however, that rather than display a mass uprising of Iraqis against the Baath regime, there were relatively few people assaulting the Hussein statue. Analysis of the pictures in the square revealed that there was only a relatively small crowd around the statue of Saddam Hussein while most of the square was empty. Those attacking the statue were largely members of the U.S.-supported Iraqi National Congress, one of whose members shown in the crowd attempted to pass himself off as the "mayor" of Baghdad, until U.S. military forces restrained him. Moreover, the few Iraqis attacking the statue were unable to destroy it, until some U.S. soldiers on the scene used their tank and cable to pull it down. In a semiotic slip, one soldier briefly put a U.S. flag on top of Hussein's head, providing an iconic image for Arab networks and others of a U.S. occupation and takeover of Iraq.

Subsequent images of looting, anarchy, and chaos throughout Iraq—including the looting of the National Museum; the National Archive, which contained rare books and historical documents; and the Ministry for Religious Affairs, which contained rare religious material—created extremely negative impressions.[9] Likewise, growing Iraqi demonstrations over the U.S. occupation and continued violence throughout the country put on view a highly uncertain situation in which the spectacle of victory and the triumph of Bush administration and Pentagon policy might be put into question, domestically as well as globally.

For weeks after the fall of the Iraqi regime, negative images continued to circulate of clashes between Iraqis and the U.S. forces, of gigantic Shia demonstrations and celebrations that produced the specter of a growing radical Islamic power in the region, and of the continued failure to produce security and stability. The spectacle of Shia on the march and taking over power in many regions of the country created worries that "democracy" in Iraqi could produce religious fundamentalist regimes. This negative spectacle suggests the limitations of a politics that can backfire, spiral out of control, and generate unintended consequences.

Indeed, in Gulf War I, the Iraqi flight from its occupation of Kuwait and the United States' apparent military defeat of the Iraqi regime were followed by images of Shi'ite and Kurdish uprisings and their violent suppression by the Saddam Hussein regime, ultimately coding the Gulf War as ambiguous and contributing to George H. W. Bush's defeat in 1992. Likewise, while the September 11 terror attacks on the United States by the al Qaeda network appeared to be a triumph of the Islamic radicals, worldwide revulsion against the attacks and the global and multilateral attempts to close down its networks ultimately appear to have seriously weakened the al Qaeda forces. Politics of the spectacle are thus complex and unstable, subject to multiple interpretations, and generate ambiguous and often unanticipated effects, such as when the Republican attempts to use Bill Clinton's sexual escapades to promote his impeachment backfired and created sympathy and support for him.

Media spectacles can backfire and can become subject to dialectical reversal, as positive images give way to negative ones. Spectacles of war are difficult to control and manage, and they can be subject to different framings and interpretations, such as when non-U.S. broadcasting networks focus on civilian casualties, looting and chaos, and U.S. military crimes against Iraqis rather than on the U.S. victory and the evils of Saddam Hussein. It is obviously too soon to determine the effects of Bush Junior's Iraq War, but the consequences are likely to be complex and unforeseen, thus rendering claims that the adventure represents a great victory premature and one possibly quite erroneous.

NOTES

1. For my previous studies of war, media, and propaganda, see *The Persian Gulf TV War* (1992) and *From 9/11 to Terror War: Dangers of the Bush Legacy* (2003b). For my daily Internet commentary on the media, Bush administration, Iraq, and other topics, see BlogLeft at www.gseis.ucla.edu/courses/ed253a/blogger.php.

2. On May 29, 2003, CBS News reported that no evidence was found (no bunker, no bodies, nothing) that Saddam Hussein or his family was at the site bombed the opening night of the war.

3. Soon after, British and then U.S. military sources affirmed that the site was not a chemical-weapons production or storage facility. For a critique of a series of "smoking gun" discoveries of weapons of mass destruction facilities and their subsequent debunking, see Jake Tapper, "WMD, MIA?" *Salon,* April 16, 2003; and "Angry Allies" *Salon,* May 30, 2003.

4. On the Baghdad bombings, see the reporting of Robert Fisk in the London *Independent,* and for the story that questioned official U.S. military accounts of the checkpoint shootings of a civilian family, see William Branigin, "A Gruesome Scene on Highway 9," *Washington Post,* April 1, 2003.

5. An April 3 *Washington Post* story was headlined "She Was Fighting to Her Death," and it was based on unnamed military sources that claimed that Lynch "continued firing at the Iraqis even after she sustained multiple gunshot wounds" and that she was also stabbed by Iraqis who captured her. In fact, Lynch's vehicle took a wrong turn, overturned, and she was hurt in the accident, not by fighting Iraqis.

6. See Mitch Potter, "The Real 'Saving Pte. Lynch,'" *Toronto Star,* May 5, 2003; the Associated Press also confirmed this story, as did the BBC on May 15 and CBS News on May 29.

7. Rogers was interviewed on Howard Kurtz's poorly named, CNN media review "Reliable Sources," on April 27, 2003.

8. For systematic analysis of the new barbarism accompanying and in part generated by the Bush administration and their hard-right supporters, see my *From 9/11 to Terror War: Dangers of the Bush Legacy* (2003b). See also, Jim Rutenberg, "Cable's War Coverage Suggests a New 'FOX Effect' on Television," *New York Times,* April 16, 2003. Rutenberg provides examples of FOX's aggressively opinionated and biased discourse, as when anchor Neil Cavuto said of those who oppose the war on Iraq: "You were sickening then, you are sickening now." FOX's high ratings during the war influenced CNN and the NBC networks to be more patriotic and dismissive of those who criticized the war and its aftermath.

9. Evidently, the museum community thought it had an understanding with the U.S. military of the need to preserve Iraqi national treasures, which ultimately were allowed by the U.S. military to be looted and destroyed while they protected the Petroleum Ministry; see www.nytimes.com/2003/04/16/international/worldspecial/16MUSE .html?pagewanted=print&position=. On the looting of the Ministry for Religious Affairs, see www.nytimes.com/2003/04/16/international/worldspecial/16BAGH.html? pagewanted=print&position=. Later reports indicated that some of the museum artifacts believed destroyed were hidden, but there were also reports of continued looting of Iraqi archaeological sites throughout the country that were not protected by the United States; see Edmund L. Andrews, "Iraqi Looters Tearing Up Archaeological Sites," *New York Times,* May 23, 2003.

REFERENCES

Kellner, Douglas. 1992. *The Persian Gulf TV War.* Boulder, Colo.: Westview Press.

——. 2003a. *Media Spectacle.* New York: Routledge.

——. 2003b. *From 9/11 to Terror War: Dangers of the Bush Legacy.* Boulder, Colo.: Rowman and Littlefield.

8

War as Promotional "Photo Op": The *New York Times*'s Visual Coverage of the U.S. Invasion of Iraq

Lee Artz

The most dramatic image of the 2003 U.S. war on Iraq was the toppling of Saddam Hussein's statue. That picture has already become a propaganda icon, declared the equivalent of the fall of the Berlin Wall by U.S. secretary of defense Donald Rumsfeld, NBC's Tom Brokaw, and other news media celebrities. The photo quickly became the most critiqued photo of the war as well. Other pictures of the event revealed that the "historic" moment was actually a staged propaganda event, orchestrated by the U.S. military, with willing U.S.-partisan participants as cast members, and ultimately close-cropped by media gatekeepers, obscuring its limited, distorted, representation of Iraqi passions ("The Photographs Tell the Story" 2003).

The falling Hussein statue was certainly an obvious favorable visual of the U.S. war, an image that warmed the patriotic hearts of millions and undoubtedly pleased the image makers in the administration. Yet, closely observing other photographs of the war suggests that in many respects the more commonplace visuals were more effective as propaganda. Visuals with less clearly aesthetic or political appeal, such as snapshots of soldiers' daily lives in Iraq, helped confirm the moral rightness and military superiority of the United States. Specifically, a survey of the *New York Times*'s coverage of the first full week of the U.S. attack on Iraq, March 24–28, 2003, discovered 241 graphic images, including drawings, charts, maps, and photographs that overwhelmingly depicted visual images supportive of the war. The *New York Times* provided readers with a slick "poster war," consisting of reassuring prowar images, including maps, drawings, and especially photographs. Such images were an important tool in the United States' domestic propaganda campaign on the Iraq War; these photographs brought home particular versions of events—versions that legitimated the United States' "preventive" war drive.

Photographs and drawings in the *New York Times* are perhaps the most revealing instances of media's complicity with U.S. propaganda because presumably the *Times* sets the standard for objective journalism. Its reputation for accuracy, thoroughness, impartiality, and independence, with its international distribution and influence among policy makers, make the *New York Times* a most authoritative news source. For scholars and historians, the *New York Times* is considered the newspaper of record. Ten years from now, the *New York Times* will be the authority on what happened today. Yet, despite its editorial dissatisfaction with the Bush administration's political strategy on Iraq, the *New York Times* lined up with the rest of corporate media in promoting the war, its position exposed by its visual coverage of the beginning of the attack, from March 20 to March 28, 2003. One could do a content analysis of the news text, identifying sources and evaluating word choice, headlines, layout, and other indicators of bias. Likewise, one could analyze selected visual images in terms of captions, size, color, layout, and other characteristics. A fuller analysis would likely even consider how photographs, other visuals, and text semantically and rhetorically constructed political arguments about the validity of the war. I also suspect that a more thorough study would further demonstrate the function of *New York Times*'s visuals in aiding and abetting the U.S. war drive. However, by limiting the investigation to one week of all war-related published graphic images (March 23–28, 2003)—regardless of size, location, color, caption, or other variable affecting persuasive appeal—this study was less ambitious but ultimately quite revealing about the political perspective of the *New York Times* regarding the 2003 U.S. war on Iraq. Without any "presumption of veracity that gives all photographs authority, interest, seductiveness" (Sontag 1977, 6), the conclusions discovered relied simply on the observation that some photographs and graphic drawings were selected, whereas others were not. The visuals that were featured purported to show us what was happening in Iraq and helped shape our understanding of the purpose of the war, the conduct of the war, and the role of the troops. The findings of this study, presented here and summarized in table 8.1, acquire more meaning if understood in the context of the power of photographs to communicate and persuade.

Politicians, propagandists, and researchers have long recognized the communicative efficacy of visuals. And using visuals to blur the "boundaries between truth and myth certainly did not begin with the current Bush administration"—for instance, Alexander the Great reportedly placed large breastplates of armor on his troops to convince the enemy that his soldiers were giants (Rampton and Stauber 2003a, 17). Graphics, posters, cartoons, films, and photographs have demonstrated their ability to convince, reassure, and challenge viewers on the justification and conduct of war (e.g., Artz and Pollock 1995). "Politicians use symbolism to engage the popular imagination which has no recourse to direct experience" (Grosswiler 1997) because "in the battlefield of public opinion . . . images are as potent as bullets" (A. Sabar, quoted in Rampton and Stauber 2003b, 21). Photographs in particular attract public attention and suggest truths. Sontag writes that photographs have an unstated but largely unchallenged presumption of validity: "they do not seem to be statements about the world so much as pieces of it, miniatures of reality" (1977, 4). Karl Rove, Paul Wolfowitz, Charlotte Beers, Hill and Knowlton, the Rendon Group, and other spin doctors can manipulate language and explanation, but pictures? Pictures are taken by cameras that capture reality. Photos record the real: "incontrovertible, as no verbal account, however impartial, could be—since a machine [is] doing the recording" (Sontag 2003, 26). Without words, photographs tell us how things really are.

Photographs furnish evidence. "A photograph passes for incontrovertible proof. . . . The picture may distort; but there is always a presumption that a given thing happened" (Sontag 1977, 5). The photograph even has a "deeper bite" than do movies or television, according to Sontag (2003), because they "freeze-frame" events in a single image: "in an era of information overload, the photograph provides a quick way of apprehending something and a compact form of memorizing it" (22). An event becomes real to those following it as news, by being photographed—that which is not photographed is not "real" to those same viewers.

Although photographs appear as objective visual statements, they are actually visual constructions. "Lighting, angle, focus, and other presentational forms communicate meaning in photographs," even for viewers conscious of the techniques used (Messaris, 182). Visuals may also be more persuasive than other persuasive devices: "A verbal slogan "strong leader" may not be as effective as a campaign picture showing the person from a low camera angle—which may evoke impressions of power toward the photo subject" (Messaris, 183). Witness Secretary of State Colin Powell's February 2003 address at the United Nations. In addition to covering the "troublesome" visual hanging in the General Assembly—Picasso's antiwar painting *Guernica*—logistic planners worked to stage the speech with the most favorable lighting, angle, and setting. Visual aids to Powell's speech, from the cartoon trucks to the vial of powder suggesting anthrax, offered striking visual evidence for his narrative claims regarding the need for war. Despite the late-night comics' rendering of Powell's graphics, most news accounts featured his visuals in effusive praise of his speech.

Visuals tend to enter our consciousness with less reflection than do textual accounts and often with more impact on our understanding; photos avoid prolonged complex debate (Robertson 1994, 105). As Barthes (1988) suggested, "Images persuade by the logic of the unconscious" (141). Consider how some war photos have presented events in such a way to sway and mobilize public sentiment: the grand photos of officer picnics during the Crimean War reassured Brits of their noble intentions; the Vietnamese girl napalmed by U.S. forces confirmed antiwar sentiments; the filmed assassination of an ABC journalist by a Nicaraguan National Guardsman clarified the brutality of the U.S.-backed Somoza dictatorship; or even, more recently, the *Top Gun* moment of the U.S. commander in chief, President George W. Bush, landing in full flight gear on an aircraft carrier, momentarily cheered by citizens anticipating an early end to the U.S. war in Iraq.

Photojournalists, of course, cannot always be in the photo-perfect place at the photo-perfect moment, as suggested by frequent reenactment shots that reach the public eye—such as the reconstruction of the raising of the (bigger) flag at Iwo Jima, which won a Pulitzer Prize. Yet, the power of photography may not depend on the singular great shot, any more than the rhetorical power of a propaganda campaign rests on one particular speech. Indeed, many weeks before Hussein and his statue fell, newspapers and news magazines were distributing hundreds of war photos—many supplied by the Pentagon. During the March–April 2003 invasion, the Pentagon had its own "Combat Camera" film crew of "combatants as journalists," providing hundreds of photos and videos to news media outlets: "photos of sleek fighter jets, rescued POWs, and smiling Iraqis cheering the arrival are easy to find among Combat Camera's public images. Photos of bombed-out Baghdad neighborhoods and so-called 'collateral damage' are not" (A. Sabar, quoted in Rampton and Stauber 2003b, 21).

Of course, if governments had their way, war photography would always drum up support for the campaign. During the first Gulf War, the Pentagon "controlled almost every aspect of the coverage the American public saw . . . disturbing images that reminded us that war is brutal or that U.S. goals questionable rarely were published in the U.S." (Howe 2002, 25), but the United States did not need to order photojournalists to record favorable images in 2003. They were simply "embedded" with the troops. The Pentagon "allowed" reporters to travel with military units, first, because it understood that media coverage would shape public perception and, second, because such coverage was being guided by former Hill and Knowlton public relations executive Victoria Clarke (now a CNN analyst) as the U.S. assistant secretary of defense for public affairs. With these "embedded" journalists, the Pentagon sent its own public relations officers, who, according to *PR Week*, helped manage the reporters by steering them toward stories and by facilitating interviews and photo opportunities (Rampton and Stauber 2003b, 21). In other words, neither the press pools of Gulf War I nor overt censorship was needed to market the war to the public.

Although objectivity seems built into photographs, they still necessarily always have a point of view. That point of view physically depends on the actual location from which reporters witness events. In this war, embedded journalists saw the war only from the point of view of U.S. troops; there was almost no U.S. reporting from Iraqi cities. "Sheer genius," commented U.S. public relations consultant Katie Delahaye Paine, saying that embedded reporters

> have been spectacular, bringing the war into our living rooms like never before
> . . . The tactic is based on the basic tenet of public relations: It's all about relationships. The better the relationship any of us has with a journalist, the better the chance of that journalist picking up and reporting our messages. So now we have journalists making dozens—if not hundred—of new friends among the armed forces. (quoted in Rampton and Stauber 2003b, 22)

It turns out to have been an effective propaganda adjustment: in 2003, news media outlets certified the Gulf War according to Pentagon outtakes—few photos showed actual fighting, as one might expect from previous war photojournalism. Indeed, the predominant message in news photos from the first weeks of the war was that of a giant training exercise: sophisticated weaponry in the setting sun; determined soldiers on scouting patrols; photogenic boys and girls in desert fatigues just wanting to have fun and just doing their jobs.

Photojournalism occupies a crucial political role in domestic propaganda for U.S. foreign policy. Using numerous studies covering foreign policy from 1950 through the 1980s, Grosswiler (1997) observes that "for most U.S. residents, knowledge and perceptions of international events depend on how those events and issues are symbolized in the media" (196). This war is no different: there can be little doubt that public attention was steered by the presentations of the media—especially the decisive and redundant images that appeared on television, in newspapers, and in newsmagazines—and those images fit the propaganda goals of the war makers. The image flow of videos, photographs, and graphic illustrations in the early days of the war held our attention, but the tension was muted. Until the staged fall of the Hussein statue, no single image was privileged; rather, the overall flow of comfortable images massaged anxiety and calmed fears. In prior conflicts, war often appeared as spectacle in media accounts (Sontag 2003), but in this case, U.S. news of the war was converted into a patriotic confection, suggesting (except for one brief, on Monday, March 31) that there was no real suffering in Operation Iraqi Freedom.

Almost uniformly, cable talk shows, network news, and major daily U.S. newspapers trumpeted the administration's daily line. For propaganda effectiveness, however, the banal visuals published in the *New York Times* during first weeks of war did as much to promote the war as did the more strident jingoism of any breathless FOX News reporter or loud talk-show pundit. Like the decision to cover up Picasso's antiwar painting *Guernica* at the UN, the *New York Times* shielded the public from other unpleasant challenges to U.S. war appeals. In the special daily supplements, the *New York Times* presented the U.S. war as a Middle East travelogue—pictures of soldiers at play in the desert reassured readers of the United States' good will and power. If the camera is the eye of history, as Civil War photograph Matthew Brady once said, then the U.S. history of the invasion of Iraq in 2003 will be told with photographs taken from the perspective of Pentagon and administration publicists.

From March 20, 2003, the day following the beginning of the U.S. invasion, through the end of April 2003, the *New York Times* expanded its coverage, adding a special twelve-page section, A Nation at War (March 23–28, 2003), to its weekday editions. In the sixty-five pages of coverage during the first full week of A Nation at War, 241 visuals were published. They included photographs, maps, drawings, charts, and other graphic renderings of war-related topics (see table 8.1).

Table 8.1. Photographic and Graphic Images Appearing Front Page and in Section B, "A Nation at War" (quantity and percentage)

Image	Quantity	Percentage
U.S./U.K. soldiers at the ready	68	28%
U.S. POWs, wounded, or families of,	49	20
Maps, charts, drawings of military equipment	36	15
Iraqi civilians	28	12
Fleeing, seeking refugee or relief	16	
Friendly (waving, smiling)	7	
Unfriendly (jeering, angry, agitated)	5	
Vox populi, including former generals	22	9
Non-U.S. persons	5	
U.S. officials and former officials	21	9
Kurds	10	4
Other persons unclassified in listed categories	9	4
Iraqi POWs	7	3
War photos (explosions)	6	2
Iraqi troops	3	1
Iraqi civilians wounded	2	—
Iraqi soldier dead	1	—

Source: *New York Times*, March 24–28, 2003.
Note: Total photos, graphics, maps, drawings, and other nontext visuals: 241.

Sixty-eight photos (28 percent of the total, the largest subject category) featured United States or United Kingdom soldiers at the ready. Although this was war, the soldiers photographed were not in active combat. Photos included soldiers riding in vehicles, walking in groups, or prone behind bunkers and other cover—*none* of these sixty-eight photos pictured soldiers shooting, firing artillery, throwing grenades, or engaging in any other violent act directed at an enemy target. Photographs published were undoubtedly real, but their content could just as easily have been simulated. Network television viewers would have seen more violence on any weeknight drama than did readers of the *New York Times* during the entire first week of the war. Photos showed soldiers having fun at war: laughing and hovering over computers; enjoying videos of attack jets; shaving their heads; reading novels; flying kites in a sandstorm; distributing water and candy to children. War may be hell, but it's not particularly unpleasant, according to *New York Times*'s news photos.

One example is the color photo in column 1 on the front page of A Nation at War, March 23. Measuring seven inches high, it features the silhouettes of four soldiers talking, standing against a picturesque background of a glowing setting sun, a red and gold sky, and a cluster of billowy gray-white clouds. A travel photo could not have been staged more carefully. A special feature of in all issues of A Nation at War was the inside, two-page centerfold (8–9). On March 23, the centerfold subtitle was "The Faces of War," and it presented ten full-color photos—including six shots of soldiers at the ready: crouching, peering, kicking down a door, unloading supplies; one in particular showed a close-up of a British marine firing a missile to destination unknown. The largest photo of the centerfold, right side above the fold, displays a dramatic bird's-eye of the aircraft carrier *USS Abraham Lincoln*, with shiny jetfighters neatly lined up on deck, a blue sea rippling below. If not already available through the Pentagon's Combat Camera, it should be purchased for military recruitment centers across the country.

Other editions of A Nation at War offer similar representations of combat-ready soldiers engaged in noncombat activities. On Friday, March 28, the front page of the section (B1) highlights female soldiers via four snapshots: one woman, with thoughtful expression, holds a small U.S. flag; a female marine carries her gear across the tarmac; a soldier with goggles, a red helmet, and a vest poses in front of a missile (an echo of the *Times* March 21 special report on military gear and apparel); and one woman, hair akimbo, inspects her gas mask. On March 26, the *Times*'s front page and first page of section B consisted of four color photos: tanks in a sandstorm; U.S. soldiers after the capture of 170 Iraqis (none of whom are shown); a photo of ten marines preparing to enter the hospital where the Iraqis were reportedly hiding (again, no Iraqis and no battle scenes); and finally, below the fold, a photo of a wounded U.S. soldier being carried on a stretcher. The featured visual on the front page of A Nation at War on March 27 focuses on President Bush waving to soldiers at a MacDill Air Force Base gathering. Bush is in sharp camera focus, the throng of soldiers blurred, and a glistening, sleek fighter jet appears across half of the pagewide spread: soldiers at the ready await orders from their commander in chief, military technology available. Long before Bush did his *Top Gun* routine on the *Abraham Lincoln,* he was posed and photographed by an eager media, including the *New York Times*—in each case, troops provided the backdrop, the visual linchpin that communicates the connection between the administration, the willing soldier, and a policy of war.

But war is not all fun and games, despite what army recruiters and more than one-quarter of all war visuals in the *New York Times* might suggest. Forty-nine photographs published during the first week of the war (20 percent of all visual images during this period) were photographs of U.S. soldiers and of families of soldiers who had been wounded or captured. Missing soldiers and known POWs appeared in austere photographs, dressed in fatigues or uniforms; families always appeared solemn—never distraught—usually in group shots (as illustrated by Jessica Lynch's family, March 27, B13). The *Times*'s photo story on March 23 demonstrates the politics of the photography. On the front page of A Nation at War, we find a prominent square color photo of smiling parents near a photo of their son in his U.S. Marine dress uniform. A larger, five-column-wide photo on page B2 shows another family scene: mom, dad, and sister are in the library watching a CNN newscast. Smaller snapshots capture mom planting red, white, and blue pansies, and dad presenting a book to his son just before deployment to Iraq. Certainly multiple interpretations of these photographs are possible, but as Berger (1989) has argued, our visual experiences are tied to our intellectual and emotional experiences (15). Given the complementary images of polished soldiers and resolute families in the context of a war against terror for democracy and freedom, sympathy is a most likely inference. And sympathy, in the vein of "Support the Troops!" was one of the main ingredients of the U.S. public opinion strategy.

The next most frequent topic of visual images was military logistics. Constituting thirty-six visuals (15 percent of total) were maps of enemy strongholds, troop movements, and geographic obstacles to the war; drawings of military equipment, including attack helicopters, tanks, gas masks, and supply vehicles; and graphics of military tactics. Maps looking like the board games *Stratego* or *Risk* helped sanitize the realities of war, violence, destruction, and death. During the first week, a large map covered the full back page of each A Nation at War section, with the exception of Wednesday, March 27, when the page was given over to an elaborate chart of the war's "progress," with smaller maps, short narratives, and miniature photos of Bush and Hussein for each of the seven days of the war. Predictably, all of the graphics assumed a United States perspective. Such features also discard any concern with the merits of the war in favor of graphics touting military prowess and strategy, echoing the White House and congressional agenda that focused almost solely on how soon the war would end and how expensive it would be. Examples include a half-page, detailed skeletal drawing of the U.S. *Apache* helicopter (March 25, B3), made infamous in Israeli attacks on Palestinians; and a half-page drawing of "Target Acquisition," complete with descriptive key and logistical information sketches of equipment and soldier so that readers would understand how enemy combatants are tracked (March 24, B3). Such graphics of military operations seem to transcend questions regarding validity or morality, just as politicians argued that once the war started, all discussion must cease until after victory.

These three topics—nonfighting soldiers, wounded soldiers, and military logistics—made up almost two-thirds of all visuals (63 percent) appearing in the *New York Times* during the first week of the war. Although one cannot conclude from a single photograph, an analysis of the content of multiple photographs often reveals a consistency that cannot be explained by chance (Hovanec and Fruend 1994, 51). In this case, the thematic consistency of visual images sympathetically representing the war underscores the accommodation that the *New York Times* made to administration perspectives. Although the United States was the invading power, in the overwhelming majority of *Times*'s photographs, soldiers appeared in nonantagonistic poses or as victims of a violent enemy—a glaring inconsistency with the actual conduct of the war, where Iraqis died in the thousands (at least 6,113 civilians died, www.iraqibodycount.net; in Gresh 2003, 2) and fought only sporadically and briefly, and almost entirely on the defensive.

In stark contrast, the *New York Times* saw "fit to print" only seven Iraqi prisoners, three Iraqi combatants, two Iraqi wounded civilians, and one dead Iraqi soldier. In all, out of 241 visuals during the first full week of the *Times*'s war coverage, only thirteen photographs (about 5 percent of the total) indicated that Iraqis were involved in the fighting at all. Another twenty-eight photographs (12 percent of all visuals) had Iraqi civilians in various states of surprise or despair. If the public relied on the *Times* for information on the war, it might be led to believe that few Iraqis fought, few suffered, and even fewer died.

As suggested by the internal consistency of war-related visuals in the *New York Times*, although "the camera is an observation station, the act of photographing is more than passive observing" (Sontag 1977, 12). Visual images are "chronologically and spatially limited anecdotes about specific incidents. All photographs are snapshots . . . the seeming naturalness of the imposed metonym masks the variability of its context" (Perlmutter 1998, 17). In the pages of the *New York Times*, anecdotal pictures of the war suggested a fairly innocuous operation, illustrating the good will and good nature of the United States and its young troops.

Although visual devices were not the focus of this study, one prominent device that helped construct the photographic images in the *Times* should be noted because of the political context of photojournalists as "embedded" reporters. The subjective shot—which takes the point of view of a chosen agent—simulates and naturalizes that as the point of view of the photographer and, more important for propaganda purposes, the point of view of the viewing public. The angle-of-view convention is part of a larger family of visual devices having to do with how the viewer is positioned relative to the people or objects in the image (Meyrowitz 1986). Point of view "determines the details shown and what is included or not included creates the viewer's impression of the subject" (Hovanec and Fruend 1994, 49). In the case of the U.S. war, "embedded" photographers—at least as represented by photojournalists contributing to the *New York Times*—took subjective shots from the point of view of the U.S. military, positioning the viewer inside the action or in many cases inside the "nonaction." Of course, "photographs, which fiddle with the scale of the world themselves get reduced, blown up, cropped, retouched, doctored, tricked out" (Sontag 1977, 4). But here it is not a question of whether a particular photograph was intentionally altered or whether photographs can be manipulated technically; rather, the significant point is that simply by determining that the camera will be pointed in one direction rather than another allows the embedded photojournalist to be manipulated politically—deflecting the public's attention from other events, perspectives, or images. As Sontag (1977) observed almost three decades ago, picture taking is an event with "peremptory rights—to interfere with, to invade, to ignore whatever is going on. Our very sense of situation is now articulated by the camera's intervention" (12). In 2003, our sense of the Iraqi "situation" was articulated by the embedded cameras of the *New York Times* and other news media as propaganda tools of the U.S. invasion.

Notably, although the *New York Times* gave special, expanded coverage of the U.S. war—including daily full-color centerfolds of U.S. military prowess— photos of the devastation of Iraq and the suffering of civilians were absent. This practice occurs in a larger, cultural context, of course. The success of

any effort to shape public opinion depends on the predisposition of the public to believe the message . . . and Americans have been conditioned to understand that the most significant threat to the American way of life is external to us. (Robertson 1994, 103)

For U.S. citizens who were still "experiencing" 9/11 (due in no small measure to media urgings), Iraq was part of the "axis of evil" and the international terror network. For over a year, Homeland Security and administration spokesmodels were warning of imminent terrorist attacks on "our way of life." In this climate—and according to this narrative—the United States was only responding defensively to the aggression of others. Under such conditions, corporate media could deny and withhold images of the destruction of Iraq, its weak and decayed infrastructure, its civilians (including children) impoverished by ten years of UN sanctions, its devastation owing to a decade of U.S. air raids, and its visits by UN inspectors to empty warehouses.

Given the administration's control over the flow of information about the war—through press conferences, news backgrounders, embedded reporters, and patriotic intimidation—and given corporate media's hegemony over public information in the United States, there was no significant public space for alternative images or democratic discussion. There was no ideological space, either. Whatever their degree of independence or subservience to the political power structure in foreign affairs, the news media once again served as "a continuous and articulate link" between government officials and the public (Perlmutter 1998, 9). In short, U.S. government propaganda—the institutionalized, systematic campaign controlling the flow of information to influence public support for the war—was successful largely because of media complicity.

When another point of view occasionally slipped through, circumventing the political and photographic frame of the *New York Times* and other corporate media—such as political satirist Bill Maher's comment on U.S. bombings, U.S. congressman Jim McDermott's questions about Bush's war plans, actor Sean Penn's visit to Iraq to witness civilian conditions, or former UN inspector Scott Ritter's revelations about Iraqi weapon destruction—corporate media joined the administration in condemning and marginalizing the critics. Indeed, to escape the drums of war in the free marketplace of ideas in the United States, citizens had to listen to the BBC or Canadian public radio, visit international websites, or subscribe to a limited-circulation domestic journal. Unfortunately, most U.S. residents were politically anesthetized by upbeat photos and military-friendly graphics, such as those in the *New York Times*, that presented the war as serious but innocuous, even fun on occasion. To paraphrase Perlmutter (1998), the news photos and graphics featured in the *New York Times* focused our attention on selected places, times, and events—to the point that items not pictured seem not to exist.

Overall, the visuals presented mirrored the policy imperatives of the administration's war drive; visuals for alternative policies did not appear.

Popular culture and an almost palpable public fear may have aroused a desire for images that would simplify the world, but the *New York Times*, as the flagship U.S. newspaper, helped justify the mentality of a nation involved in an invasion. The *New York Times* furnished vivid fantasies about the war that met the needs of U.S. government propaganda and denied the public images necessary for making informed evaluations and choices about U.S. war aims and actions. This does not seem to be a recent development: in his analysis of the *New York Times*'s coverage of earlier U.S. foreign policy, Berry (1990) found that the paper was unable to critically report the formulation and execution of foreign policy (143–44).

In the case of the 2003 U.S. war on Iraq, the *New York Times* contributed to the manipulation of public perception through its publication of prowar visuals. One is led to conclude that with the *New York Times* as the most shining example of American journalism, U.S. corporate media function best as institutions of propaganda, not news and public information.

REFERENCES

Artz, L., and M. Pollock. 1995. "Limiting the Options: Images as Argument in U.S. Media Coverage of the Politics of the Gulf War." In *The U.S. Media and the Middle East: Image and Perception,* edited by Y. Kamalipour. Westport, Conn.: Greenwood.

Barthes, R. 1988. *Image-Music-Text.* Translated by S. Heath. New York: Noonday (originally published 1977).

Berger, A. A. 1989. *Seeing Is Believing: An Introduction to Visual Communication.* Mountain View, Calif.: Mayfield Publishing.

Berry, N. O. 1990. *Foreign Policy and the Press: An Analysis of the "New York Times" Coverage of U.S. Foreign Policy.* Westport, Conn.: Greenwood Press.

Gresh, Alain. 2003. "Wave of Chaos." *Le Monde Diplomatique,* September, 1–3.

Grosswiler, P. 1997. "The Impact of Media and Images on Foreign Policy: Elite U.S. Newspaper Editorial Coverage of Surviving Communist Countries in the Post–Cold War Era." In *New Media and Foreign Relations,* edited by A. Malik, 195–210. Norwood, N.J.: Ablex.

Hovanec, C. P., and D. Fruend. 1994. "Photographs, Writing, and Critical Thinking." In *Images, in Language, Media, and Mind,* edited by R. F. Fox, 42–57. Urbana, Ill.: National Council of Teachers of English.

Howe, P. 2002. *Shooting under Fire: The World of the War Photographer.* New York: Artisan.

"A Nation at War." 2003. *New York Times,* March 23–28, B1–B12.

Messaris, Paul. 1994. "Visual Literacy vs. Visual Manipulation." *Critical Studies in Mass Communication* 7, no. 2: 180–98.

Meyrowitz, Joshua. 1986. "Television and Interpersonal Behavior: Codes of Perception and Response." In *Inter/Media: Interpersonal Communication in a Media World,* 3rd ed., ed. G. Gumpert and R. Cathcart, 253–72. New York: Oxford University Press.

Perlmutter, D. D. 1998. *Photojournalism and Foreign Policy: Icons of Outrage in International Crises.* Westport, Conn.: Praeger.

"The Photographs Tell the Story." 2003, April 15. Retrieved from http://information clearinghouse.info/article2842.htm.

Rampton, S., and J. Stauber. 2003a. "How to Sell a War: The Rendon Group Deploys "Perception Management" in the War on Iraq." *In These Times*, September 1, 14–17.

———. 2003b. "The 'Sheer Genius' of Embedded Reporting." *Extra!*, September/October, 20–21.

Robertson, L. R. 1994. "From War Propaganda to Sound Bites: The Poster Mentality of Politics in the Age of Television." In *Images, in Language, Media, and Mind,* edited by R. F. Fox, 92–107. Urbana, Ill.: National Council of Teachers of English.

Sontag, S. 1977. *On Photography.* New York: Noonday Press (originally published 1973).

———. 2003. *Regarding the Pain of Others.* New York: Farrar, Straus and Giroux.

9

Murdoch's War—A Transnational Perspective

Daya Kishan Thussu

If the Gulf War of 1991 created the twenty-four/seven global television news culture and launched CNN to a global public, the "war against terrorism" has catapulted Rupert Murdoch's television news networks into the international spotlight. With FOX News in the United States, Sky News in Europe, and Star News in Asia, Murdoch's media are relayed to television screens around the world. The Australian-born media magnate's majority stake in News Corporation (one of the world's biggest media and communications conglomerates) has given him extraordinary powers to influence the coverage of the open-ended and global "war," including the U.S. military intervention to topple the Iraqi government in March–April 2003.

The reach of Murdoch's global television empire is worth a brief tour. In the United States, his media interests are now extensive, ranging from film studios to television networks. By producing such internationally successful programs as *The Simpsons*, the FOX network is already well established in the world's most competitive media market, giving the three traditional networks—CBS, NBC, and ABC—a run for their money. In cable and satellite homes too, Murdoch's presence is growing and not just in the area of entertainment television. With more than two million viewers regularly watching FOX News in the United States, it has now overtaken CNN as the key cable news channel in the country. As the Federal Communications Commission further deregulates television, FOX is likely to increase its hold on the U.S. media market. In Europe, British Sky Broadcasting (BSkyB), with majority ownership by News Corporation, is one of the most profitable broadcasters. In Latin America, Sky network has agreements with the Mexican television giant Televisa and other regional broadcasters for direct-to-home (DTH) operations, while Canal FOX and FOX Kids Latin America are among networks catering to audiences across Latin America.

The Asian branch of this global empire is represented by STAR (Satellite Television Asian Region) television, which proudly claims to be "setting the pace of media in Asia," broadcasting forty services in eight languages and reaching more than three hundred million viewers in fifty-three countries. Over 120 million people watch STAR every week, according to its own estimates. Though most viewers choose STAR for its entertainment programs, there is also an increasing audience for its news output. STAR network has a news operation in India—Star News, with the twenty-four-hours news now entirely in Hindi, the language most widely used in the country (also available in Europe, the Middle East, the Philippines, and Thailand)—as well as an English-language Pan-Asian news operation, Star News Asia, operating from Hong Kong. For the huge Chinese market, the Murdoch's stable has Phoenix News in Mandarin, available in East Asia as well as mainland China. Both Star News and Phoenix also have a dedicated following among the huge Indian and Chinese diasporas, respectively.

News Corporation has used an array of strategies, including localization of editorial content and managerial staff, to consolidate its position in Asia—the world's biggest television market. In India, for example, its operations were coordinated in the crucial, early years by Rathikant Basu, a former director general of Doordarshan, India's state television network. After losing a great deal of money for over ten years, Murdoch's India operations started to make a profit in 2002, and by 2003, according to the trade press, it had become the most popular private channel in the country—with an average of forty out of the top fifty shows every week.

Apart from owning substantial chunks of satellite television, Murdoch also controls the largest number of English-language daily newspapers around the world, as well as such powerful international publishers as HarperCollins. This makes News Corporation one of the world's largest media empires, truly global in its reach and influence. What distinguishes it from its rivals such as AOL-Time-Warner and Disney Corporation, however, is the fact that it is the only media conglomerate created, built, and dominated by one man—Rupert Murdoch, the septuagenarian chairman and chief executive officer of News Corporation (Page 2003). As Robert McChesney has noted, "More than any other figure, Murdoch has been the visionary of a global corporate media empire" (1999, 96).

A deeply conservative political agenda has characterized the creation of this media empire (Ackerman 2001; Page 2003). In Britain, for example, Murdoch has consistently used his newspapers—the *Times* and the *Sun* (Britain's largest selling popular newspaper)—to champion the privatization of broadcasting, thus undermining the BBC and all that it stands for, prompting the BBC director general Greg Dyke to caution against the escalating influence of Murdoch's media in Britain (Wells 2003).

In the United States, Murdoch's media has been an enthusiastic supporter of the Republican cause, including the deregulation of broadcasting. Analyzing for nineteen weeks (between January and May 2001) the FOX News Channel's flagship daily program *Special Report with Brit Hume,* the media monitoring group FAIR (Fairness and Accuracy in Reporting) found an overwhelming slant on FOX News toward Republicans and conservatives: of the fifty-six guests with declared political affiliations interviewed on the program during the monitoring period, fifty were Republicans. Of the others, sixty-five of the ninety-two guests (71 percent) were avowed conservatives (Rendell 2001).

MURDOCH'S MEDIA WAR

Given this background, it is scarcely surprising that Murdoch's media have acted as frontline cheerleaders for the U.S. military action in Iraq. In line with other major U.S./U.K. news outlets, Murdoch's media played a central role in preparing and then retaining public opinion in favor of the invasion. In the words of Ignacio Ramonet, director of *Le Monde Diplomatique*, their key contribution was "to justify a preventive war that the United Nations and global public opinion did not want, a machine for propaganda and mystification, organised by the doctrinaire sect around George Bush, produced state-sponsored lies with a determination characteristic of the worst regimes of the 20th century" (quoted in Pilger 2003).

It may be worth reflecting for a moment on the use of language during the recent conflict in Iraq. The phrase "Gulf War II" has become fashionable not only in media but, worryingly, in academic discourses as well. This is inappropriate at least on two counts: first, even if one accepts the two major U.S. military campaigns in Iraq—in 1991 and 2003—as "war," though invasion would appear to be a more accurate description of what actually happened, this was not the second but the third Gulf War: the first one being the nearly decade-long Iran–Iraq War, which claimed more than a million lives and was aided and abetted by the West, supporting their then-favorite Arab leader, one named Saddam Hussein. Second, by calling it Gulf War II, the media are being disingenuous, since the latest U.S. invasion of Iraq is not just about "regime change" in Baghdad; rather, it has far-reaching implications for the entire Arab region, as well as a wider, Islamic and developing world.

Even before the U.S. invasion, Murdoch himself appeared to be keen on the "war," telling *Fortune* magazine that it could fuel an economic boom in the West. In an interview to the Australian news magazine *Bulletin* in February 2003, he expressed unconditional endorsement for the proposed military actions of U.S. and U.K. leaders, praising George W. Bush as acting "morally" and "correctly." No wonder, virtually all of the 175 editors working for Murdoch's newspapers unequivocally supported the invasion of Iraq (Greenslade 2003).

However, it was television rather than newspapers that set the agenda for Operation Iraqi Freedom, with FOX News playing an important role in legitimizing U.S. invasion. During the "war," the twenty-four-hour news network became little more than the loud mouthpiece of the round-the-clock, operational Office of Global Communications in the White House. FOX's unrelenting and literally flag-waving patriotism (with the U.S. flag fluttering in the corner of the screens) and the description from its "embedded" reporters of U.S. war machine as "heroes" and "liberators," met with triumph in the ratings war. Even before the bombs started falling on Baghdad, one of the main presenters on FOX News, Bill O'Reilly, dismissed even mild skepticism about the desirability of military action or any disagreement on military tactics, telling viewers that the United States should go in and "splatter" the Iraqis. In this gung-ho approach, the network appeared to present the "war" as a spectacle, with celebrity reporters such as the Contra-scandal star Colonel Oliver North, filing live from Iraq.

Moreover, in this version of televised "regime change," military action was couched in the language of a war of liberation and sometimes presented in the form of an entertainment show, drawing on visual techniques borrowed from Hollywood. The rescue of Private Jessica Lynch, who became an icon of the conflict, provided an example of mixing entertainment and information, no doubt influenced by the Hollywood film *Saving Private Ryan*. It is now known that Lynch's courageous "rescue" by U.S. Special Forces from Iraqi captors, was in fact a morale-boosting event staged for television cameras. Weeks after the actual incident, a BBC documentary showed that the Iraqi doctors had looked after her well. One of the doctors who treated Jessica told the BBC, "It was like a Hollywood film. They cried, 'Go, go, go,' with guns and blanks and the sound of explosions. They made a show — an action movie like Sylvester Stallone or Jackie Chan, with jumping and shouting, breaking down the doors" (BBC 2003).

The toppling of a statue of Saddam Hussein in a square in central Baghdad, conveniently next to the hotel where the world's media were staying, was another example of a staged event, giving the impression that U.S. troops were removing the statue at the behest of crowds of cheering Iraqis. In reality, it was the culmination of a well-orchestrated propaganda operation at the most crucial time of the invasion, highly symbolic in its significance, not just for Iraqis, but for the wider Arab world.

FOX News, like other U.S. and U.K. television networks, was willingly part of the operation's news management, which included arranging for embedded television journalists to report the progress of the invasion from the perspective of Pentagon. Unfounded allegations were bandied about on news channels such as FOX to justify the invasion: that Iraq was linked to the 9/11 attacks; that it possessed vast "weapons of mass destruction"; and that it was ready and willing to use them.

In addition, FOX News amply demonstrated an unambiguous dislike for any dissent. When Michael Wolff, a regular contributor for *New York* magazine broke ranks at the daily press conference at the million-dollar press center in Doha, Qatar, arguing that he was not covering the war but "the news conference about the war," FOX News attacked him for his lack of patriotism. One of its regular commentators, Rush Limbaugh, gave out Wolff's e-mail address on air, and in one day alone, according to Wolff, he received three thousand hate e-mails (Wolff 2003).

Yet FOX News continues to flash its proud corporate slogan—"Real Journalism, Fair and Balanced"—though some have said that the only word with any truth in the slogan is "and." It was reported in August 2003 that the network was suing a liberal political satirist, Al Franken, for using these words, albeit in jest, in the title of his new book, *Lies and the Lying Liars Who Tell Them: A Fair and Balanced Look at the Right.* Ironically, the controversy only helped boost the sales of Franken's book.

TOWARD THE "FOXIFICATION" OF TELEVISION NEWS

Such a one-dimensional approach to news reporting is not just confined to FOX News alone, given the reach of Murdoch's media. In the market-driven broadcasting environment, it might justifiably be feared that FOX's success could lead to "FOXification" of television news in other parts of the world. Already, other Murdoch networks, particularly in Asia, regularly use news reports and footage from FOX News.

If jingoism and blatant political partisanship can work in the United States, why not elsewhere? After all, newspapers and magazines have definite editorial slants and dedicated readerships precisely for this reason. Why should broadcasters not be free to project certain viewpoints? However, in the United Kingdom, Sky News has to operate within the remit of "due impartiality," proposed by the government-appointed, though autonomous, Independent

Television Commission, making it difficult for Sky News to openly pursue a political position. Given the cultural influence of the BBC and the public service broadcasting ethos, Sky News has tended to follow the standards set up by the BBC News journalism. However, Sky is under constant pressure from its owner to treat news from conflict zones as drama and as an event. During the coverage of the invasion of Iraq, Sky News, though less belligerent than FOX, acted as a morale booster for the British troops in the theater of war.

There were also examples of faking reports for dramatic impact. According to a BBC documentary, *Fighting the War,* Sky News correspondent James Forlong (since suspended) reported a missile-launch exercise from a docked British submarine as if it were a launch from a vessel in action. It was actually an exercise conducted for the benefit of the camera crew. The news report, aired on Sky News between March 31 and April 2, 2003, ended with images of an underwater missile launch, but the Sky reporter had used archival footage of a different launch and the submarine in the report did not fire while the news crew was aboard. The report, part of a pool report made available to other news organizations, was also broadcast by Britain's ITV News.

Such instances reflect the pressure that journalists are under to conform to a more entertainment-driven news agenda. Dissatisfied with what he perceives as its staid presentation and "liberal bias," Murdoch wants Sky News to become more populist. "Sky News is very popular and they are doing well but they don't have the entertaining talk shows—it is just a rolling half-hour of hard news all the time," Murdoch told the *New York Times.*

These changes are also visible on Murdoch's India news operation, Star News, which until April 2003 broadcast news in both Hindi and English, procured from New Delhi Television (NDTV), India's most respected news and current affairs company. Star News has since changed its editorial focus. As the contract between Star and NDTV came to an end, Star News became revamped, although some would say dumbed down. In its new spruced-up, youthful, and flashier incarnation, launched in the middle of Operation Iraqi Freedom, the news network, now produced in-house, tended toward *infotainment.* Besides showing reports and live footage from its sister outlets—FOX News and Sky News—it reproduced, often verbatim (though in Hindi translation), the standard Pentagon line on the progress of the "war."

Its only claim to fame during the Iraq invasion was that its correspondent in Baghdad was able to broadcast a live interview with an Indian businessman after he was freed from spending thirteen years in various Iraqi prisons, all while his family was still in Mumbai. The poignancy of this story was highlighted by the fact that the family, which had fled Kuwait during the Iraqi occupation of 1990, had presumed him dead. This human-interest story dominated Star coverage of a major conflict, which not only changed the government in Iraq but also had long-lasting regional and international repercussions.

The Murdoch influence was clear in this shift from a serious to a more popular news agenda, driven by the logic of maximizing profit. As television increasingly defines how public opinion is shaped—in its national, regional, and international spheres—such trends can only be described as worrisome. Elsewhere, I have tried to define this "Murdochisation of media" as "the process which involves the shift of media power from the public to privately owned, transnational, multimedia corporations controlling both delivery systems and the content of global information networks" (1998, 7). I characterized "Murdochisation" by a combination of the following factors: a convergence of global media technologies; a tendency toward a market-driven journalism thriving on circulation and ratings wars; transnationalization of U.S.-inspired media formats, products, and discourse; and lastly, an emphasis on infotainment, undermining the role of the media for public information (Thussu 1998, 7).

Five years on, and with growing FOXification of television news, the contours of this media landscape appear to be clearer. Murdoch's growing political influence as a multimedia mogul and his extensive control of both information software (program contents) and hardware (digital delivery systems) make him a hugely powerful player whose empire straddles the globe with wide-ranging media interests—from newspapers, to film, broadcast satellite and cable television, interactive digital television, television production, and Internet.

In the notoriously competitive current news environment, the framing of news in terms of infotainment is likely to become more widespread. As the boundaries between news and entertainment and between news reports and commentary get narrower, we are likely to see more of Mr. Murdoch's media. This bodes ill at a time when there is pressing need for sober comment and analysis rather than rash and jingoistic journalism.

REFERENCES

Ackerman, Seth. 2001. "The Most Biased Name in News: Fox News Channel's Extraordinary Right-Wing Tilt, A Special FAIR Report." *Extra!* August.

BBC. 2003. "War Spin." *Correspondent*, BBC 2, British Broadcasting Corporation, May 18.

Greenslade, Roy. 2003. "Their Master's Voice." *Guardian*, Media, February 17, 1–3.

McChesney, Robert. 1999. *Rich Media, Poor Democracy: Communication Politics in Dubious Times*. Champaign: University of Illinois Press.

Page, Bruce. 2003. *The Murdoch Archipelago*. New York: Simon & Schuster.

Pilger, John. 2003. "The War On Truth." *Znet*, July 31.

Rendall, Steve. 2001. "Fox's Slanted Sources: Conservatives, Republicans Far Outnumber Others." *Extra!* August.

Thussu, Daya Kishan. 1998. *Electronic Empires—Global Media and Local Resistance*. New York: Arnold.

Wells, Matt. 2003. "BBC Chief Warns over Murdoch Dominance." *Guardian*, August 25, 1.

Wolff, Michael. 2003. "You Know Less Than When You Arrived." *Guardian,* Media, March 31, 1–3.

10

Glossy: American Hegemony and the Culture of Death

Leila Conners Petersen

In 1996 I interviewed the Egyptian minister of culture, Dr. Gaber Asfour, and the minister of education, Dr. Hussein Kamel Bahaa El Din, about their efforts at keeping extremist Islamic fundamentalism from dominating the Egyptian cultural landscape. At that time, their hope and focus were on, first, cultural programming that included operas, plays, and television programming; and, second, a closing of the information technology gap by accelerating education in the sciences. They were doing this through new labs built in schools and through Internet-ready vans that would drive into the desert and into small villages, where children and adults could plug into the wider world.

All their efforts at education, however, were being challenged by a certain Saudi individual who was flooding the streets of Cairo and beyond with glossy magazines that preached anti-Western and anti-American propaganda. This man, Osama bin Laden, was outpublishing and outdesigning both the Ministry of Culture and the Ministry of Education. Asfour and Bahaa El Din were in a print war with bin Laden, trying desperately to create materials that appealed to the man on the street and that told of a broader and more accepting view of the world. They did not have the budget, though, to make their materials as glossy, with so many colors and pictures! Bin Laden's printed materials were seductive compared to the government's, which were printed on lower-quality paper and with fewer colors. Furthermore, bin Laden's editions were continual, building up influence for years. In addition to the grinding poverty experienced by so many in Egypt, bin Laden's print campaign helped create, less than a decade later, many willing minds able to accept his violent agenda.

In the minds of millions, glossy media can prepare a fertile soil for violence and war. It takes time, but once the mental landscape has been primed, it only takes small efforts in print, video, or television to propel an agenda through large populations, even when it means making the ultimate sacrifice.

Egypt and other countries on the receiving end of bin Laden's propaganda are not the only places that are negotiating a radical taste for violence and war. In America, our mediasphere has also created a fertile soil for war, in a less-intentional but no less-powerful way. Indeed, our media culture is a glossed-up "culture of death" that has cheapened the concept of death and has distanced us from it; and in so doing, it has made war easier to accept.

Any global hegemony, America's included, is supported by three powerful forces: military might, economic might, and social strength. American society is, at its best, inclusive of a variety of cultures: it is energetic, creative, flexible, experimental, and brave. It is entrepreneurial and open. However, there are aspects of our culture that are less optimistic and actually corrosive. Any quick review of American media today will give a snapshot of a culture obsessed with violence and death. Indeed, for decades, we have been in a downward spiral away from the celebration of life and toward a *schadenfreude* (pleasure attained from the pain of others) ever more detailed and destructive.

America's nightly television dose of over one thousand acts of fictional violence and murder that (in all but 10 percent of programs) shows those acts out of context and with no consequence has weakened us, not only in that it results in real-world aggression from our children and our later adults, but that it has also hobbled our national discussion, and lack thereof, on war and its consequences. Violence is even more accentuated in the even-bigger video-game market. "Single shooter" games occupy hundreds of hours of our youth's free time. These games have realistic settings in which one "wins" by killing well. The games have become so realistic that the Pentagon has even created a single-shooter game that monitors the ability of the players for recruitment purposes.

Indeed, we see the blood on corpses in programs such as *CSI* and *Law & Order*; yet, we don't see the pine boxes carrying our dead home from Iraq, nor do we see the hundreds wounded in hospitals there and in those here at home. The dichotomy of our fictional, up-close, and in-millions-of-colors encounter with death and the dearth of image and information on the costs of our war in Iraq shows most starkly our lost connection to the real meaning of death and, with it, what it means to go to war, to kill others, and to be killed ourselves.

I need not repeat the statistics of what hundreds of reports have stated regarding violence in the media and in our culture. The main point here is that the violence of our American cultural landscape is noted not for a discussion on whether it is right or wrong, not for a discussion on censorship, and not to answer the question of whether someone or something is to blame for it. It is noted here simply as a point of fact: It is within our cultural norm to have killing central to our nightly television entertainment; it is our cultural norm to view corpses, the act of killing through shooting, maiming, and other violent behavior; it is our cultural norm to practice killing other people with the use of highly sophisticated weaponry through video games. It is an accepted cultural norm to allow children to view acts of violence and participate in acts of violence through video games over long periods every day, repeated throughout the year, and throughout a child's and then an adult person's life.

In light of this proximity to fictional death on television, we do not visually witness the horror of our daily loss of our brave men and women. Can it be because, as the National Television Violence Study determined, "televised violence leads to a desensitization to violence" and therefore apathy in the face of war? The Senate Committee of the Judiciary's Study on Children, Violence, and the Media said:

> The majority of the existing social and behavioral science studies, taken together, agree on the following basic points: (1) constant viewing of televised violence has negative effects on human character and attitudes; (2) television violence encourages violent forms of behavior and influences moral and social values about violence in daily life; (3) children who watch significant amounts of television violence have a greater likelihood of exhibiting later aggressive behavior; (4) television violence affects viewers of all ages, intellect, socioeconomic levels, and both genders; and (5) viewers who watch significant amounts of television violence perceive a meaner world and overestimate the possibility of being a victim of violence.

In short, as Americans, we live stuck in a dual emotional state of being at once distanced from death but, at the same time, fearful of what we know not.

And so the agenda of the American empire grows nicely from this sad soil. Our social desensitization–fear axis has formed one of the many supports of our expanding American empire that is propped up not by international agreement and diplomacy but by the brute strength of unilateralism and military engagement. In the media, the logic of this lonely and expansive agenda shaped by the Bush II administration has been easily digested; and the management of public opinion since the tragic events of 9/11 and the subsequent wars in Afghanistan and Iraq is done by one-liners. "Wanted dead or alive" becomes reason enough to invade a country because it triggers decades of fear-based assumptions formulated from deeply grooved responses to violent television and other media entertainment. All a president needs to do in a press conference is utter the phrase "empire of evil," and the American people will sign up for war, carpet bombings, and perhaps even a nuclear attack.

And the death that has ensued from the war in Iraq and Afghanistan has not yet penetrated our national psyche, as American news has yet to provide context for the real pain and suffering that are being endured by not only our military, press corps, and humanitarian workers but by the Iraqis, the Afghanis, and so many others. Granted, the task at hand is now difficult, in a "Dead Bodies Beat Hot Bodies Every Time" world (*Washington Post* article title, November 2003, on sweeps week). How can the news get through, especially if a mind has just come off of two hours of fear-based programming?

Instead of greater detail on regional histories and the telling of complex interaction between governments, corporations, and organizations, news shows have instead believed that audiences would appreciate increased slick and beautiful presentation. Glossy is everywhere and content is nowhere—and content is getting tough. So much of our televised political dialogue is violently akin to kids fighting in the elementary school sandbox. Now, the ability to discern truth in news that tries to be entertainment is next to impossible, between the cut-up title sequences and story graphics. Since Iraq, what seems to be the killer app in news programming is that the news is now read by a person who is standing up.

That the corporations that own the news media have yet to figure out how to explain the news of empire and still make a profit is not surprising. As Paul Kennedy said,

> a country needing to reformulate its grand strategy in the light of the larger, uncontrollable changes taking place in world affairs may not be well served . . . by an inherent "simplification" of vital but complex international and strategical issues through a mass media whose time and space for such things is limited, and whose raison d'etre is chiefly to make money and secure audiences, and only secondarily to inform.

It is difficult to make the business of media and the higher purpose of media complementary. Making money as well as informing and educating the public seems to be, especially now, at cross-purposes. For example, try selling a show that educates the public about the carbon cycle and how humanity's impact on it has lead to global warming. Sounds interesting? Not scary enough? (Although it is scary.) The head of documentary programming of a network once said, "If you do get to do a show on the environment, it will usually consist of coverage of poisonous snakes or shark attacks."

So at a time when America is blindly transitioning from a republic to an empire without an enlightened public debate in a new world order that Bush Jr. describes as "the civilized world fighting the uncivilized world," media needs to consider a basket of considerations and externalities that go beyond profit that will then allow for programming that educates the public about complex issues. Furthermore, media production should spend time and money making this serious content interesting and attractive, as so often this type of programming is decidedly not.

Most important, we need a media that helps create in our imagination a better world. We need to pierce through the simplicity and the fear and seed our mental environment with ideas that go well beyond death: ideas that are positive, beautiful, and constructive and that allow for a greater understanding not only about ourselves but about other people and places around the world. We need to deem as unacceptable and insufficient the endless litany of one-liners that reduces our complex world to a simple polemic. If we do not, our political and national dialogue will be further weakened and, with it, our ability to seek out the truth and take action based on it, which is a central activity on which our democracy depends.

11

War, Propaganda, and Islam in Muslim and Western Sources

Karim H. Karim

Propaganda about Islam is disseminated by many sources. Various Muslim groups attempt to present their own particular perspectives through the media and other means. Some of these declarations are in competition with those of other Muslims, and certain messages attempt to put right what is viewed as the distortion of the image of Islam and Muslims by outsiders. Western governments, who increasingly find themselves in conflict with Muslim-majority states, have often been the sources of material on Islam that serve their specific interests.

DIVERSITY AMONG MUSLIM PERSPECTIVES

The followers of Islam constitute a vast diversity of peoples residing in almost all countries of the world. Traditionally, they have lived in the Middle East; northern, western, and eastern Africa; the Balkans; Central Asia, South Asia, Malaysia, and Indonesia. They have migrated in the last few centuries to other parts of Asia, Africa, and Europe, and to the Americas and Australasia. Apart from the forty-seven Muslim-majority states,[1] there are several other countries in which large numbers of people follow Islam, particularly in Asia and Africa. In India, even though Muslims form only 10 percent of the population, they number over one hundred million.

Muslims view themselves as belonging to a global community called the *ummah*. However, it is incorrect to view the "Muslim world" as a monolith in which all believe and act in the same manner. The followers of Islam are composed of a variety of cultures, linguistic traditions, and even religious beliefs. Whereas all of them agree that there is only one God (monotheism) and that

Muhammad was a prophet of God, there are differences in other aspects of Muslims' religious creeds. Some of these differences have existed for over a thousand years, and others have appeared more recently. However, the propaganda distributed by a number of Muslim organizations seeks to impart the impression that adherents of Islam are alike in all their beliefs.

Governments of some Muslim-majority countries often refer to their policies as "Islamic," which is probably the most misused word in the discourses of both Muslims and non-Muslims. In the absence of a single religious establishment to which all Muslims adhere, each group can claim that its actions follow the teaching of the religion. However, when the governments of two Muslim-majority states go to war against each other, the propaganda messages of both usually draw support for their respective positions from Islam. For example, during the 1991 Gulf War, both Iraq and Saudi Arabia obtained sanction for the legitimacy of their respective positions from different sets of Muslim religious leaders.

The al Qaeda terrorist network is widely held to be responsible for destruction of the twin towers of the World Trade Center and the subsequent death of around three thousand people on September 11, 2001. This network is composed of a number of people who constitute a minute part of the over one billion followers of Islam. Unlike the majority of Muslims, they have chosen to use terrorism against the people they view as their enemies. Members of al Qaeda see not only the West as a potential target but also fellow Muslims who disagree with al Qaeda's ideology. Al Qaeda's propaganda presents the justification for its actions as based on Islamic teaching, even though prominent Muslim religious scholars have condemned the militants' narrow interpretations of Islamic scripture.

Al Qaeda was established by Osama bin Laden and his close associates. They built training camps in war-torn Afghanistan with the support of its former Taliban government. The Taliban was also composed of people who had a rigid understanding of Islam; they abolished most human rights in Afghanistan and terrorized its population. Most other Muslims around the world were horrified with the repression carried out by the Taliban and their dogmatic approach to Islam. However, there are some Muslims in various countries who are attracted by the propaganda of the militants because it seems to speak to their insecurities about a world that appears to be hostile to Muslim interests.

JIHAD

The notion of jihad has been exploited by a series of Muslim leaders for centuries and has been the subject of considerable propaganda in support of various ends. *Jihad* means "effort in the cause of God." Such effort can be of many nonviolent means, but jihad tends often to be thought of only as fighting for religious purposes. This is similar to the Christian concept of "just war," which is what George H. W. Bush used to justify U.S. involvement in the 1991 Gulf War. The rules of jihad and just war have their origins in the early Jewish (Davidic) code of war (Vaux 1992).

Jihad is a much-contested issue among Muslims. It emerged in the time of the prophet Muhammad as a means of defending the small Muslim community against its powerful enemies. In the following periods, a number of Muslim military leaders used it against other Muslims for political and economic gain. It has been adopted to fight colonial forces since the eighteenth century. After gaining independence, the propaganda of certain leaders reinterpreted jihad within national contexts as an economic war against their country's state of poverty (Peters 1979, 119).

However, militant Muslims have used the concept of jihad in their violent opposition to governments of Western as well as majority-Muslim states. A key document of the group that assassinated Egyptian president Anwar Sadat in 1981 referred to jihad as a religious obligation that Muslims had disregarded. It made selective use of Islamic scripture, legal writings, and historical sources to make its case to justify its program to overthrow the Egyptian government by force. In response, Egypt's chief scholar of religious law also chose material from scriptural and legal sources to refute the militants' position. Arguing from a nationalist perspective, he stated that "the character of jihad . . . has now changed radically, because the defence of the country and religion is nowadays the duty of the regular army, and this army carries out the collective duty of jihad on behalf of all citizens" (Jansen 1986, 60). Jihad continues to be used by various groups to support their own particular positions and their own particular methods. Additionally, Western propagandists exploit it to portray their enemies who espouse the concept of jihad as adhering to ancient and barbaric notions of war.

MODERNITY

Muslims have been attempting to deal with the influence and presence of the West in their lives for over two hundred years. Many lands where Muslims lived were colonized by European powers. The subject populations resented the loss of their independence and the displacement of their cultures. Whereas a number of rebellions were carried out against colonial powers, significant attempts were also made to engage with Western ideas of modernity from Muslim perspectives. (There is an important distinction between Westernization and the adoption of modernity: the first is the uncritical acceptance of almost all aspects of Western culture, and the second involves a selective acceptance of innovative ideas within the context of one's own cultural and intellectual heritage).

One of the major debates among Muslims is about the extent to which traditional practices can be changed to accommodate modernity. There is a tendency among some to view facets of their particular ethnic cultures as "Islamic" even though these traditions existed long before the arrival of Islam. Conservative Muslims see the religion as almost completely unchangeable, even though a series of changes have occurred during the last fourteen centuries since the establishment of the faith. Those who propose the adoption of modernity seek for ways in which traditional practices can evolve to keep up with changing circumstances, without compromising the principles of Islam.

Such discussions have become especially urgent, as Muslims have been migrating to Western countries. They find themselves having to engage continually with Western ways of life. Some Muslims living in the West have abandoned many of the traditional aspects of their lives; others have attempted to modernize within the context of Islam; and yet others have sought to cling as much as possible to what they perceive as a "pure" Islamic existence. As may be expected, many contradictions reside within the lives of the last group, as it resists change while living in an environment that it views as being un-Islamic.

As a result of globalization, these dilemmas exist for Muslims living in their homelands. Western influence continues to penetrate traditional Muslim lands, even after the end of colonialism. Technology, consumer goods, and ideas from the West constantly circulate around the world. Television and the Internet as well as other forms of communication—such as short-wave radio, newspapers, magazines, books, recorded music, and film—carry Western propaganda globally. The intercontinental movement of people, which has grown vastly with easier air travel, is another source of spreading messages.

However, many Muslim groups are using transnational media to disseminate their messages as well (Eickelman and Anderson 1999; Karim 2003b). This form of communication can be viewed as "globalization from below" (Karim 2002). Yet, the amount of media content in such channels is small compared to the overwhelming dominance of the "North–South flow," from North America and Europe to southern countries (Rampal 2002). Some governments of Muslim-majority countries have attempted to counter the Western images of their cultures and of Islam through satellite television, but their messages are swamped by the content of the large number of other channels available to global viewers.

The differences and diversity among the followers of Islam are often lost to the Western audiences, who are used to seeing images of the stereotypical

Muslim. For example, even though the repressive Baathist government of Saddam Hussein had adopted modernist approaches to the development of Iraq and often persecuted conservative Muslims, their government was viewed by many in the West as an "Islamic government." Such a lack of understanding on the part of Western populations tends to often favor the propagandic interests of Western governments. The widespread impression in the American public that Saddam Hussein was responsible for the attacks of September 11 assisted the administration of George W. Bush when it was making the case for the 2003 invasion of Iraq. Many Americans believed that there was a link between al Qaeda and the Iraqi government even though there was little evidence to support this view.

WESTERN IMAGES OF MUSLIMS

Certain historical bases explain the widespread misperceptions about Islam and its followers. Basic Western notions about the characteristics of Muslims are many centuries old and affect the frameworks within which the media use to portray present-day events involving Muslims. (The same can be said about some Muslim perceptions about people in the West; however, the worldwide presence of Western media make the images that they project much more problematic for the development of intercultural understanding.)

According to Jack Shaheen, American television tends to have four primary stereotypes about Arabs:[2] "they are all fabulously wealthy; they are barbaric and uncultured; they are sex maniacs with a penchant for white slavery; and they revel in acts of terrorism" (1984, 4). The four core Western images of Muslims—that is, those of greed, barbarism, lust, and violence—have persisted since the earliest contacts of Europeans with Islam and can be seen in the medieval descriptions of the prophet Muhammad (Karim 2003a, 63–64).

These stereotypes have been applied historically to Muslims of various ethnic and cultural backgrounds: Persians, Turks, Africans, Indians, Malays, and others. Norman Daniel (1960) traces how writers in medieval Europe frequently used such stereotypes. Edward Said (1978) has demonstrated that, even with the emergence of nonreligious perspectives to the study of non-European peoples in the nineteenth century, the age-old stereotypes of Muslims frequently continues to shape the views of social scientists and historians. These attitudes were reflected in the European paintings of Muslims, who were often depicted in scenes of intense brutality (Kabbani 1986). Reeva Simon's (1989) research indicates how the core stereotype of the violent Muslim is prominent in the portrayal of Middle Eastern characters in British and American crime fiction.

The historically entrenched image of the "bad Muslim" has been quite useful to Western governments planning to attack Muslim-majority lands. If public opinion in their countries can be convinced that Muslims are barbaric and violent, then killing them and destroying their property appears more acceptable. This form of justification has been used in the medieval Crusades, when European Christian powers attacked Muslims in the Holy Land; in the colonial period, when Western nations colonized Muslim countries; and in more recent times, when military attacks and wars have been launched against Muslim-majority states.

This form of propaganda is usually spread through the media.[3] Despite the journalistic principle of objectivity, the media of a country usually reflect their government's foreign policy in the reporting of news (Malek 1996). The coverage of events in Muslim-majority countries by Western media is generally carried out within the frameworks set by powerful Western governments (Karim 2003a; Poole 2002; Said 1981).[4] Some academics have played a political role as well, by presenting the image of a few militant Muslims as being representative of Islam—namely, those who grab headlines through their acts of terrorism.

CONSTRUCTING THE GENEALOGY OF MUSLIM ASSASSINS

The Cold War against Communism had provided an enemy in the shape of the Soviet Union. The military–industrial complexes spent billions of dollars on weapons, producing profits and other advantages for elite sections of society. The diminishing danger from Eastern Europe in the late 1980s seemed to produce what John Esposito has called a "threat vacuum" in international relations (1992, 7). A number of academics began to present Muslims as the new major threat to the West. The effort on the part of some was to build the case that the West and the Muslims could never be reconciled, because Islam was completely opposed to Western values (see Barber 1995; Huntington 1996).

A number of scholars, acting more as propagandists than as academics (e.g., Bernard Lewis and Elie Kedourie), have attempted to show that militants among contemporary Muslims are merely the present-day incarnations of terrorists from the beginning of Muslim history. For example, Kedourie (1987) developed a genealogy covering over fourteen hundred years to demonstrate that Islam was inherently terroristic. Exploiting the existence of the core Western stereotype of the violent Muslim, Kedourie sought to trace the "Islamic" pedigree of contemporary Muslim terrorists. He did so by relating that the "first political assassination to take place in Islam" was that of Ali, the cousin of the prophet Muhammad, in 661; that Hasan-i Sabbah in eleventh- and twelfth-century Iran "may be considered as a foremost exponent of the theory and practice of terrorism"; that Jamal al-din Afghani, a nineteenth-century Muslim reformer "certainly believed in assassination"; that during the 1940s and 1950s the Muslim Brethren in Egypt, the Fedayan-i Islam in Iran, and a Communist group in Algeria engaged in terrorism; that the successive presidents of Egypt, Gamal Abdel Nasser and Anwar Sadat, had either contemplated or carried out assassinations as young army officers; that "the Palestine Liberation Organisation is the best-known body in the Muslim world to derive its doctrine and practice from a European model" of terrorism; that members of a Muslim group attempted to kill President Assad of Syria and that another one succeeded in assassinating Sadat in 1981; and that "Khomeini's Iran . . . exemplifies the idea of a 'terrorist state'" (1987, 13).

What would be considered laughable is a similar tracing of assassinations, from Julius Caesar to John F. Kennedy, to demonstrate violent tendencies in the ways that the West has historically treated its leaders. However, the lax manner in which some Western academics approach the history of non-Western peoples and the long-standing image of the violent Muslim allows this form of propaganda to be acceptable as scholarly evidence. It is rather unfortunate that journalists accept arguments, such as those of Kedourie's, uncritically and adopt them as frameworks in their reporting about Muslims (see Karim 2003a, 139–57).

Another example of the misuse of Muslim history for present-day ideological purposes by Western propagandists is the regular appearance of the legend of "The Assassins" in the media. The tale, which was first popularized in Europe by the Crusaders and by Marco Polo, has become standard in Western discourses about "Islamic terrorism." This story, much embellished in the course of time, is about Ismaili Muslims who had managed to acquire a number of forts in northern Iran and in Syria/Lebanon during the eleventh century. Under attack from vastly superior military powers, such as the Seljuk sultanate and the Crusaders, they sometimes used the tactic of assassinating the military and administrative leaders of their enemies.

Medieval European writings claimed that the assassins who took part in what seemed to be suicidal missions were convinced into risking their lives after being drugged with hashish. They were led to a paradisiacal garden populated with enchanting damsels; eternal residence in this garden was promised to them upon their death. (The etymological origin of the word *assassin* in European languages is consequently attributed to *hashish*.) Media narratives frequently repeat this lurid account even though it has been found to be lacking in historical evidence (Daftary 1995; Hodgson 1955).

It seems that some Western journalists tend to use references to "The Assassins" as a propagandic tool to emphasize the endemically violent nature of contemporary Muslims. In its April 21, 1986, issue, *Time* magazine had cover story titled "Targeting Gaddafi," which attempted to make the case for the imminent bombing of Libya by American forces. A two-page article presented a profile with the headline "Gaddafi: Obsessed by a Ruthless, Messianic Vision." It sought to link his known support for terrorism and with an "Islamic" fanaticism:

> His messianic vision, like the turbans in which he wraps himself, does not camouflage his vicious methods and his ruthless fanaticism. He believes his own erratic ends are justified by any means, however bloody. He has become the modern-day incarnation of the society of Assassins, which flourished from the 11th to the 13th century in the Middle East, only his victims are random and spread over the entire map. The primary tool of his effort to achieve Islamic unity and the elimination of Israel is terrorism. Gaddafi regards himself not only as the last great hope of pan-Islam but as the scourge of the West, which he fervently believes has humiliated the Arab world for centuries. It is a humiliation he intends to avenge.

The writer, conflating the Libyan leader's Pan-Arabism with Pan-Islamism, had clearly intended to create the image of an arch "Islamic" terrorist, who had to be stopped. Gaddafi's link with "The Assassins" does not seem obvious, but it is thrown into the mix, with the description of his exotic headdress and his violent tendencies, to create the picture of a rogue leader of a Muslim state. All this went to provide justification for the U.S. military's impending attack on Libyan targets.

It is remarkable how widely "The Assassins" legend was used in post–September 11 coverage. Articles in the London-based *Financial Times* and the Toronto-based *Globe and Mail* sought to link al Qaeda to the historical group. A senior reporter with the Canadian Broadcasting Corporation drew on the tale in the *Foreign Assignment* program. The legend also appeared in a news backgrounder on MSN's online *Slate* magazine. Nor were the scriptwriters of the popular drama television series *The West Wing* on the NBC network immune to "The Assassins" bug: an episode titled "Isaac and Ishmael" referred to the tale.

Rather than provide a better understanding of the elusive present-day threat of al Qaeda, journalists seem bent on further mystifying the terrorist network by repeated reference to a medieval group. This reflects a frequent tendency to see Muslims as belonging not the present age but as stuck in the past, that they can only be understood in the setting of their violent and barbaric history. It reduces al Qaeda, Saddam Hussein, and "The Assassins" to the same common denominator, which then makes it easier to make the case for government actions, such as the invasion of Iraq. The work of Western propagandists is made easier by the propaganda of Muslim sources, such as Osama bin Laden and Saddam Hussein, who couch their policies in "Islamic" rhetoric. Whereas the latter use Islam to justify their violence, the former use it to demonize their Muslim enemies. The primary victims of this propagandic war are the hundreds of millions of Muslims who view their religion as a source of harmony between people but are often viewed en masse as terrorists.

NOTES

1. A "majority-Muslim country" is defined here as one in which more than 50 percent of the population is Muslim.

2. A number of Western journalists tend to think of all Arabs as being Muslim, despite the significant number of Arab Christians who live in the Middle East and in the West.

3. Not only does the representation of the violent Muslim serve a propagandic purpose, it is also highly profitable. The utility of presenting Muslims in negative ways is exploited extensively by producers of films, television drama and comedy programs, advertising, comics, toys, computer games, and carnival and other live entertainment.

4. For discussions of attempts by Western journalists to resist stereotypical portrayals of Muslims, see Karim (2003a, 189–91).

REFERENCES

Barber, Benjamin R. 1995. *Jihad vs. McWorld*. New York: Random House.

Daftary, Farhad. 1995. *The Assassin Legends: Myths of the Isma'ilis*. London: I. B. Tauris.

Daniel, Norman. 1960. *Islam and the West: The Making of an Image*. Edinburgh: University of Edinburgh Press.

Eickelman, Dale, and Jon Anderson, eds. 1999. *New Media in the Muslim World: The Emergence of Public Sphere*. Bloomington: Indiana University Press.

Esposito, John L. 1992. *The Islamic Threat: Myth or Reality?* New York: Oxford University Press.

Hodgson, Marshall G. S. 1955. *The Order of Assassins*. The Hague: Mouton Publishers.

Huntington, Samuel. 1996. *The Clash of Civilizations and the Remaking of World Order*. New York: Simon and Schuster.

Jansen, Johannes G. 1986. *The Neglected Duty: The Creed of Sadat's Assassins and Islamic Resurgence in the Middle East*. New York: Macmillan Press.

Kabbani, Rana. 1986. *Europe's Myths of the Orient*. Bloomington: Indiana University Press.

Karim, Karim H. 2002. "Globalization, Communication and Diaspora." In *Mediascapes: New Patterns in Canadian Communication,* edited by Paul Attallah and Leslie Regan Shade. Toronto: Nelson Canada.

———. 2003a. *Islamic Peril: Media and Global Violence*. 2nd ed. Montreal: Black Rose.

———, ed. 2003b. *The Media of Diaspora*. London: Routledge.

Kedourie, Elie. 1987. "Political Terror in the Muslim World." *Encounter*, 12–19.

Malek, Abbas, ed. 1996. *News Media and Foreign Relations*. Westport, Conn.: Ablex Publishing.

Peters, Rudolph. 1979. *Islam and Colonialism: The Doctrine of Jihad in Modern History*. The Hague: Mouton Publishers.

Poole, Elizabeth. 2002. *Reporting Islam: Media Representations and British Muslims*. London: I. B. Tauris.

Rampal, Kuldip. 2002. "Global News and Information Flow." In *Global Communication,* edited by Yahya R. Kamalipour. Stamford, Conn.: Wadsworth.

Said, Edward. 1978. *Orientalism*. New York: Pantheon.

———. 1981. *Covering Islam*. New York: Pantheon.

Shaheen, Jack. 1984. *The TV Arab*. Bowling Green, Ohio: Bowling Green State University Popular Press.

Simon, Reeva S. 1989. *The Middle East in Crime Fiction: Mysteries, Spy Novels, and Thrillers from 1916 to the 1980s*. New York: Lilian Barber Press.

Vaux, Kenneth L. 1992. *Ethics and the Gulf War: Religion, Rhetoric, and Righteousness*. Boulder, Colo: Westview.

12

Enemy Image: A Case Study in Creating a Mata Hari

Asra Q. Nomani

When Muslim terrorists hijacked three planes and crashed them into the World Trade Center on the morning of September 11, 2001, the world witnessed the phenomenon of enemy image making. Hartmann (1982), Keen (1986), and Fiebig-Von Hase and Lehmkuhl (1997) outline how countries create images of the enemy to build national identity and unify citizens behind a common perceived threat. The White House painted Osama bin Laden and the Taliban as the demagogues of evil. Many Muslims created a caricature of U.S. president George W. Bush as a cowboy. As a veteran journalist born in India and raised in West Virginia, I jetted to Pakistan to write dispatches for *Salon* magazine in an effort to bridge the misunderstanding that was evoking the notion of a clash of civilizations, between Islam and the West (Huntington 1998). Unwittingly, I became a case study in how enemy image making unfolds.

A staff reporter for the *Wall Street Journal* since 1998, I became the target of a disinformation campaign, orchestrated in part by officials of the Pakistani government. They wanted to use my birth, in Bombay, India, to blame India, Pakistan's historical adversary and neighbor, for the kidnapping of my friend and colleague, *Wall Street Journal* correspondent Daniel Pearl. Disinformation is a systematic, clandestine campaign of lies and distorted information meant to mislead public opinion (Nelson 1996, 156). U.S. officials took to referring to me as "Mata Hari," after the exotic dancer from France, who was executed in 1917 for being a double agent (even though her guilt was based on flimsy evidence). Both Danny's case and mine reveal how journalists themselves become the face of the enemy in the propaganda wars between nations. For Danny, the misrepresentation resulted in a lethal series of events that led to his murder. For me, the image making put my family and me at risk, tarnished my reputation, and forced me to wonder if I could ever safely return to Pakistan (Nomani 2003). By dissecting the process of how I became the enemy, it's clear that, just as in the West, a lax media perpetuates disinformation and contributes to enemy images. The disinformation campaigns also often amount to libel, or written defamation (Rosini 1991, 3).

After reporting in Pakistan for about three months, I had innocently rented a house in the port city of Karachi to write a book. Danny and his wife, Mariane Pearl, came to visit me on January 22, 2002, for a planned three-day visit. After September 11, Danny, the South Asia bureau chief for the *Wall Street Journal*, had traveled to Pakistan from India with Mariane, who was also a journalist. Danny came to town to interview a religious leader, Sheikh Mubarak Gilani, suspected as the spiritual guru to Richard Reid, the "shoe bomber" caught trying to board a flight with explosives in his shoes. Gilani has denied any link to Reid. Danny didn't return home from the interview, and four days later his wife and I saw the first photos of Danny held hostage. The kidnappers, calling themselves the National Movement for the Restoration of Pakistani Sovereignty, sent an e-mail with nationalistic demands and the subject line "American CIA Officer in Our Custody."

The kidnappers—and later the Pakistani media—tapped into a convenient label put on journalists to discredit them. From Cuba and Peru to Afghanistan, governments throughout the world plant stories in the media calling journalists spies, in an effort to discredit them, says Joel Simon, deputy director of the New York–based Committee to Protect Journalists (CPJ). To dispel that threat, the CPJ Washington representative Frank Smyth has testified that the CPJ wants the the U.S. Congress to enforce a policy banning the use of journalists as spies (Smyth 2002).

On January 30, 2002, veteran Pakistani journalist Kamran Khan penned an article in the *News,* the English sister newspaper to *Jang,* the country's largest Urdu-language newspaper, tapping into the distrust and enmity that has defined relations between India and Pakistan since the partition of the subcontinent in 1947. Each country regularly blames the other country for terrorist acts. The headline read, "Indian Connection in U.S. Newsman Case," and it drew one of the first caricatures of Danny and me in the media:

Some Pakistani security officials—not familiar with the worth of solid investigative reporting in the international media—are privately searching for answers as to why a Jewish American reporter was exceeding "his limits" to investigate [a] Pakistani religious group. These officials are also guessing, rather loudly, as to why Pearl decided to bring in an Indian journalist as his full time assistant in Pakistan. Ansa Nomani, an American passport holder Indian-Muslim lady who had come from Mumbai to Karachi with Pearl, was working as his full-time assistant in the country.

Khan didn't file this account for the *Washington Post,* where he was a stringer, and he didn't have his facts right. Danny and I had met as journalists at the *Wall Street Journal*'s Washington bureau, in 1992. I was never his assistant, nor had I traveled from India with him. The insinuations about Danny were lethal in a country where many Pakistanis alleged "a Jewish conspiracy" behind the September 11 attacks, which is also a phenomenon in enemy image making (Fiebig-Von Hase and Lehmkuhl 1997, 115). Mariane says that Khan issued a "death sentence" to her husband by revealing that he was Jewish (Pearl 2003). In retrospect, Khan admits that the article was a "misjudgment" (interview, January 1, 2004). Khan says that an intelligence source told him the details about Danny and me and that he printed such details because they seemed relevant. About raising suspicions about Danny, he says he feels "very sad. . . . I thought these [intelligence] people had a complete handle on things. . . . I couldn't have imagined that this story was headed to its tragic end."

That day, the kidnappers sent a second e-mail, claiming that Danny was a spy for Israel's Mossad intelligence agency, not the CIA.

> We have interogated mr.D.Parl and we have come to the conclusion that contrary to what we thought earlier he is not working for the cia. in fact he is working for mossaad. therefore we will execute him within 24 hours unless amreeka flfils our demands.

The kidnappers raised the specter of journalists' being spies and, thus, the enemy:

> We warn all amreekan journlists waorking in pakistan that there are many in their ranks spying on pakstan under the journlist cover. therefore we give all amreekan journlists 3 days to get out of pakstan. anyone remaining after that will be targetted.

According to police, either that day or the next day three Arab men walked into the compound where Danny was held and literally slaughtered him. The kidnappers had tapped public suspicions about Jews and Americans, to turn Danny into the enemy. What Danny's murder reveals is the slippery slope between creating an enemy image and destroying the enemy. Khan acknowledges that he erred in writing inaccuracies about me as well: "I'm not feeling very happy about that. . . . India is a four-letter-word in Pakistan. I hope things will change, but the 'India' word is enough to create a web." He admits he didn't fact-check: "I didn't get that deep into it," to find out the truth.

Enemy images are most often used to blame external forces for internal problems, such as, in this case, homebred militant Muslims. Many Pakistanis believe that Mossad works with India's intelligence agency, the Research and Analysis Wing, or RAW. In the *Frontier Post*, Pakistani journalist Naveed Miraj wrote that Danny had "lived for three nights with an Indian-American woman named Asra Q Nomani before he was kidnapped" (January 30, 2002). The headline read, "RAW Hand Seen in Abduction of U.S. Journalist." The story said, "It is feared that Indian Research and Analysis Wing (RAW) has staged the episode to defame Pakistan."

The campaign to use me to blame India for Danny's kidnapping involved the egregious act of lying, for Cliff and Ramsay (2000, 3) describes a *lie* as "a statement intended to deceive others." The government fed the mystery about me, saying that I had been arrested, even though I was staying in Pakistan on a valid visa, living in my house with Mariane, and talking to high-ranking Pakistani police and intelligence officials every day in an effort to try to find Danny. *News India-Times,* a New York–based newspaper with a correspondent in Islamabad, reported that

> on February 2, an official had stated in Islamabad that during the investigation of Pearl's kidnapping, security agencies had discovered that Nomani had rented a house in Karachi, where Pearl lived with her. He said that Nomani was arrested for unauthorized stay in Pakistan, and that she was in custody of a security agency. Asked if he had any information on her whereabout, [the government's chief spokesman, Maj.] Gen. [Rashid] Qureishi said: "Several people are being interrogated, but I cannot give details on that." ("Jaish Linked to Kidnapping of U.S. Reporter," February 15, 2002)

On February 3, 2002, another article appeared in the *News* by Tariq Butt, a journalist based in Islamabad: "Baffling Questions about Indian Lady in Pearl Case." The article said:

> Security agencies are probing several baffling questions pertaining to the unauthorized stay of an American passport holder Indian Muslim lady, Asra Q Nomani, with whom the kidnapped Wall Street Journal reporter Daniel Pearl had been living in Karachi.

My stay wasn't "unauthorized," and Pakistani police and intelligence investigators knew it from the first moment that I handed them my blue U.S. passport to inspect. The article said that the Pakistani consulate in New York had denied me a visa. That was true. After September 11, 2001, I had gotten drenched in a sudden rainstorm waiting for the Pakistan consulate's press counselor, a well-coifed woman named Rizwan Khan, to step out of the consulate's building on Manhattan's Upper East Side. I handed her a written appeal for my request for a visa. When I called the next day, she told me that Pakistan had decided that it had issued too many journalists' visas and was not issuing anymore. I was surprised. Other consulates and embassies were issuing journalist visas, but I learned that Pakistan was denying visas and visa extensions to even U.S. journalists with connections to India, such as Rajiv Chandrasekran of the *Washington Post.*

Veteran foreign correspondents told me that getting a visa was sometimes as simple as applying in a different branch of a country's diplomatic missions. When I applied in Washington, D.C., the press attaché asked me a few questions and granted me a visa. As my eyes scanned the article in the *News,* I was shocked to read the full content of the letter that I had handed to the New York consulate's press counselor:

> Salon.com . . . has hired me to send dispatches of the true humanity of this crisis unfolding in the region of my birth.

The article included the address for my maternal ancestral home, Latif Manzil, in the village of Jaigahan, in the state of Uttar Pradesh, India. I had printed the information on my business card. It also included the Brooklyn phone number that I had written on the letter as my contact number. The article claimed that I had "disappeared" after arriving in Pakistan. In fact, I had extended my visa once in Islamabad and twice in Karachi, the last time with the government's information ministry.

Rizwan Khan, who was pulled from her post, said that she doesn't know how my letter appeared in the media. She said she didn't release it to the media. "That must have been some dirty game played somewhere," she said (interview, January 2, 2004).

A later article in *Dawn,* Pakistan's largest English-language newspaper, revealed that Pakistani officials in New York had sent "an official letter" about me after Danny's kidnapping, stating:

> "She was denied a visa by the press counselor. It is not known how she had managed to reach Pakistan," said an official letter sent from the Pakistani officials in New York to the government.
>
> Referring to the Indian connection in the U.S. newsman case, the official correspondence said: "May I inform you that Asra Nomani, the American passport holder—Indian Muslim woman who accompanied Daniel Pearl—had applied for visa Pakistan visa on Sep 19, 2001, on the ground that she wanted to visit Pakistan, her ancestor's birth place.
>
> The letter gave her residential address in India and New York and a note that the information might be of help in the investigations in the Pearl case.

Throughout the investigation, I had worked closely with Danny's wife, Mariane, to try to find Danny. In Paris, she became involved in a documentary project for which a friend and colleague went to Pakistan to shoot video.

The filmmaker shot images of the jail that held Omar Sheikh, a former London School of Economics student who was charged with plotting Danny's kidnapping. Our friend was stopped while leaving Karachi, and seven of his video cassettes were seized. I called government officials from Paris on Mariane's behalf. When I spoke to Information Secretary Anwar Mehmood, he recognized my name. I assured him: "I'm not a spy for India." The next day the tapes were released through an order by the Internal Bureau, a Pakistani intelligence agency. The next day, an article appeared in *Dawn* with the byline "By Our Staff Reporter," quoting Mehmood and Information Secretary Nisar Memon about the tapes' representing a security breach. Most of the article discussed suspicion over my role, detailing the letter sent earlier in the year from the consulate to Islamabad. It said:

> At an official meeting held here, concerns were voiced over the filming of such sensitive places and suspicious role of a journalist of Indian origin, Asra Nomani, in the case.
>   Last week, Asra Nomani had made a number of calls from Paris to some officials of the information ministry for securing the release of the video tapes made by Jennings, the sources said. . . .
>   The mystery of how Asra Nomani managed to get a visa, despite initial refusals by the Pakistani authorities and her role in getting the seven movies confiscated by the customs authorities released is a cause of concern, one of the participants of the official media meeting told Dawn.

All along, Pakistani investigators and *Wall Street Journal* editors chose to not set the record straight for fear attention on me would be detrimental to the investigation. With the misinformation unchallenged, the defense lawyers for Omar Sheikh raised the specter of my involvement in Danny's kidnapping. Sheikh was convicted and sentenced to be executed. The propaganda so spun out of control, however, that on September 25, 2002, a newspaper called the *Daily Times* published an article with the headline "Daniel Pearl Case: Who and Where Is Asra Nomani?" It listed my home address and phone number in Morgantown, West Virginia. Reporter Anjum Gill quoted Omar Sheikh's defense lawyer, Rai Bashir, as saying that Sheikh's appeal would focus on me: "Mr. Bashir has said he suspects Ms. Nomani of working for the Indian intelligence agency RAW" ("US Newsman Allowed to Take Sensitive Video Tapes," May 12, 2002).

It noted my "sudden disappearance from the scene," even though police and intelligence officials knew about my departure from Pakistan, with Mariane and two *Wall Street Journal* colleagues after we found out Danny had been murdered. It said my "actual name" is "Quratulain Nomani," a reference to my middle name, and it alleged that I was once in Pakistan "posing as a student of mysticism" while actually "gathering information about jihadis," Muslim militants. It claimed that I had tried to get a visa to Pakistan by "pretending to be a *Wall Street Journal* correspondent." It charged that I had hi-tech satellite equipment installed in my home in Karachi, even though the most hi-tech technology I had was a five-track CD player I'd gotten because I knew how much Danny liked music. It also claimed that Danny's kidnappers had been in contact with me, even though they had only contacted my mobile phone once, to try to talk to Mariane.

Najam Sethi, the editor of the *Daily Times*, is no stranger to disinformation campaigns meant to discredit individuals, just as the journalist Kamran Khan is. The CPJ has defended both of them against attacks to discredit them. Sethi spent time in jail after a Pakistani government official claimed he had made anti-Pakistan comments during a trip to India. "When I came out of prison, my wife said, 'I have a file on you of articles your friends have written.' They called me a RAW agent, a terrorist, a monster," he said (interview, January 1, 2004). He attributes his experience to a lack of journalistic standards and of ethics in a profession mired with low salaries and poor training. "I've been through this. My own paper does this. I hang my head in shame. Everyday I have to apologize to someone. The phone rings, and I apologize. I go to my editorial board meeting. I say, 'Why do you do this?' They look at me like I'm an idiot. I say you shouldn't hurt one person with lies."

The solution is to train journalists so that they can counter misinformation campaigns with good reporting skills that allow them to separate fact from fiction. Andrew Finkel, a journalist who has worked in the Turkish media, notes that a constant violation of professional journalistic standards in Turkey contributes to "reporters and columnists who indulge in sloppy practices or outright libel." These practices make worse a tradition of state-sponsored deceit dating back to the late nineteenth century. He wrote, "That half-truths and disinformation can be enlisted in the interest of the state is a notion that dies hard" (2000, 147).

Sethi, the Pakistani newspaper editor, says that it's a journalistic tradition in Pakistan to publish first and make corrections later. Truth telling, journalism, and, ultimately, the public's interest would best be served by questioning the enemy images with the simple act of fact-checking. After Danny's death, Pakistani intelligence agents and media continued to play games with the truth and lives. On July 1, 2002, *Jang,* the popular Urdu newspaper, ran the headline "Life of American Citizen Working for Mossad in Danger, Is Impersonating a Journalist." It said: "Karl Vick, an American citizen working for Mossad and impersonating a journalist in Karachi is apparently in danger. He is also not adhering to the instruction being given to him by the U.S. consulate in Karachi on June 27 and booked a room in a five-star hotel and showed himself as a correspondent of *Wall Street Journal.*" Vick was a staff reporter for the *Washington Post,* often sharing a byline in the *Washington Post* with Khan, the reporter for the *News* and *Jang.*

While this analysis focuses on a case study in Pakistan, the same type of demonizing of Pakistan occurs on the other side of the border, in India. Disinformation and enemy image campaigns are a way of demonizing the opposition, or "using domestic media and control over the levers of power to create hatred for leaders and peoples of other nations in order to prepare the population for war" (Nelson 1996, 156). Journalists often enjoy a privileged position in society, one immune from public scrutiny. But in the business of enemy image making, no one is safe, including journalists. The *Wall Street Journal* and a foundation set up by Danny's family, the Daniel Pearl Foundation, have developed training programs for journalists in Pakistan. All journalists would serve not only society but also ourselves if we would develop our professional and ethical standards so that we don't allow ourselves to be used as vehicles for communicating disinformation in the propaganda wars between nations.

REFERENCES

Cliff, Lionel, and Maureen Ramsay. 2000. *The Politics of Lying: Implications for Democracy.* Basington, Engl: Houndsmills.

Fiebig-Von Hase, Ragnhild, and Ursula Lehmkuhl. 1997. *Enemy Images in American History.* Providence, R.I.: Berghahn Books.

Finkel, A. 2000. "Who Guards the Turkish Press? A Perspective on Press Corruption in Turkey." *Journal of International Affairs* 54.

Hartmann, Frederick H. 1982. *The Conservation of Enemies.* Westport, Conn.: Greenwood Press.

Huntington, Samuel. 1998. *The Clash of Civilizations and the Remaking of World Order.* New York: Simon & Schuster.

Keen, Sam. 1986. *Faces of the Enemy: Reflections of the Hostile Imagination.* San Francisco: Harper & Row.

Nelson, Richard Alan. 1996. *A Chronology and Glossary of Propaganda in the United States.* Westport, Conn.: Greenwood.

Nomani, Asra Q. 2003. *Tantrika: Traveling the Road of Divine Love.* San Francisco: Harper San Francisco Publishers.

Pearl, Mariane. 2003. *Mighty Heart: The Brave Life and Death of My Husband Daniel Pearl.* New York: Scribner.

Rosini, Neil J. 1991. *The Practical Guide to Libel Law.* New York: Praeger Publishers.

Simon, Joel. 2003. Personal interview, December 17.

Smyth, F. 2002. "Testimony by the Committee to Protect Journalists." Subcommittee on International Operations and Terrorism. Comments at the Senate Foreign Relations Committee, May 2.

13

Anatomy of a Bonding: An Embedded Reporter's Account of the Bonding Process with the Soldiers

Ronald Paul Larson

I was standing about three feet away from Specialist Daniel Starkey, his .30-caliber machine gun hanging by a sling over his right shoulder, its barrel forward. Our backs were to our Humvee, and we stood facing a crowd of about two-dozen loud, curious, and excited Iraqis. Most were boys, not yet teenagers. About a half-dozen older men stood behind the crowd, watching interestedly. It was Friday, April 11, 2003. We were somewhere in the middle of An Nasiriyah, a southern Iraqi city of a third of a million people. Our officers had left Starkey and a few other soldiers in the street to guard the Humvees while the officers went into nearby buildings searching for building supplies.

At first, the kids wanted food or water. We convinced them, falsely, that we didn't have any. Then they wanted their picture taken. I took a dozen photos. After that, they asked us where we were from and what our names were. Then they noticed the name tags on our helmets and flak jackets. A dozen kids produced scraps of paper out of nowhere and wanted us to write our names on the pieces of paper. The children closed in, one little girl brushed up against Starkey's machine gun. He gently warned her away.

The situation was not really dangerous, but it was stressful. The constant attention of the kids was beginning to take its toll. Several times Starkey and I looked at each other with a sort of "When is this going to end?" look. By this time, I had grown to know and like Starkey. We slept on cots next to each other in our tent. He was originally from Ohio, and I was from Wisconsin, so we had the Midwest in common. He was married and had two young boys, was a serious Christian (like many other soldiers), and liked to dip tobacco.

We were both subject to the same stress and dangers of ambush. We were "on the same side" not only as Americans but as human beings. True, I was a journalist, and he was a soldier; but as far as I was concerned, that didn't really matter too much. Those were only our jobs. He was a guy from Ohio, and I was a guy from Wisconsin, both of us facing a crowd of Iraqis with our backs to a Humvee.

Fortunately, I escaped from the mob of children. An army civil-affairs officer came by and introduced me to an English-speaking Iraqi engineer. I interviewed him about the fighting in An Nasiriyah and about his feelings regarding Saddam and the war. About a half-hour later our officers returned, and we climbed into our Humvees and moved on to another location.

My experience with Starkey was not unique. I had similar experiences with other soldiers. As an embedded journalist, I had an unusual opportunity to not only report on the war but on the American soldiers who fought it. Instead of being some nosy reporter intruding into the soldier's world, I was part of that world, a person allowed to enter it through official sanction. Eventually, after days and weeks of living with the soldiers, of suffering through sandstorms, and of preparing for the possibility of ambush or attack, I bonded with them. I came to know and like many of them, and I developed a personal relationship with several. This bonding with the soldiers gave me some of my most rewarding personal experiences. It was also a potential source of professional complications.

I should begin by noting that the unit I was embedded with, the Thirty-sixth Engineer Group, was not a combat unit. It was a support unit of about a hundred soldiers that commanded army engineer construction battalions in Kuwait and southern Iraq. The unit entered Iraq four days behind the frontline troops. Although we saw and heard combative weapons fire twice, in both cases it was miles away and there was no immediate danger. My unit never came under direct enemy fire. There was always the threat of danger, usually in the form of ambush, but it never materialized. The story of the Thirty-sixth was one of overcoming physical hardship and being prepared for danger. This should be kept in mind. I suspect that the strength of my bonding with the soldiers could only have been less than that in a combat unit, where the dangers were greater and more apparent.

I arrived at my unit on March 20, the first day of the war. When I first arrived at the unit, I was given a tour of the encampment by Captain Brian Chapuran, the unit's adjutant (the one in charge of legal issues). I was introduced to most of the officers and the first sergeant. After the introductions, a young female lieutenant took me to the "D-Fac" (dining facility) to eat lunch. I was about to take my first bite of a cheeseburger when we got the first scud alert. This began the bonding. I was with the soldiers when, for them, the war began. Not only was I walking around in a heavy protective suit and mask as the other soldiers were, but I was subject to the same dangers from scuds. It also became clear that I lost some or all of my neutrality in terms of physical safety. I was an American, I was with American soldiers, and people from another country were trying to kill all of us.

As the first weekend of the war passed and the scud alerts continued but lessened, I gradually began to meet the enlisted soldiers and come to know them. I initially set up my laptop on a back table in the tent of Captain Patrick Hogeboom, the company commander. I sat at one end of the table; he sat in the middle; and his executive officer, First Lieutenant Julie Campbell, worked at the other end. Although I didn't plan it, I found it advantageous to work so closely with the company commander. As I wrote and filed stories about the opening days of the war, he and I talked about our lives as well as any professional issues that arose. I found myself building a positive relationship with the man who was in charge of the headquarters company (not the Thirty-sixth Engineer Group itself); that is, I was with the man who could get things done.

I also built relationships with some of the enlisted soldiers who worked in the headquarters tent, such as Sergeant Chad Shier, an ex-marine who was the nuclear-biological-chemical noncommissioned officer (NCO). This provided practical benefits right away. When I first tried to file a story using my satellite phone at an army camp prior to being placed with the Thirty-sixth, it didn't work. As a result, I put my stories on a floppy disc and gave them to an army public affairs NCO and had him send them via military e-mail. With the Thirty-sixth, Captain Hogeboom and Sergeant Shier let me use their laptops to send my stories the same way.

One of my priorities, although I didn't consciously realize it, was to build trust between myself and the soldiers. On the second or third day of the war, an enlisted African American woman who had learned of the antiwar demonstrations in the United States asked me what kind of reception I thought she would get back in the states after the war. I remember her saying that she was afraid she would be spat on. I was surprised by this question. I thought that the one thing we learned from the Vietnam War, if nothing else, was to distinguish between the soldier and the policy. I assured her that people who disagreed with the president's policy would not take it out on the soldiers. It was only at this point that the issue of the soldier's feelings about the war came up. Before this, it never occurred to me to ask the soldiers about their opinions of the war. I decided to not pursue the question. Not only did I have my hands full working on stories between scud alerts, but in retrospect, I realize I was more concerned about building trust with the soldiers. I thought that if I suddenly started asking them whether they were for or against the war or what their personal feelings were, I might scare them and create suspicion. After all, they didn't know me or how I would report things. For all they knew, I might have exposed those who said they were against the war, thus getting the supposed soldiers into trouble. The fact that I was against the war may have played into this. I thought that if they were honest with me, I would have to be honest with them; and if they supported the war, they might see me as an adversary. Had I been a more experienced journalist, I may have found a way to ask this kind of question without any negative consequences to my relationship with the soldiers. I knew enough to know, however, that the more they trusted me, the more information I might get.

It was the move into Iraq on March 24, 2003, that pushed my relationship with the soldiers to another level. Danger, or the threat of danger, is a great bonding mechanism. Our first night in Iraq we saw what we presumed to be American artillery or rockets shelling Iraqi positions. Although it only lasted a few moments, it was quite a display of firepower, and it reminded us that we were in "Indian country" as Colonel Michael Biering, the commanding officer of the Thirty-sixth, put it.

The next day, March 25, we suffered through what one officer called the "sandstorm from hell." Soldiers who were fixing and putting up tents against a gusting wind in the morning found themselves filling and placing sandbags around the tents in a blizzard of desert and wind in the afternoon. This was another great bonding moment. After shooting some video and taking photos of the sandstorm and of soldiers filling sandbags, I helped them.

Two days later, the Thirty-sixth moved north to Tallil Air Base, a captured Iraqi airbase outside An Nasiriyah, and the unit remained there for the rest of the war. A sense of threat and vulnerability filled the first days there. Although U.S. combat forces had passed through the area several days before, the airbase was not fully secured, and we suspected that unknown and possibly dangerous forces were near. The marines had encountered some resistance in capturing An Nasiriyah, and it was in this area that the 507 Ordnance Maintenance Company was attacked and Jessica Lynch and others were captured. It was at Tallil where most of my stories were written and where my relationship with the soldiers took its final form.

I knew from my own previous military experience that the officers and enlisted lived in separate worlds. I quickly realized that, to do my job, I would have to live in both worlds at the same time. The difficulty of doing so first presented itself in the question of where I would sleep. Officers and enlisted slept in different tents. During the first two weeks, I alternated between the two options as we moved from place to place. Once we settled at Tallil Airbase though, I had to find a place and stay there. I let the company commander assign me to one. It was with the enlisted men. At first I wondered if this meant that the officers disapproved of me. The captain said that it was merely a question of space. I was assigned to the tent that, at the time, had the fewest people in it.

Shortly after our arriving at Tallil, some of the officers asked me to call them by their first name, an indication of their willingness to become familiar. Having been an enlisted soldier when I was in the army, I was a little uncomfortable about this but did it anyway, using their first names only when no enlisted soldiers were around.

Perhaps because of their deference toward authority, it took the enlisted soldiers longer to warm up to me. Initially, most called me *sir*. I had to tell them to call me Ron. It took some soldiers a while, but many eventually did. Some never felt comfortable with that and always called me *sir*. Whether a soldier ended up calling me by my first name was entirely dependent on how close we became. And this is exactly the point.

I bonded with all the soldiers to one degree or another but became particularly close with a few. As elsewhere in life, you find those people you most get along with, and you begin establishing a friendship. There was a group of enlisted men who dipped tobacco and had what they called a "dip circle." I really liked some of the guys in this group and grew closest to them (Starkey was one of them). I eventually took up dipping tobacco and joined their circle. We would usually meet after dinner. Fortunately, this time also coincided with women's shower hours, and the showers were across the street. Our circle was able to watch female soldiers, often dressed in gym shorts, walk to and from the shower. This was more or less the high point of the day (at least for me).

I also spent a fair amount of time with the chaplain, Major Timothy Bedsole. He was an affable middle-aged Southerner who had a cappuccino machine, and we enjoyed each other's company. He also was in the habit of driving around the airbase in his Humvee to meet the other chaplains and see what was going on. I accompanied him several times in the hope of stumbling upon a story and never failed to find one. Time with him always seemed profitable, both personally and professionally.

I suspect that the possible pitfall of close bonding for a journalist may be clear. If you are friends with somebody, then you don't want to write anything that would make that person look bad. I especially didn't want to report anything that would get soldiers into trouble or make their lives more difficult.

As far as the senior leadership was concerned, this was never really an issue. I was never close enough to the colonel, the major, or the senior NCOs to consider there being any kind of a personal relationship. However, this was not true of some of the junior officers, such as the captains and the lieutenants; and likewise for the lower-ranking enlisted, the sergeants and below. Even though I wasn't friends with the senior officers, I still developed a concern for their well-being and the reputation of the unit. I didn't want to report anything that would make the unit as a whole look bad.

What would be the effect of my reporting anything that made the officers and men look bad? It might have made my life very difficult, both personally and professionally. Depending on what I wrote and who it was about, the soldiers' attitudes might have turned hostile, and they might have refused to be interviewed, give information, or assist me in sending my stories.

Of course, my life was dependent on protection from the soldiers. This was more of an issue in combat units than it was in a combat-support unit, such as the one I was in. I don't think soldiers would have "fragged" me, or allowed me to ride into an ambush, for an unflattering story. The soldiers would have been putting themselves at risk as well. This was not a realistic threat. The real threat to me, or any other reporter, was to objectivity—a too-close identification with the soldiers. We were all Americans in a foreign land and in danger. It was quite difficult not to psychologically surround the wagons and see yourself as an *us* against a *them*. I suspect this is a natural reaction. Had I been with troops from another country, I think my sense of difference would have been greater, but the same bonding mechanisms would have been at work. In fact, I remember hearing about a female journalist from Latin America embedded with the marines who strongly opposed to the war but who "fell in love" with them and was supposedly unapologetic about it.

Fortunately, I believe my bonding with the soldiers never seriously affected my reporting. I never had to make a choice between my friendship for a soldier and my obligations as a journalist. In my opinion, nothing that might have cast individuals in a bad light ever rose to the level of news. Overall, I think the bonding was positive. Soldiers became helpful and forthcoming with information and opinions. Although some view being embedded as a potential problem for journalists, I do not regard the bonding with the soldiers as a failing of embedment; rather, I see it as merely one of its characteristics, one that can be positive but one that needs to be taken into account.

When I look back, the most meaningful experiences to me were interactions with the Iraqis and the U.S. soldiers. Whether it was standing in the street waiting for officers to conduct business, whether it was a Civil Affairs mission delivering food and water, or whether it was the two young boys who shouted "We love you" at my Humvee as I was driving out of Iraq, all of my interactions with Iraqis were rewarding in one way or another—even the time an Iraqi tried to rip my video camera out of my hands.

But, it was only with the soldiers that I had an opportunity to establish personal relationships. I don't know if these relationships will continue into the future. Like summer-camp friends who at the end of the summer promise to keep in touch, they will probably fade with time. I do know that they will continue for some time, however. I promised the soldiers copies of the photos and video I took. I feel enough of a bond to think I owe them that much.

14

The War on Iraq: A Reporter's Observations

Dana Hull

Last spring, when my editors at the *San Jose Mercury News* in California said that reporters were needed to go cover the war in Iraq, I jumped at the chance. I lived in Amman, Jordan, as an exchange student in high school and graduated from college with a degree in international relations, and I often wished for a reason to return to the Middle East.

But I was emphatic on one point in particular: I did not want to be "embedded" with American troops and thus be put into a position where my survival would depend on protection by the soldiers who I would be reporting on. The pros and cons of embedding have been hotly debated within the world of journalism and beyond, and that debate will continue for years to come. Some of my colleagues said that being embedded was the safest way to cover the war and that it would give me a rare, bird's-eye view of the battlefield. Others urged me against it, warning that military commanders could control when I filed my stories, on the premise that my satellite phone—which can be used to connect to the Internet—would give away troop movements.

I wanted to go to Iraq more than anything, and I worried that by refusing to embed I was blowing my one and only chance to report from the region. But I know myself well. I didn't want to have the raw reality of war—American soldiers and Iraqis being killed or wounded—scorched into my psyche. When I thought long and hard about the types of stories that most interested me, reporting on the advance of American troops through the sand-whipped desert wasn't high on the list. I wanted to spend as much time as possible with Iraqi civilians, talking with them about their lives over the past decade in their homes and schools and mosques. I worried that if I embedded, my experience

would be skewed—that all I would see was Iraq from the inside of a tank. So
I took a deep breath and told my editors that I wanted to cover not the war but
the war's aftermath and the occupation.

I arrived in Baghdad in late May, after a surreal twelve-hour drive in the
dark of night from Jordan. It felt like crossing from Germany to Eastern Europe, or going back in time. Jordan's glitzy five-star hotels and Western shops
gave way to a country devastated by the Iran–Iraq war, the first Gulf War, and
nearly twelve years of crippling sanctions. The road from Amman to Baghdad was desolate for hundreds of miles. But as we approached the Iraqi border, we came upon scores of old cars, many filled with refugees who had fled
during the bombing and were now trying to get home. Newly purchased satellite dishes were strapped on the roofs of beat up old Toyotas with cracked
windshields. Black-market gasoline stations—usually just a young boy and a
jerrycan—lined the road.

I quickly found that propaganda works both ways in places like Iraq. Saddam Hussein's image towered over everything else at the border crossing. A
feared despot, he was larger than life: enormous paintings of Hussein were
everywhere, from government ministry buildings to the grounds of the
mukhabarat, or Iraqi Intelligence Service.

But nearly everywhere I went, Saddam's face had been scratched out or
vandalized. I arrived in Iraq as a great purge was underway. Outside of the
communications tower was a large painting of Saddam talking on a telephone; his face was obliterated by a yellow smiley face. American civilian
officials with the Coalition Provisional Authority were racing to remove
Hussein's face from Iraqi money; the newly printed currency now features
images of archeological sites. A booming black market in all things Saddam
was underway: soldiers and journalists alike paid fifty dollars or more for
Saddam Hussein wristwatches, thinking that one day they'd be collectors'
items on eBay. I could never tell if the Saddam paintings and statues had
been marred by Iraqis seeking revenge or by American soldiers under orders
to erase the Iraqi leader's omniscient presence from the nation's collective
consciousness.

Reporting in Iraq was unlike anything I've ever done before. I hired a
twenty-seven-year-old Iraqi woman named Ban Adil to work with me as a
translator and guide, and she was indispensable. Ban had a three-year-old
daughter and was five months' pregnant when I met her; she desperately
wanted to work as a translator and save money so that she and her husband
could buy a house. She has a master's degree in English literature and theater from the University of Baghdad, and she is a huge Samuel Beckett fan.
Her mother is Shiite, her father Sunni, and Ban has one foot planted firmly
in each world.

Every day was a mad race to discern the truth, with different versions of events coming at us from all sides. There was an enormous disconnect: I went to briefings with military and occupation officials where they talked about the enormous progress being made, but the Iraqis that I interviewed insisted that their lives were getting worse. L. Paul Bremer, the American occupation chief, had set up shop in one of Hussein's former palaces—an irony not lost on the Iraqis. Many of them had never been inside of Hussein's numerous palaces, and most were dying to see them. But American reporters and military contractors could come and go through the gates.

I wanted to find out why the electricity kept going off, why the water quality was deteriorating, and why women and young girls were afraid to walk to school. American officials often gave rosy assessments that were completely at odds with what was happening on the ground. Iraqis were wonderful to talk with, but I was always hearing what they said through the lens of a translator. I kicked myself that I didn't speak Arabic but started to learn key phrases. *Wayn Kahrabaa?* (Where is the electricity?) became a running joke.

Some days were wildly successful, and some days completely fell apart. Ban would arrive at the hotel where I was staying each morning with a stack of the day's Arabic-language newspapers, and we would drink tea while she read them. Iraq, which used to be dominated by the state-controlled media, has seen an explosion in new media in recent months. Though some publications are more reputable than others, nearly a hundred newspapers have sprouted up, and Iraqis are able to watch satellite television for the first time.

The Arabic-language papers often reported on incidents that we never would have heard about otherwise, and such sources were the only real way to learn about the deaths of Iraqi civilians. One day a paper had a short story that said a family attending a wedding in the town of Samarra had been accidentally shot and killed at a checkpoint. A colleague of mine went to Samarra and confirmed that the incident was true. But when I asked an American commander about this incident at a military briefing, he simply said that they were "looking into it," and he refused to provide any details. I realized that the military would not have commented on the shootings in Samarra unless I had asked about them in a public forum. It was a key lesson to learn: asking questions at briefings forced the American commanders to give some sort of response, and other journalists then heard the question and were more likely to follow up on the story themselves.

I also learned a great deal from my colleagues in the Arab world. They attended the briefings also and asked questions about incidents that I was totally unaware of. The enormous language gap was not just a problem for the U.S. military but for journalists as well. Few American journalists speak Arabic, and nearly everyone relied on translators to help them navigate the maze

of Iraqi society. But each translator came with his or her own ethnic and political point of view, and some reporters were never sure if the translations
were accurate. But at the same time, some stories in the Arabic press had to
be taken with a grain of salt. One day Ban arrived excited: there was a story
in the paper that a woman had hidden a knife under her black *abaya* and
stabbed an American soldier in the neck. It would have been the first attack
on U.S. forces by a woman, and we were both intrigued. We raced to the
neighborhood where this incident supposedly happened and interviewed
shopkeepers, soldiers, children, and women on the street. No one had heard
of the incident, and with surprise Ban ultimately surmised that the story was
completely false.

The U.S. military closely monitors the number of American soldiers who
are killed or wounded in Iraq. Central Command, or "Cent Com," sends out
press releases by e-mail whenever a soldier is hit by a roadside mine or is
fired on by a rocket-propelled grenade. But there was no equivalent tally for
Iraqis, and it was impossible to know with certainty how many Iraqi civilians
had been killed, even by accident. People whom I interviewed on the street
insisted that it was in the thousands—everyone knew someone who had died
during a raid or while crossing a checkpoint. President Bush announced that
"major combat" in Iraq ended on May 1, but the combat continued and escalated as the summer wore on and as the searing temperatures continued to
rise. It was a guerilla war, though few would say so at the time.

One morning Ban and I watched Al-Jazeera, the popular Arabic-language
satellite channel. Al-Jazeera was enormously controversial. The station had a
horrible reputation among the U.S. military: many soldiers felt that the reporting was not only predominantly false but inflammatory, and some insisted that the station reported attacks on U.S. soldiers just minutes before
they occurred. But the station's reporters were fearless and had contacts all
over Iraq. They were also furious: during the fighting in Baghdad, American
forces had attacked Al-Jazeera's headquarters, and one of their reporters had
been killed—an incident that many believed to be intentional.

The Arabic script that crawled along the bottom the screen said that a
twelve-year-old boy had been shot and killed while playing on his roof in
west Baghdad. Ban and I flipped through the other Arab-language channels,
and no one else had the story. Was it true, or was it hype? Ban and I decided
to drive to the western edge of the city and see what we could find, even
though I thought it might be a futile effort.

News in Iraq travels by word of mouth, from cousin to cousin to neighbor
to shopkeeper to friend. It's an oral grapevine that spreads faster than wild-
fire. We stopped on the side of the road and asked a cigarette vendor if he'd
heard anything. He pointed us to another neighborhood, where Ban chatted

with a taxi driver who sent us to another neighborhood. We stopped and talked to some kids who were fixing a bicycle. They immediately knew what we were talking about, and one of the boys hopped into the car with us.

A moment later, we were at the home of the boy's uncles, and I then realized that I was at a family wake. It was true: a twelve-year-old boy, Mohammed, had been shot and killed by U.S. soldiers while he was on the roof. His devastated mother was hiding in a back bedroom with female relatives and wailing with grief. The father was angry and stunned, sitting with men in the front garden and drinking cup after cup of hot, sweet tea. Mohammed's twin brother, Mustafa, was visibly distraught: as his large eyes filled with tears and as he crawled, sobbing, into his father's lap, my heart broke.

The family was surprised to see us: we were the only Western journalists who had come to the house, and they repeated their story. When U.S. soldiers rumbled into the neighborhood around 10:30 PM, Mohammed ran to the roof, his mother said. He was standing on the outdoor stairs between the second floor of the family's home and the roof when a U.S. soldier saw him from below.

Witnesses said the soldier, who was standing on the street behind the house, swung his gun upward. "We saw him aim and we said, 'Baby! Baby! Don't shoot!'" said Hashim Abdullah, a neighbor who witnessed the shooting.

Up above, on the stairs, Mohammed started to walk down, Abdullah said, but was shot squarely in the chest after taking only two steps. He fell face first into the stairwell, filling it with blood. At least five other shots were fired, the witnesses said. Two bullets pierced an upstairs window; another bullet lodged in the hallway leading to the twin's bedroom.

It was brutal. Mohammed was the youngest known Iraqi civilian to be killed by American troops since May 1. But U.S. soldiers had an entirely different understanding of events: they claimed that Mohammed died with an AK-47 in his hand.

"It was dark and the soldier saw a silhouette on a rooftop. He had to make a decision and he engaged. It's a tough call to make. I'm sure the soldier regrets it," said Major Scott Slaten, a spokesman for the army's First Armored Division.

"But what is a twelve-year-old boy doing on a rooftop with an AK-47? We've seen some cases where adults are using the child to carry their weapons. In the dark, when there is no electricity, a twelve-year-old and a twenty-year-old often look the same," Slaten said. "We all hate that this has happened. But we're not admitting guilt in any way, shape, or form. He had a weapon."

I'll never really know what happened that night.

Another story has stayed with me. Scores of Iraqi men were arrested in the days that followed the fall of Baghdad, on April 9, and many of them have complained bitterly about their treatment in the U.S. prisons that were hastily set up near the Baghdad airport.

Qais Mohammed al-Saliman, fifty-four, is an Iraqi engineer who returned to Baghdad in early May after having lived in Denmark since 1990. On May 6, he was arrested when U.S. troops stopped the car he was in, on a popular street along the Tigris River. He said he was never told why he was being detained, and he insisted that he was an engineer eager to help rebuild his country. He speaks English well and has a Danish passport.

"They treated me badly. It was very hot, and they put me on the ground with a heavy shoe on my back," he said, in an interview after his release in his mother's home. "Then a TV truck came, and they pretended to arrest me again for the media. It was like staging a play."

I wish I could prove Qais's story, but he didn't know which network the television crew was with or even who arrested him. Was he lying? I didn't know, but I found it hard to believe that he would make such a compelling anecdote up. As always, I found myself straddling the line between gut instincts that said he was telling the truth and creeping doubt that kept me awake at night.

I left Iraq in mid-July, as the battle for Iraqi "hearts and minds" continued to hit major snags and the insurgency against U.S. forces intensified. I still get e-mail from both the American military and the occupation authorities. Most recently, a release touted the fact that American officials were going to remove four large statues of Saddam Hussein's head from one of his palaces (see table 14.1). It was a brilliant public relations move, and they were lining up pool photographers and camera operators to take pictures of the event. The press release, dated December 2, 2003, was titled "Saddam's Heads Roll" and is printed in full below:

Baghdad, Iraq—With a crowd cheering in the background, the first of four bronze-plated Saddam Hussein heads came down today from its perch atop the Republican Palace.

"The time has come for these heads to roll," said L. Paul Bremer III, Administrator of the Coalition Provisional Authority. He added, "These statues stood as a reminder of the megalomania of the former dictator. We're sick of them."

Once all of the statues are removed one will be destroyed immediately. The others will be kept for now to determine whether they should be melted down, or perhaps kept for historical interest. It will take approximately two weeks to remove all four statues.

More than a dozen contractors bid for the opportunity to remove the statues.

I was stunned and full of questions. Would they save any of the statues for a museum of Iraqi history? Who was in the "cheering crowd"—Americans who worked in the palace complex or Iraqi officials? Who made the decision

Table 14.1. Basic Information on Structure of Hussein Statue

Statue weight	2.72 metric tons (3 tons, or 6,000 lbs.)
Statue base	3.63 metric tons (4 tons, or 8,000 lbs.)
Statue size	65.00 cubic meters (67.50 cubic yds., or 2,295 cubic ft.)

Source: Press release from U.S. forces, dated December 2, 2003, "Saddam's Heads Roll."

to remove the statues? Was the staged event designed to provide a psychological boost for soldiers who were still searching for Hussein, or were Iraqi authorities saying that they wanted the statues removed?

The next day, the photograph of the heads was on the front page of the *New York Times*.

A few weeks later, the world learned that Saddam Hussein had finally been caught, "like a rat" in a "spider-hole," outside of Tikrit. I was on a plane that day, flying from New York City to my home in Oakland, and I watched the cable television shows. Over and over and over again, I saw the same footage, of a military doctor checking Hussein for lice and swabbing the inside of his mouth for DNA. It was compelling and thoroughly humiliating footage. But I wasn't in Iraq anymore—I couldn't interview Iraqis to see what they really thought. I'm thankful that I had the opportunity to do so when I was there.

15

America: The Fourth Reich

Barrie Zwicker

It should not be denied any longer: America is hurtling along the road to full-fledged fascism.[1] Recognizing this is the necessary first step in deflecting the juggernaut and creating the possibility of more peaceful tomorrows. It is not only legitimate but necessary to correctly employ the power of naming.

Fascism, according to the *Collins English Dictionary,* is "any (#1) rightwing (#2) nationalist ideology or movement with (#3) an authoritarian and (#4) hierarchical structure that is (#5) fundamentally opposed to democracy and (#6) liberalism." Add "(#7) racism and (#8) brutality" and you have Hitler's Third Reich in a nutshell.

By any sober analysis America has become right-wing and nationalist. At the same time I am soulfully aware of the tremendous numbers of Americans ashamed, appalled, afraid, and angry about the direction of their government and too many of their fellow citizens.

Signs of growing authoritarianism in the United States of America are evident, especially to those outside the self-absorbed cocoon of U.S. culture. The signs include the supine attitude toward authority of most of the mainstream media.[2]

Contrary to incessant rhetoric about democracy, the U.S. power structure is considerably hierarchical. Money power forms the main rungs of the hierarchy. According to the *New York Times* (June 15, 2003), the Republicans were confident of raising at least $170 million for George W. Bush's 2004 election campaign, redefining what the *Times* called "standards" for fund-raising. Both the hierarchy of money and the antagonism to democracy are spelled out in Greg Palast's *The Best Democracy Money Can Buy* (2003).

That the U.S. establishment is opposed to liberalism—no matter how you define *liberalism*—can hardly be debated. We already have six grounds for applying the term *Fourth Reich.* But consider another twenty parallels between the United States of America today and Hitler's Germany:

Anti-Communism, anti-Marxism, antisocialism are visceral. The *core opposition* to the regime is from the strong, conscious left.

A fundamentalist faith in capitalism, specifically the systematized form of
greed known as monopoly capitalism. Corporations are at the center of the
power structure.

Corruption at the top is endemic.

The number of people consigned to the grave by military and paramilitary
actions in both cases is in the millions. Backdate the Fourth Reich to the end
of the Second World War and the number murdered by U.S. forces equals or
outnumbers the toll in the Holocaust. Three million in Vietnam alone. The
brutality is a matter of record for those who are willing to look at it. See
William Blum's *Killing Hope*[3] for one researcher's record.

Most of the Fourth Reich's victims are Asians, indigenous peoples of Latin
America, and more recently "towelheads." The racism is clear.

In each case the leader was illegally installed into power, Hitler in 1933,[4]
George W. Bush in 2000.[5]

The ambition of world domination. The Third and Fourth Reichs invade as
many countries as can be gotten away with. A blitzkrieg approach is favored.
For Hitler: Austria, Czechoslovakia, Poland. For George W. Bush:
Afghanistan, Iraq, next?

Seizure of other countries' oil. Grabbing Russia's Baku oil fields was a major objective of Hitler.[6]

The "pitiful giant" syndrome is invoked. "Our enemies are powerful," it
goes, so we must arm endlessly "in self-defense." Often accompanied with
the high-sounding: "Our enemies taunt us, and we are patient, but our patience is not endless."

Preemptive, or "preventive," war is policy and practice.

Highly orchestrated propaganda campaigns are a reich staple. Hitler's stylized mass rallies come to mind. The propaganda of the Fourth Reich is suited
to the television age: sophisticated and media-savvy deluxe. Embedded journalists, for instance. An example from the 2003 invasion of Iraq was the much
publicized return of petite blonde soldier Private Jessica Lynch to her family,
in full uniform. Props included a hometown band and Blackhawk helicopters.

Where the media are not sufficiently proregime and self-censoring, censorship and intimidation of them. Brutal intimidation under the second Bush
regime includes bombing Al-Jazeera facilities in Afghanistan and Iraq, the
latter censorship by assassination.

Use of religion. Invocations of God's approval for the reich, and its works.
William L. Shirer quotes the führer's minister of church affairs as declaring that

the Nazi Party "stands on the basis of Positive Christianity, and Positive Christianity is National Socialism. . . . National Socialism is doing God's will."[7]

An ever-encroaching police state is a sure sign you're living in a reich.

Illegal actions. International and domestic laws are breached, resisted, and undermined, with rejection or subversion of multilateral agreements and organizations. Hitler pulled Germany out of the League of Nations altogether. In America's case, the United Nations is sidelined or embraced according to the Empire's needs.

"Terrorism" and terrorism—wholesale and retail[8]—are central to a reich's operation. The kind in quotes refers to inflated or imagined threats of terrorism, drummed into the domestic public's mind. Use of fear (e.g., orange alerts) is an important tool of a reich.

Alarms of "terrorism" by a reich are hypocritical to the nth degree considering the wholesale terrorism a reich unleashes on others. Third Reich Stuka dive bombers over Spain, V-2 rockets into London. Fourth Reich "daisy cutters," cluster bombs, "bunker busters," DU munitions in Yugoslavia, Afghanistan, and Iraq. Skies full of helicopter gunships, in a string of countries going back to Vietnam.

Finally there's the actual retail terrorism created by the reich: the clandestine formation, training, funding, and control of functioning terrorists, serving as dark pawns of the reich. This is one of the lesser-known parallels. Shirer again: "For months prior to July 1934 the Austrian Nazis, with weapons and dynamite furnished by Germany, had instituted a reign of terror, blowing up railways, power stations and government buildings and murdering."[9]

British investigative journalist John K. Cooley, in his book *Unholy Wars,* shows—for a careful reader who connects the dots left by the CIA, Pakistan's ISI (virtually an arm of the CIA), Saudi intelligence, and the bin Laden family—that the CIA was deeply involved in the creation and subsequent operations of al Qaeda.[10]

A preoccupation with *secrecy.*[11]

Secrecy is a precondition for deception.

Now deception, above all, is the key to everything for a reich. The leaders are marinated in a complete obsession with lying and deceiving at every turn.[12]

Deceptions are the regime's key to mobilizing public opinion. Deception is needed to fool the citizenry into relinquishing their civil rights and thereby their many avenues of dissent. Deception precedes and leads to the police state. Deception precedes and leads to war. At every step deception is required for a reich's gaining and maintaining power and carrying out all its other nefarious actions. Without successful deceptions the reich agenda simply cannot proceed. If the deceptions can be unmasked early enough and sufficiently, the reich collapses. No reich so far has collapsed this way. In an information age, it might be possible.

The masterpiece deceptions are those so big that ordinary, decent, honest people cannot (or will not) comprehend or face that such deceptions exist.[13]

Of these deceptions, the penultimate is what the anarchist Bakunin described as "the propaganda of the act." And finally the ultimate fake act is the election-stealing or war-triggering fake event, especially one involving foreign "terrorists."

This makes pivotal the parallel between the Reichstag fire of 1933, on the one hand, and the events of 9/11, on the other.

The Reichstag fire of February 27, 1933, was in its day as iconic as were the events of September 11, 2001, in ours. The Reichstag fire was blamed on a Communist, who was subsequently decapitated. And by extension, the fire was blamed on all Communists. The historical evidence is that the Nazis arranged the conflagration. In the *Rise and Fall*, Shirer writes, "Beyond reasonable doubt it was the Nazis who planned the arson and carried it out for their own political ends."[14]

The idea for the fire, writes Shirer, almost certainly originated at the top, with Goebbels and Goring.[15]

Vice Chancellor von Papen recalled that when he arrived at the blazing parliament buildings, Goering was already on the scene shouting "This is a communist crime . . ."[16]

"Hitler lost no time," Shirer writes, "in exploiting the Reichstag fire to the limit." The very next day he prevailed on the president to sign a decree "for the Protection of the People and the State," suspending the seven sections of the constitution that guaranteed individual and civil liberties. It was described as a "defensive measure against Communist acts of violence against the state."[17]

The parallel with the events of 9/11 is stunning. The official narrative, introduced with Goring-like speed, emerged within two hours: the "attack on America" was portrayed as the work of "terrorists," one evil man, Osama bin Laden, and a small group of coconspirators, the 2001 equivalents of the 1933 Communists.

The number and magnitude of anomalies surrounding 9/11 can point to only one conclusion: 9/11 was a completely made-in-the-USA inside job, a manufactured incident planned and run by some among the top leadership. Take just three anomalies:

1. During a drama in the sky in which four large scheduled passenger airliners flew wild courses for almost two hours while being tracked by radar, not a single U.S. jet interceptor turned a wheel until it was too

late. At the very least, this would have to involve serious incompetence on the part of one or more persons or units in the vast military and civil aviation establishments. And yet as I write this, just short of two years after the events, not a single person or unit from these establishments has been seriously questioned, let alone reprimanded.

2. The president was addressing an elementary school class in Florida at the time of the "attacks." His chief of staff, Andrew Card, whispered in his ear that "America is under attack" (such a brief message itself was odd). Yet the U.S. president continued for about twenty minutes to listen to a student talk about her pet goat. His behavior in this instance and in many others that day was bizarrely inappropriate. Even school children would know that when a person in authority learns of a major emergency, that person drops inconsequential tasks and begins to address the emergency.

3. Why did World Trade Center building number 7 suddenly and totally collapse at 5:25 PM on September 11? It had not been damaged earlier. Two small areas of fire, on its seventh and twelfth floors, appeared just before its collapse. Building 7 held offices of the FBI and the CIA. It was the first structural steel building ever to collapse with fire alone as the alleged cause.

Where there's a design, there's a designer. One of the most designing groups at the top of the U.S. empire is that clique of neocons who constitute the Project for a New American Century (PNAC).

Its members include Paul Wolfowitz, U.S. deputy secretary of defense; Richard Perle, resident scholar at the American Enterprise Institute; and William Kristol, editor of the *Weekly Standard*. Key PNAC members called for years, even decades, for a muscular expansion of U.S. military and economic might.

PNAC in September 2000, one year before 9/11, released a document, *Rebuilding America's Defenses*. The document states that mobilizing the U.S. public behind an imperialist agenda will be long a difficult "absent some catastrophic and catalyzing event like a new Pearl Harbor."[18] You can't get much clearer than that by way of proof that "superhawks"—fascists—at the pinnacle of U.S. power were consciously thinking of the need for 9/11.

Revealing the fraud of 9/11[19] in my opinion is the single most important task faced by civilization today. That it was dared is the supreme Achilles heel of the Fourth Reich. If enough people could be awakened to the enormity of the crime and to whom its perpetrators are, they would become a politically relevant constituency. Then the possibility of a cleansing transformation would emerge. Every worthwhile initiative you can name, be it environmental, social, political, or economic, would benefit from politically relevant exposure of the Great Deception.

In America there's a community of peace and environmental and justice activists, which includes theists, atheists, artists, workers, intellectuals, and plain folk—old and young. This community is unidentified, unrecognized, and therefore disenfranchised by the mainstream media. It may number thirty million, equal to the population of Canada. It appears to be the responsibility imposed by history on this community not only to recognize its own existence, importance, and power but to exercise that power nonviolently, before it's too late, to save their country and the world from full-fledged fascism.

Many Americans have told me they're aware of the possibility of the suspension of the U.S. Constitution (there would be a startling, deceptive pretext, of course) and other goose steps toward a führership. Should those steps be taken, it could be too late to prevent awful and perhaps permanent catastrophe.

The Fourth Reich and its outposts, including the ones within each of us, is perhaps humanity's last major challenge. Understanding and sufficiently dismantling it would probably lead to a period of chaos. But from that could emerge another world, still imperfect but one less in imminent danger of Armageddon. In it we might finally face a reasonable future.

NOTES

This chapter was adapted from remarks delivered to the World Association for Christian Communication, North American Region, University of British Columbia, Vancouver, B.C., July 30, 2003.

1. Alternative and some mainstream media are increasingly applying the "f word" (fascism) to the United States of America. See, for instance, "Is America Becoming Fascist?" in *Adbusters,* September/October, 2003, 33.

2. Most especially seen in the cover-up, rather than in the coverage of, are the most overarching crimes of the power elite. For instance, an objection by those who deny that there could be top-level fascistic conspiracies is that "surely the media would have a lot to gain from blowing the lid off such operations." This betrays a lack of understanding of the essentially subservient place of the media in this society, Feral House, 2003. For instance, Walter Karp of *Harper's* magazine is quoted on the hazards for journalists who engage in "source journalism" (namely, the top journalists who live by their relationships with high authorities) of challenging the official story on JFK's assassination (quoted in *The Assassinations: Probe Magazine on JFK, MLK, RFK and Malcolm X,* edited by James DiEugenio and Lisa Pease [Feral House, 2003], 303–4). These hazards include "lost access, complaints to editors and publishers, social penalties, leaks to competitors, a variety of responses no one wants." Karp continued: "It is a bitter irony of source journalism that the most esteemed journalists are

precisely the most servile. For it is by making themselves useful to the powerful that they gain access to the 'best' sources."

3. Black Rose Books, 1998, paperback edition.

4. See William L. Shirer, *The Rise and Fall of the Third Reich* (Touchstone Press, 1990), 199.

5. See Michael Moore, *Stupid White Men* (Regan Books, 2001), chap. 1.

6. Shirer, *Rise and Fall,* 798.

7. Shirer, *Rise and Fall,* 239.

8. To my knowledge the terms *wholesale terrorism* (meaning "state-sponsored") and *retail terrorism* (meaning "acts of terror committed by non-government-sponsored individuals or groups") were originated by Noam Chomsky and Edward S. Herman in the 1970s.

9. Shirer, *Rise and Fall,* 280.

10. *Unholy Wars: Afghanistan, America and International Terrorism* (Pluto Press, 2000), 107, 120–21, 225.

11. For an exploration of the deeply corrosive effects of obsession with secrecy, see Daniel Ellsberg, *Secrets: A Memoir of Vietnam and the Pentagon Papers* (Viking, 2002).

12. British historian Ian Kershaw, in his magisterial two-volume biography *Hitler 1889–1936: Hubris* and *Hitler 1936–1945: Nemesis* (Penguin Books, 2001) details dozens of Third Reich deceptions. In *Nemesis,* "Distortions of the truth were built into the communications system of the Third Reich at every level—most of all in the top echelons of the regime" (549).

13. It was part of the evil genius of Hitler that he knew, as he wrote in chapter 10 of his *Mein Kampf,* that "the broad mass of a nation . . . will more easily fall victim to a big lie than to a small one."

14. Shirer, *Rise and Fall,* 192.

15. Shirer, *Rise and Fall,* 192.

16. Shirer, *Rise and Fall,* 192.

17. Shirer, *Rise and Fall,* 194.

18. To view the entire document, log on at www.newamericancentury.org, search for "Pearl Harbor," choose number 5.

19. There are many revealing websites. Among the better ones are www.911pi.com, www.cooperativeresearch.org, and www.globalresearch.ca. The best single periodical is *Global Outlook* (Shanty Bay, ON, Canada).

War on Iraq and Media Coverage:
A Middle Eastern Perspective

Mahboub E. Hashem

On a nice moony night before the start of the second Gulf War, my friend Ali and I were dining at the Dubai Marina in the Jumeira District of Dubai City, the United Arab Emirates. Ali is an Iraqi who hadn't been in Iraq for more than twenty-five years because of Saddam Hussein's regime. During our conversation with regard to the situation in the Gulf, Ali said, "You know, Mahboub, I wish the Americans would invade Iraq, kill few Iraqis, and rid us of Saddam in the process. I am fed up with the way he has been treating us." Well, Ali was among the very few Arab people who were courageous enough to speak their minds and think that way about Iraq.

For a large majority of Arabs as well as other peoples around the globe, including Americans, Australians, British, and Spaniards themselves, war meant terror, disaster, death, and carnage on a large scale. It did not mean a game of "shock and awe," to be played right from the start. Thus, those peoples objected to the U.S. policy of waging another war against Iraq, which was thought to waste resources and add to the Iraqis' suffering. In fact, the killing and maiming of thousands of individuals, the destruction of Iraqi infrastructure, and the looting of private and public properties, including one of the most famous museums on Earth, have cost the Iraqis and the entire world billions of dollars. This war on Iraq is closely related to the Middle Eastern crisis between Arabs and Israel.

The world has lived through many acute crises around the globe. However, the Middle Eastern crisis is the deepest, most critical, and most complex so far. This crisis has come about since the creation of the state of Israel on Palestinian land in 1948. The injection of Israel into that region, with its influence in Western capitals (especially Washington) and its aggressive expansionist policies, has not only added a new and more potent element of settler and military confrontation with neighboring Arab states but has displaced millions of Palestinians. Since 1948, Arabs and Israelis have fought several wars, which have made the situation worse and further exacerbated this crisis. This crisis has also added to the complexity of international relations and has affected recent dialogue among world alliances. Because of this crisis and its complexities, global problems have become more difficult to solve, and the prospects of dealing with them effectively have become more obfuscated and confused than ever before (Riker-Coleman 1999).

President Bush Junior, who had his hands off of this crisis at the beginning of his term, has exerted deliberate efforts to transform any negotiated peace into a peace under arms and force, starting in Iraq. Thus, his war to "liberate Iraq from Saddam" in 2003 was not seen by Middle Eastern people as the Gulf War in 1991 was, to liberate Kuwait from the aggression of Saddam by his father, President Bush Senior. The reason is simple. Not only did Bush Senior manage to rally a large number of coalition partners, including many Arab nations, but he also got the UN's approval to wage war on Iraq in the early 1990s. Bush Junior, however, not only failed to have more than a few of the "willing" nations support his war policy, but he was also unable to secure the UN's approval to wage war on Iraq in March 2003. Thus, the first war on Iraq was seen as legitimate and was fought to actually liberate Kuwait from Saddam's aggression, whereas the second and most recent war on Iraq was perceived as illegitimate and was fought to occupy, rather than "liberate," Iraq.

In times of war, media coverage serves a crucial role of informing peoples of the world. However, the media tend to highlight immediate events and disregard relevant historical context. In addition, instead of being "watchdogs," the media became "lapdogs" and went to bed with their sources in this war. For instance, American media have presented this war on Iraq as a great triumph for the U.S. military and Bush Junior administration. Their coverage was mainly to prove the superiority and accuracy of the improved U.S. weapons systems and to speak highly of the only superpower of the world. By the same token, Arab media described the war as an act of aggression by a superpower nation against a great majority of people, the will of the UN Security Council, and the Arab League without much mention about Saddam's actions.

This chapter examines available print and electronic media coverage in the Gulf region with regard to the second war on Iraq. In addition, it includes discussions of the war coverage with about two hundred students and faculty from about sixty nationalities at an American university in the region. Those discussions took place during various mass media class sessions and panels of discussion with regard to this war. Therefore, the major points consist of the following: the historical context of the second Gulf War; the U.S. foreign policies toward the Middle East and the Arab–Israeli conflict; media coverage; and Middle Eastern perspective on war and terrorism.

HISTORICAL CONTEXT OF THE SECOND GULF WAR

There is no doubt that the Middle Eastern region has been one of the most important and dangerous areas to international peace. The growing economic interdependence among nations and the richness of the Persian Gulf have given it added significance. The Gulf's large deposits of oil, which are vital to the economies of the industrialized nations, have made it the subject of foreign intervention, mainly by Americans, British, French, Germans, and Russians. The number of nations relying on its oil has been growing and has become a subject of great concern to international consumers and world leaders. The principal concern of consumers is to ensure that enough oil is preserved to satisfy their daily needs and services. The interest of world leaders stems from concern about maintaining good relationships between oil-producing countries and the industrialized bloc of nations, to guarantee enough oil at reasonable prices. Iraq ranks second to Saudi Arabia in terms of its oil reserve and has thus been seen as one of the wealthiest Gulf nations. It has therefore become clear that the continual acts of violence and wars in that region would prevent easy access to region, increase the price of oil, and jeopardize the security and interests of the international community (Hashem 1993).

The people of Iraq are thought to have descended from the Sumerians, who established the first civilization five thousand years ago, between the Tigris and Euphrates. They are, in fact, inheritors of a great civilization and possess vast human and natural resources. In addition, the Iraqis have been known as wealthy, educated, and hospitable people throughout history, except for the past two decades, during which they remained generally poverty-stricken while their oil wealth has been extracted to benefit the West, owing to Gulf wars and harsh UN-imposed sanctions (Hashem 1993).

Over the past decades and before Saddam's regime, Iraq went through a series of coups and regime changes in the 1950s and 1960s. In 1958, Iraq was declared a republic instead of a kingdom, and then-president Kassem allowed a multinational group of firms to work with Iraq. In 1959, another coup took place, in which Saddam Hussein was wounded and fled to Syria and then to Egypt, where then-president Jamal Abdul-Nasser accused him of helping the CIA. After five years in power, Kassem's regime was toppled by another coup, which brought the Baath Party to power with the two brothers (Abdel-Salam and Abdel-Rahman Aref) serving as president, respectively. The British, French, and Americans helped that coup to succeed. In the late 1960s and early 1970s, Ahmed Hassan Al-Baker and Saddam Hussein grabbed power in Iraq. Both of them started to finish their opposition. In 1972, the Iraqi government nationalized its educational system and the oil industry. At the time, this move helped the Iraqi government gain much in popularity (Kadhim 2003).

The Iraqi regime has always had a double-standard policy: despotism against its own people and friendliness toward foreign governments. Foremost among Iraq's allies had been the Soviets at a time when the Iraqi regime had been killing Communist Party members at home. As to the West, the major interest had always been to keep the oil flowing without any other concern. Up to the early seventies, no one in the West had given a thought about consumption of fuel or the cost of electricity, that is, until the energy crisis hit home in 1973 with the oil embargo. Then conservation of oil in the West and in many other parts of the world became the order of the day. Despite attempts to reduce dependence on oil-producing nations, demands continued to grow, especially in the United States (Kadhim 2003).

Iraq's nationalization of its oil industry hadn't made much difference early on, but when the price of oil quadrupled in the mid-1970s, Iraq boomed and became a primary destination for international business. At that time, Saddam Hussein was president and had a strong hold on government by killing anyone who opposed his opinions or policies. He began to court the French, hoping to gain more leverage with the Soviets. He met with French prime minister Jacques Chirac, whose goal was to secure Iraq's future oil reserve for France; as a result, nuclear reactor contracts were signed on both sides (Kadhim 2003).

Iraq used its oil money to build a modern state with new hospitals, schools, rails, roads, and businesses all over the country. These facts gave Iraq, like its neighboring country Iran, a more Western look than ever before, until 1979. Then Westernization took a major blow in the region with the ousting of the Shah regime by a fanatic Muslim cleric, Ayatullah Khumaini, in Iran. Suddenly the United States lost its closest ally in the Middle East. Therefore, as a secular dictator and friend to the West, Saddam Hussein became preferable to a fanatic religious leader, even though he was power hungry and did not hesitate to kill dissidents in public if he thought that doing so would strengthen his hold on the country (Kadhim 2003).

In 1980, Iraqi forces crossed the borders into Iran, and an eight-year war of attrition started, with the blessing of the U.S. government. When the United States realized that Saddam Hussein was losing the war with Iran, it sent him Donald Rumsfeld, the current U.S. secretary of defense, to offer help with weapons in return for oil. During the eight-year war with Iran, U.S. ships escorted oil tankers under the American flag in the Gulf to keep the oil flowing into the West. About one million people died in that war, and the West never raised any objection. During that same time, Kuwait had started to pump more oil than it had ever done before, which angered Saddam Hussein and gave him a pretext to invade the small country later on (Zarif 2003).

In 1981, Israeli warplanes destroyed Iraq's nuclear reactor, which was bought from Jacques Chirac to produce electricity. Other than electricity, many world leaders alleged that Saddam Hussein intended to produce nuclear weapons to establish a balance of power with Israel in the region. The Soviets, Americans, Germans, and French had supported Saddam's regime. In fact, Saddam acquired chemical and biological weapons and was on his way to acquiring nuclear weapons as well. Iranians were the first victims of Saddam's poison gas, followed by Iraqi Kurds because they rejected to fight Iranians in 1988.

In 1990, Saddam Hussein invaded Kuwait, basing his claim on history, which reveals that under the Ottoman Empire, Kuwait was a province of Basra, meaning an integral part of Iraq. Six months after that invasion, George Bush Senior (GBS) was able to gather a large coalition force, which began striking Iraq in January 1991. Kuwait was quickly liberated, and the road to Baghdad was open, but GBS did not want to finish Saddam Hussein for political reasons and called on Iraqis to overthrow him. Thus, many Iraqis rose against Saddam in anticipation of U.S. help to unseat him. However, they were let down, and hundreds of thousands of Shiites in the south, as well as Kurds in the north, were slaughtered by the remaining forces of Saddam. Since then, the Iraqis have suffered more than a decade of siege, harsh UN sanctions, and intermittent aircraft bombing by U.S. and British forces. GBS and the majority of Americans remained indifferent to the suffering of Iraqis and showed no concern about how tarnished the U.S. image would be in the minds of those Iraqis and other people in the region (Hashem 1993).

In 2002 and 2003, George W. Bush (GWB) and his administration had tried hard to make a strong case for invading Iraq. They had scared their own people as well as others by excessive talk about the September 11, 2001, attacks on the World Trade Center and a wing of the Pentagon, even though none of the attackers were from Iraq. Thus they tried but failed to link those attacks to Saddam Hussein. GWB was then successful in getting a new UN resolution allowing UN inspectors to go back into Iraq to find and destroy what was allegedly left of Iraq's weapons of mass destruction (WMD). However, those inspectors did their best and got access to whatever sites they requested but found nothing, because those weapons and their programs had been destroyed in the past seven years, owing to continual inspection until 1998. In addition, GWB managed to get the U.S. Congress to okay his invasion of Iraq and send U.S. troops into the Middle East hoping the UN Security Council would also agree. However, the majority of the UN Security Council was against the invasion of Iraq to topple Saddam's regime, having established no clear links between Iraq and the September 11 attacks nor having found any hidden WMD. But GWB, with a few of the "willing" nations, went to war against Iraq anyway.

In sum, the influence of the West in the Middle Eastern region was at first occasioned by strategic concerns for future imperial possessions elsewhere. But with the injection of the state of Israel and the rise of that region's oil production in the twentieth century, Western economic interests grew dramatically. The effect of Western influence was to undermine local governments by actively creating militarized states and laying foundations for subsequent military influence. As a result of militarism and foreign intervention, most forms of political expression have been minimized or marginalized. The United States, with few of its allies, have tried to impose their own solutions on the region by an unconditional support of Israel and certain repressive regimes in the Gulf region while excluding others who did not agree with their policies. Islam remained as a central unifying element of a significant majority in the Middle East and, thus, led to the rise of fundamentalism, which scared the West, especially after the Iranian revolution of 1978–1979 and the fall of the Soviet Union, from 1989 to 1990. Militarism, foreign policies in the Middle East, and regional wars have cost Iraq and its neighbors a heavy price, culminating in a tremendous toll on human life, economic stability, and regional trust (Riker-Coleman 1999). Now we turn to the discussion of U.S. foreign policies and their effects on the Middle East.

U.S. FOREIGN POLICIES TOWARD THE MIDDLE EAST AND THE ARAB–ISRAELI CONFLICT

The Iraqi invasion of Kuwait on August 2, 1990; the subsequent war on Iraq in Operation Desert Storm, in 1991; the resulting UN sanctions on Iraq for over a decade; and the latest invasion of Iraq, in March 2003, to free the country from Saddam Hussein are still fresh in people's memory and have had a great impact on the Middle East, the United States, and the rest of the world community. The U.S. foreign policies toward the Middle East are believed to have led to several regional wars in the Middle East and to the creation of many fundamentalist groups around the world. In addition, those policies are also believed to have contributed greatly to the instability of the Middle Eastern region and added to the misery of many peoples, including Americans. More important, it is widely believed in the Middle East that the U.S. policies and invasion of Iraq, even though successful in toppling the Iraqi dictator, have created chaotic conditions that could lead to a Talibani-like regime's coming to power in Iraq and somewhere else in the Muslim world.

The U.S. policies and actions in the Middle East have been based on two major interests: the first and most obvious is oil. Despite various conservation efforts and reduced imports since the 1970s, the United States remains highly dependent on foreign energy sources. Referring to the Persian Gulf oil reserves, former secretary of defense Elliot Richardson once said, "Continuing access to these reserves by all consumer nations is a matter of great interest to us. . . . Access to raw materials and overseas trade and investments are essentials to the vitality of the U.S. economy and to the continued prosperity and security of our friends and allies" (Hashem 1993, 1).

The second U.S. interest in the Middle East consists of the survival and security of Israel. The commitment to Israel seems to be based on biblical and historical emotions. A great majority of Americans believe that Israel and the United States share and cherish the common values of freedom and democracy. In addition, Americans seem to have certain obligations toward Israel because of the Holocaust. Hence, Israel has become the largest recipient of U.S. foreign aid ever since the decline of the British power and the assumption of Western leadership by the United States. Furthermore, since its creation on Palestinian territory in 1948, Israel has been perceived as a dominant factor in America's internal politics and, as a result, in U.S. Middle Eastern policies. A simple explanation for Israel's great influence in Washington is the strength of its lobby and the activities of its supporters throughout the United States (Hashem 1993).

To protect its interests in the Middle Eastern region, the United States has felt a great need to solve the Arab–Israeli conflict. As a result, it has always maintained close relationships with powerful regional allies in the Gulf, besides Israel. Thus, it has kept successful relationships with oil-producing countries, such as Saudi Arabia and other smaller Gulf nations. The United States, instead of reaching a comprehensive settlement of that conflict, opted, as Israel had suggested, to reaching dyadic resolutions with neighboring Arab states. The first peace treaty was established between Israel and Egypt in the early 1970s. The second one took place between Israel and Jordan in the 1990s. However, the United States has, to date, failed to mediate any lasting solution between the Palestinians, Syrians, and Lebanese on one side and Israel on the other. The major causes of its failure have been the Arabs' perception of U.S. bias toward Israel and the inability of a succession of U.S. administrations to keep their promises, deal with the intransigence of certain Middle Eastern governments, and apply serious pressure on Israel to reconcile with its Arab neighbors on the basis of UN resolutions. The U.S. inability of applying serious pressure on Israel to abide by UN resolutions, as any other state, stems from domestic political factors and agendas that have rendered U.S. efforts useless (Hashem 1993).

However, the Arab League organization, which is composed of twenty-two Arab nations, failed to prevent the invasion of Kuwait in 1990 as well as the invasion of Iraq in 2003. These two invasions made it weak, inefficient, and unable to implement any landmark political or economic decisions reached at the Amman and Beirut summits. Among those decisions was the peace proposal between Arabs and Israel. In addition, the war on Iraq has dealt a serious blow to this organization and had many Arab leaders thinking about fixing it. Because of the Arab League's weakness, the resulting two wars on Iraq, and the UN-enforced sanctions on Iraq, the people of Iraq have become poor, desperate, hungry, and angry at Saddam's regime, at the Arabs, and at the invading forces in general. To Iraqis, the invaders seem to have gotten Iraq into a power vacuum, owing to the failure of a coherent, implementable postwar plan (Kawach and Nowais 2003).

Some of the U.S. journalists have criticized the U.S. foreign policy in the Middle East. Foremost among them is Norman Solomon (2003a), who stated that, despite the various polls showing how the latest war on Iraq has improved GWB's image in the United States, such polls also reveal that U.S. credibility and favorability ratings have suffered greatly abroad, not only in countries opposing the war, but also in countries that fought side by side with U.S. forces. In addition, Thomas Friedman has stated that, from the start, GWB "has been long on road maps and short on drivers. If he wants to go on the road he paved, he has to step-up his Mid-East diplomatic game, with sustained energy, focus, and toughness" (2003, 9). GWB has not been doing that, for a long time after the Clinton administration; thus, he has lost trust and credibility among the Arabs. From the buildup to the war to the bombing and the final days, he and his team have constructed a simple, heroic narrative of freedom and asked the world to ignore the much messier human devastation and tragedies of this war. For instance, there are many untold stories on the U.S. media, stories that, sadly, have little to do with the heroic legend that the U.S. administration tried to create to secure its reelection in 2004 (Friedman 2003; Solomon 2003b).

Propaganda tactics have prevented media consumers to get any story straight on any of the most recent events. This war supposedly came about because Iraq has been hiding WMD. And yet the war has come and gone, revealing nothing to threaten U.S. security. In addition, Pitt and Ritter (2002) stated that the case for war against Iraq had not been made. It is doubtful that Saddam has retained any functional biological, chemical, or nuclear weapons programs, which were thoroughly dismantled by the UN inspectors. Many people around the globe have been asking some interesting questions these days. Those questions have dealt with whether information concerning Iraqi WMD has followed the top-down formula so that GWB could go to war against Saddam Hussein. On a recent U.S. television show, a caller asked whether information that the American administration wanted to spread around had been given to information agencies so that they may come up with something to back it up with. These facts have given more credibility to Scott Ritter and other UN inspectors, who had been against the second war on Iraq from the start and had confirmed on many occasions and on several television shows that, during the seven years that UN conducted weapons inspections in Iraq, Saddam Hussein's chemical, biological, and nuclear weapons programs had been effectively destroyed (Pitt and Ritter 2002).

In a different story, Saddam Hussein had been subconsciously linked to Osama bin Laden by the Bush administration. This story had been fostered mostly in the U.S. media in a deliberate attempt to justify and bolster support for the war on Iraq. Scott Ritter and William Rivers Pitt had demonstrated the lack of any plausible link between the Iraqi dictator and al Qaeda because Osama bin Laden had called for the death of Saddam Hussein and seemed more in agreement with the Bush administration than with Saddam. In addition, they had listed many ways in which it could not be possible for Iraq to pose any credible threat to the United States or any of its allies after destroying its WMD programs. Furthermore, Ritter had compared the invasion of Iraq to Hitler's invasion of Poland. He told the *Berliner Zeitung* newspaper that Americans had died "for a lie" and that he did not see any difference between the invasion of Iraq and the invasion of Poland in 1939. Both invasions were based on what he said was an artificial argument of self-defense. GWB had used the September 11, 2001, attacks as Hitler had used the 1933 burning of the Reichstag to repress domestic dissidents. However, Ritter was considered by many fellow Americans as nonpatriotic or a traitor who received money from Saddam Hussein to speak on his behalf.

Even though the connection of Saddam Hussein to Osama bin Laden has never been supported with hard facts and has appeared to be an artificial creation, it has been continually mentioned and discussed by the U.S. media, but not the connection of GWB to Hitler. Instead, the U.S. media constantly helped the Bush administration's propaganda machine by supporting the story connecting Saddam to Osama through the use of innuendos and rumors, to play on Americans' fears and revenge fantasies. Thus, American mainstream media news reporting and repetitions of the same story for an extended period, while ignoring other similar stories, have been instrumental in the marketing of this second war on Iraq.

When Americans asked questions about the war on Iraq, they were interested in specific sorts of answers, as many news reports and television talk shows had revealed. Americans wanted to hear something about "Arab rage" and the "innate Arab hatred of America." If anyone responded that Arabs generally harbor no such feelings, American listeners openly scoffed. When Americans ask the question about "why they hate us," Americans would be content in hearing what they want to hear. Instead of allowing others to answer this question the way they perceive the facts, Americans expect others to answer it by saying "because you are a rich superpower and others are jealous of you." Americans, including their media professionals and diplomats, maintain and reassure that the September 11 attacks, as well as other terrorist activities around the world against Western interests, have nothing to do with U.S. foreign policies and Israel nor are about Palestinian-occupied territories—for example, per Dennis Ross's and Dan Rather's assertions on several television shows (Dennis Ross, the U.S. Middle East envoy/ambassador during the Clinton Administration who had been negotiating a settlement between Israelis and Palestinians; Dan Rather, CBS news anchor). This way they confuse the facts and shape public discourse according to what they want, by hiding their foreign policies and Israel in the process. Because the U.S. media rarely question their politicians' foreign policies, especially toward Arabs, and continue to systematically portray Arabs as an essentially hate-filled people, those same media will keep being instrumental in helping their government market expensive wars in the Middle East and somewhere else, such as this war on Iraq, which made U.S. occupation much easier to manage.

Distrust of the United States has been running high over the war on Iraq and over Washington's perceived pro-Israeli bias and support policies. Hence, Arabs have been afraid of American imperialism and their demands for painful reforms, which could threaten domestic stability. Coupled with these concerns has been the usual dose of conspiracy theories involving regional archrival Israel. Since the establishment of the state of Israel, in 1948 on Palestinian territories, the U.S. government has displayed an unconditional support for the policies of Israel. Thus, U.S. government officials have been against criticizing the Israelis, no matter what they do. Israelis have learned that lesson pretty well and have been using American weapons to hunt down Palestinian political and military leaders, destroy Palestinian properties, and devastate Palestinian lands without any denunciation from U.S. officials. In addition, when Prime Minister Ariel Sharon warns U.S. officials on several occasions not to "appease Arabs" as Hitler was appeased by West Europeans on the eve of World War II, U.S. officials listen without any objection.

Arabs don't understand how Israel can get away with using U.S. weapons, such as the F-16 and cluster or smart bombs, to destroy Palestinian and other Arab targets in the Middle East. They cannot understand the inability of

Americans, who claim to fight for human rights, to stop Israeli aggression, expansion, and settlement policies in Palestinian territories. In addition, they also cannot understand why the United States has been scrutinizing what some Arab regimes do while it has been turning a blind eye to what Israel has been doing. Thus, they keep asking themselves how this behavior can help the United States in solving the Arab–Israeli conflict in the Middle East.

Arabs believe that Americans can critically analyze current events and listen carefully to others' assessments of those events from their own American-based perspectives. For instance, the inability to understand U.S. double standards in the Middle East and the unconditional support of Israeli policies have led many Arabs to say that "it was not Bin Laden but Israel and the American government who destroyed the World Trade Center and a part of the Pentagon on September 11, 2001." Do Americans understand this? Obviously not, because one of my American friends, a college professor at an American institution in the Gulf, came to tell me one day "how absurd his students were for saying that Israel and the CIA were behind the destruction of the World Trade Center and a part of the Pentagon." This professor, who lived in the Middle East for quite a while, did not realize that his students meant that the Israeli actions over the years and the Americans' unconditional support of those actions coupled with their negligence of Palestinian's basic human rights have been at least partially responsible for the September 11 attacks.

Americans, rather than assume "others hate them because they are rich and powerful," should run a critical analysis of their government's foreign policies. Americans will then realize that their government not only uses double standards but also supports foreign dictatorships and repressive regimes while supporting diversity, democracy, and freedom at home. This analysis can then help Americans see for themselves what their government policies have been costing them to have double standards and support dictatorships in dealing with different others. In addition, a cost-benefit analysis of U.S. actions and foreign policies is sine qua non to effective governing. This could be performed with a critical analysis. In fact, it would be irresponsible to ignore the magnitude cost of identifying with the wrong policies abroad in the lives and resources of Westerners in general and Americans in particular. The double standards of U.S. foreign policies in the Middle East have resulted in the expansion of the recruiting base for terrorism from the ethnic Arab region in the Middle East to the entire Muslim population of the globe. The Muslim world perceives recent developments between Israel and the Palestinians differently from the way that the U.S. media describe them. Muslims identify with their brethren Muslims no matter where they come from. Thus, they see the United States as the only superpower and cannot believe that it is unable to stop Israeli expansion of Jewish settlements on Palestinian territory, even during peaceful negotiations between the two parties. This fact has facilitated the spread of the rumor among Middle Eastern Muslims "that it was not bin Laden but the Jews who destroyed the twin towers and part of the Pentagon" (Arjomand n.d.).

MEDIA COVERAGE

U.S. Media

The main role of the U.S. media is that of a watchdog, not a lapdog. Therefore, the military considers them adversaries, and, as such, they have to be on a leash. However, the U.S. media seem to have ceased to fulfill their main role lately. They have become more like "lapdogs" and have gone to bed with their sources. In that regard, the majority of them were used as tools to perform a public relations function for their sources, not like a Fourth Estate, watching every move and critically reporting the news about their hosts. During this last Gulf war on Iraq, the military held daily news conferences that stifled the appearance of open and free access to the real battlefield. The U.S. media reporting included minute details comparing the two Gulf wars on Iraq by stating the number of bombs and flight sorties and by excluding the killing and suffering of civilians during the two wars and sanctions. For instance, extensive reports concerning the difference between fighting the Iraqis in 1991 and in 2003 were given utmost importance. In the first war on Iraq, the U.S. military ejected Saddam Hussein's forces from Kuwait and declared victory in forty-three days. In 2003, in just twenty-one days and with a smaller force, America decisively won the war. Military aircraft flew 15,825 strike sorties and dropped 27,250 weapons. Coalition ground forces fired tens of thousands of artillery and mortar projectiles, rockets, and tank-gun rounds. In less than half the time of the 1991 Gulf War and with less than one-third of the strikes and with one-tenth the number of bombs, victory was achieved on the battlefield, and the regime was overthrown. By the time the war was over, Pentagon comptroller Dov Zakheim estimated (at an April 16 news conference) that U.S. forces had exploded an estimated $3 billion worth of bombs, bullets, missiles, shells, rockets, and mortars. Was this type of coverage necessary? Sure, but how about whether the result was worth the efforts, the killing of many innocent people, and destruction of a country? Why didn't they discuss these issues at length and with minute details, as they did with other military news?

According to Solomon (2003b), Americans have caught only glimpses of the carnage, because their media sanitized their war coverage. A few newsmagazines provided some grisly pictures, and a few reporters wrote vivid accounts of what the U.S. military did to Iraqis on the ground. Most of what the

American media covered consisted of great successes, such as reporting that there weren't many casualties among the American forces and that the Iraqis could not destroy the oil fields nor could they cow the American troops by sending in their suicide bombers. Even though there have been some unfortunate deaths of civilians there, nobody witnessed scud missiles flowing over Israel. In addition, Solomon (2003c) stated that the American media considered Americans and their allies as sacred people, at a time when President Bush Junior has had blood of many Iraqi children on his hands after launching an aggressive war in violation of the UN charter and the Nuremberg principles, which were established long ago.

Allowing certain media personnel to become embedded with units, the army appeared to have done a good service to media and their consumers. However, this embedding function, no matter how good it was, gave the media a tunnel vision and allowed their reports to be controlled and censored (Kawach and Nowais 2003, 4). In addition, the U.S. efforts to spy on UN delegates before the latest war on Iraq, to win votes in favor of war against Iraq, prompted the London-based *Observer* to report a story concerning this fact, on March 2, 2003. However, the U.S. media failed to mention anything about that story until later. As Solomon (2003a) mentioned, "When war and peace hang in the balance, journalism delayed is journalism denied" (2).

Dr. James Zogby (2003) characterized U.S. media as "dancing to White House tune" because they had been "uncritical conveyors of the White House efforts" and policies for more than a year, to build a strong case against Iraq and thus establish public support for the war. Some of the White House tactics used to build a good case for the war were as follows: continuing the war on terror, enforcing the UN Security Council resolutions concerning WMD in Iraq, and ridding Iraq of a terrible and dangerous dictator. Zogby emphasized that, instead of respecting the journalistic profession and questioning the truth that is presented to the public, the U.S. media and their journalists "behaved more like compliant campaigners." He cited an incident concerning a challenge to U.S. information agencies by UN weapons inspectors, who characterized the U.S. information with regard to WMD in Iraq as "pure rubbish and a waste of time." The U.S. mainstream media ignored that challenge, did not cover it, and "seemed more inclined to beat the drums of war than to investigate the White House's claims" (Zogby 2003, 9).

In addition, during the war, that behavior never changed, which led some media critics to think that the U.S. mainstream media appeared more as "staterun" media than as free and critical media. Constituting the order of the daily coverage were briefings by the White House, the Pentagon, the State Department, and by military commanders; in-studio commentaries by military experts or analysts; and certain interviews with embedded journalists.

Reporters and anchors that praised the military and their own coverage of war show live long-distance shots of bombs exploding over Baghdad. "Only a few journalists have expressed their outrage over their industries' abandonment of their role. Ashley Banfield, one of the U.S. rising stars in TV journalism, accused news outlets of 'wrapping themselves in the American flag,' shielding the American people from the horrors of war, and failing to probe deeper into the war and search for the truth" (Zogby 2003, 9).

In sum, Zogby stated that everything the White House said was reported without a question. The fact that Afghanistan and Iraq remain quite dangerous and unstable has been rarely discussed, and no questions have been asked about what may be the broader goals of this continuing war. Success has been neither measured nor evaluated. "It is just reported as such" (Zogby 2003, 9). These facts have been proven to be a major mistake and misjudgment on the part of the mass media personnel, for no WMD have been found in Iraq so far. To avoid such fatal incidents between nations and keep media away from such mistakes, it is crucial to question the omnipotence of the mass media and whether they are playing their assumed role or not. There is a pressing need to ask about the true effectiveness of this last war and occupation of Iraq. There is also a need to pressure media personnel, writers, scholars, and leaders of the world to go back in history and address the real story behind the relationship between Iraq and the United States that is more than a small question of weapons of mass destructions and change of a leader.

Arab Media

A growing number of twenty-four-hour satellite-based Arab news channels in the Middle East has been witnessed since the late 1990s. Most of their programs consist of news talk shows, press briefings, historical videos, national and international music videos, and other various programs. These channels have been active during this second Gulf war. None of these channels existed during the first Gulf war, in 1991. Most of them showed how unfair, unjust, and uninformed the invading forces were during this second war. They showed Iraqi residential neighborhoods, hospitals, and schools that were hit by the so-called smart weapons. Becoming the highlight of their daily coverage were the results of such strikes—namely, the many civilians who suffered or were killed. In addition, their coverage included the casualties, setbacks, and suffering of the invading forces (Fandy 2003, B01).

The Arab news coverage of the war drew on the Arabs' past, such as on the Crusaders, Mongols, Ottomans, colonial powers, and the Arab–Israeli wars. Their news coverage consisted of a mixture of narrative and images. Because the Arabic language is mostly metaphorical, rich in meanings, and different from the English language (which usually separates photography and narration), what seemed to be ranting and raving by Arabs to Americans did not seem to bother Arabs at all. A case in point was the showing of American POWs on their newscasts (Fandy 2003, B01; Urayyid 2003, 10).

Besides their coverage of the war on Iraq, Arab media continued to cover the Palestinians' legitimate struggle against the Israelis' illegitimate occupation of Palestinian land. Even though Israel was not an active participant in this war, it was looming large in the horizon, for Arabs have always believed that the United States had been going to war against Iraq for the sake of Israel. The Arab media depicted a relatively unarmed people in Iraq and a Palestinian nation facing the best equipped, armed, and trained forces on the face of the earth to defend their honor, freedom, and land. The Americans and British forces were described as Israelis were, as occupiers of Arab territories. The Iraqis and Palestinians were seen as "freedom fighters," "resistance forces," "mujahideen," or "fedayeen." For instance, Arab media repeatedly showed an Iraqi peasant standing with a rifle near a downed Apache helicopter, which meant that a simple farmer could cause harm to Western invaders. Thus, if every Iraqi does the same, the invaders would go back home and have no chance to succeed. This iconic Arab picture is borrowed from the ex-Egyptian president Jamal Abdul-Nasser, who fed the Arab world pictures of peasants shooting at planes during the Suez war (Fandy 2003, B01; Urayyid 2003, 10).

The Arab media have repeatedly showed how the American officials and media spoke of the alleged Iraqi WMD and failed to mention anything about Israeli WMD. In addition, whenever Israel attacks Palestinians, American media barely mention anything about Israeli aggression. However, whenever Palestinians hit Israelis, those same media keep on covering the same incident for an extended period of time. Arab media have also discussed how American officials and media ignored, for the most part, what Israeli military had been doing to humiliate Arabs, through destroying their neighborhoods and severely limiting their access to clinics and hospitals. They explained how American media reporters have ignored Israeli tanks destroying ambulances, targeting Palestinian health facilities, razing houses to the ground, ravaging strawberry fields, tearing olive trees from the ground, and killing foreign photographers to destroy evidence of the Israelis' aggression against an entire population.

Besides being more visual and drawing on their past in their coverage of the war, Arab media imitated the Western modes of representation. For instance, Arab media, like the American media, had used "war rooms," staffed with retired generals who discussed the war and how it should proceed. Many Arab reporters and producers, like their Western counterparts, knew what their listeners and readers wanted to see and read; and they gave it to them.

Repetition and emphasis of certain events, rather than others, had been the essence of propaganda in this war. Arab and Western mass media kept on repeating the same propagandistic statements to please their own listeners. For instance, an Al-Jazeera reporter in Baghdad falsely claimed on the first day of war that "here in Baghdad, a city accused of hiding weapons of mass destruction is being hit by weapons of mass destruction." In addition, night after night, mass media showed the Iraqi information minister Muhammed Said al-Sahhaf telling lies about how to teach the American and British "uluge" (a lesson) and that Iraqis were no less than the Vietnamese. They could make it costly in body bags, and the invaders will run home (Fandy 2003, B01). Thus, while Western media helped GWB to wage war on Iraq through propagandizing, Arab media helped al-Sahhaf to keep propagandizing, even after the statue of Saddam Hussein was toppled, on April 9, 2003.

MIDDLE EASTERN PERSPECTIVE ON WAR AND TERRORISM

From a Middle Eastern perspective, Americans and Israelis are close allies fighting together to safeguard Israel as the only regional power. They do not want to see any other powerful country threaten the existence of Israel or even establish some kind of a balance of power with it in the Middle Eastern region. It is believed that American media have contributed to this fact by failing to create any balance in their coverage of the Middle Eastern events. They have failed to portray the Israeli government's efforts to oppress and imprison an entire population, and they have led Arabs to doubt U.S. commitment to peace in the Middle East. Arabs could not believe the United States to be acting as an even broker and standing up to the Israeli government. The majority of Arabs believe that the U.S. goals to free Iraq and set up a democratic government are not genuine. Their real goal is to control Iraq's oil fields and set up permanent military bases to impose their will and hegemony on the Middle Eastern region for the sake of Israel before their own. Some Arabs also believe that Israel seems to dictate to the United States, rather than the other way around, with regard to the Middle East. Hence, they are very doubtful about U.S. intentions, and they see the Western media much as they do their hosts, treating the war on Iraq as a war against a corrupt dictator and one of liberation. By the same token, the majority of Arabs and their media, without considering what Saddam Hussein did to his own people and others in the region, perceive this war as an aggression and occupation of Arab land by force.

Arabs believe that, besides maintaining the supremacy and stability of Israel, the main reason of U.S. involvement has been to secure the flow of Gulf oil into the West. Therefore, several U.S. administrations have been determined to eradicate all factors that could endanger the security of Israel and of the oil fields in the Middle East. The invasion of Iraq was perceived as a first step in that direction. In addition, Arabs perceive the United States' wanting to enfeeble all countries in the region for these two major reasons. Thus, the United States has been using various tactics of threat, pressure, force, and intimidation on many Middle Eastern nations to pressure them to conform to its demands and facilitate the implementation of a peace treaty between Arabs and Israel. However, by doing so, the United States seems to complicate the situation further and block any real opportunity of a just and durable peace in the region.

Arabs also believe that the United States, contrary to what it applies to them, has given Israel the green light to pursue its policies of the occupation, destruction, and settlement building on Arab land. All that Arabs can hope from the United States, if they conform to its demands, is no more, no less than a pressuring of Israel to comply with UN resolutions, because without obliging Israel to fulfill these resolutions, peace cannot be achieved in the region. In addition, Arabs think that as long as the United States keeps on exerting pressure on some and not on others, it will make matters worse, thus driving the peace process into an impasse unless tangible changes are realized by a durable agreement (Munif 2003, 8).

A careful analysis of U.S. diplomacy in the Middle East reveals a series of implicit threats to Arabs, as well as a U.S. determination to draw a new map of the region in light of the change in Iraq and the prospect of renewed peace talks between Israel and the Palestinians. The U.S. plan for the Middle East is believed to imply a complete transformation of the entire region in all fields. The change will envisage reaching the political, economic, social, and cultural aspects. However, these changes are perceived to serve the interests of Israel but not those of the Arab countries. Therefore, Arabs believe that they must join efforts to counter the U.S. hegemony, which has nothing else other than the security of Israel. This may be accomplished through instigating a dialogue with Washington on the grounds of mutual understanding and common interests. To reach this goal, cooperation must be the guiding principle, rather than force and intimidation (Munif 2003, 8).

Contrary to the U.S. perception of this war, Middle Easterners saw American and British officials, especially GWB, as bloodthirsty. Their launching of an aggressive war on Iraq in violation of the UN charter and against the wishes of a great majority of nations and peoples around the globe was a clear testimony to that effect. The picture of the maimed child who lost his entire family cannot go away from the heads of Arabs. For instance, Arabs saw the war hitting civilian homes, killing many children and elderly alike. They saw "dumb" bombs demolishing hospitals and schools, rather than smart bombs precisely hitting military installations. They witnessed Washington's deadly orders more than they saw faulty perceptions and public relations claims. They saw more than a half-million Iraqi children dead because of U.S. foreign policy decisions between and during the two wars on Iraq. They saw that not a single person out of the September 11 hijackers was an Iraqi. Yet the American administration kept on trying to find a link.

Besides seeing Saddam Hussein as an evil despot who brought great damage and suffering to his own country and people, Arabs saw Ariel Sharon as a bloodthirsty leader who did not abide by any UN resolution. The pictures of Palestinians massacred in Sabra, Shatila, Janeen, and many other camps under the orders and watch of Ariel Sharon are still fresh in the minds of many Arabs—yet GWB and his team have considered Ariel Sharon "a man of peace."

In addition, Arabs saw the UN Security Council not as an effective international organization but simply as an instrument for Washington's will and intentions in the world. Thus, many of them have become desperate and believe that the UN has not only lost its value and credibility but should also be done away with. Arabs have also been aware of how several UN Security Council resolutions underlined the need for regional security in the Gulf region, yet nothing was done to spare the region much destruction, devastation, and tragedy. Desperation has led many Muslims in the region and elsewhere to commit themselves to the utmost sacrifice, suicide bombing, which they believe is the only way to get the West as well as their own leaders to understand what they have been going through after many years of humiliation.

Furthermore, the tactics used by the United States to defeat extremism have been inefficient in the eyes of most Arabs. Hence, they believe that Americans have not learned any good lesson from their past, for they keep using the same old tactics with more improved versions of their weapons. Arabs also believe that U.S. force may reap instant benefits, but in the long run, it creates a more fertile breeding ground for extremism, fanaticism, and terrorism. In fact, Arabs have been witnessing these phenomena spread largely as a response to a lack of justice and political participation in their region. They also believe that these phenomena can be removed only by addressing the root causes that gave raise to them rather than through the use of force alone.

In sum, the principal sources of Arab anger during Iraq's invasion have been as follows:

1. the United States' defying the UN Security Council resolution;
2. the U.S. government's ignoring large numbers of worldwide demonstrations by a majority of Arab citizens, as well as those of the United States, Britain, Spain, Italy, France, Germany, Russia, Australia, and many others;

3. chaos and looting that prevailed after the war, which were believed to be intended by U.S. forces;
4. lack of security and civil services in Iraq;
5. turning a blind eye to everything Israel has been doing; and
6. the destruction of Baghdad's infrastructure.

Arabs have been asking themselves, Why did the "invaders" protect the oil fields and oil ministry but not Baghdad's museum and hospitals? They think that the United States has replaced one type of powerlessness by another, and this has been very disappointing to them.

Arabs perceive reform in their states as a painful process, but the United States has been clear on this issue. This process should include fighting corruption, terrorism, and protecting property rights. In addition, Arabs need reform geared toward greater participation, respect for the rule of law, and appreciation of basic human rights. Reform, however, must be homegrown, because Arabs believe that democracy cannot be imported nor imposed at the point of a gun. Offering native models of reform, fighting corruption, eradicating terrorism, protecting property rights, ensuring political participation, and appreciating basic human rights may be nonexistent at the present, may take a slow start, and may require the international community's help so that the Arab nations can succeed during the process of democratic reform. Among Arabs, there exists a tangible distrust of GWB and his team. GWB does not appear evenhanded in the Middle Eastern affairs, and it would be helpful to him to find some semblance of any of the assumed WMD, which he claimed to exist in Iraq. Arabs believe that he fabricated and used this claim time and time again to provide valid reasons for waging war on Iraq. GWB and his team have failed in finding any WMD so far, and their efforts to eradicate terrorist activities remain as elusive as ever. Therefore, how can he convince Arabs that he is sincere, especially in asking them to undergo certain reform or in solving the Arab–Israeli conflict through his "Road Map"? Is he going to pressure Israel to comply with UN resolutions and give up land conquered in the 1967 war for peace with its Arab neighbors? Or is he playing a political game for his 2004 reelection campaign? These are some of the most important questions on the minds of many Arabs. The answer to these questions and the attitude of GWB are going to matter with regard to GWB's quest for reform in the Arab world. Otherwise, we are going to yet again witness a dialogue of the deaf in the Middle East, as we have become used to it (Arjomand n.d.).

However, as Urayyid (2003) stated, Arabs have to also realize that they have not been raising their children to enjoy freedom of thought and creativity, nor have they been encouraging them to surpass their own generation. Instead, they have continued to glorify rhetoric about their historical achievements and civilization. Crowds filled the streets in virtually every Arab city to protest the latest war on Iraq. However, the reality in Iraq during Saddam's regime and under the watch of Arab and many international leaders was shameful to Arabs and to many Americans who had been supporting this dictator for so long. Saddam had been a horrific and inhumane dictator who had tortured his own people for three decades by means of rape; severing tongues, ears, arms, legs, and genitals; and by imprisoning family members, many of whom "vanished" while in prison. He made Iraqis afraid of anyone, to a point where they had been afraid of their own shadows. All of this was happening at a time when Arab media treated this problem as an internal Iraqi matter, without daring or intending to cover it. What amazes Arabs is that all of this was taking place with the United States' blessing, until it stunned the world with its war to "liberate" the Iraqi people. Why did the United States do this right now and not in 1991, when Bush Senior ended the war on Iraq abruptly and Saddam Hussein was about to fall? The United States could have saved millions in more than a decade. Why didn't the Arab leaders do something about this? And why did Arab leaders keep quiet about Saddam Hussein's deeds? These legitimate questions need honest answers so that people can learn some lessons from the past.

In addition, Urayyid (2003) said that many Arabs have mixed feelings about what had happened. There is a feeling of relief at the end of the Iraqis' suffering, yet there are also feelings of anger and shame that Arab leaders had to wait for a foreign nation to invade an Arab state to put an end to Saddam Hussein's regime. There is also a feeling of distrust, that it took so long to act against such a dictator; and there is a feeling of fear of the unknown, concerning this late action and what it may cost Arabs in terms of their attitudes, culture, and traditions. Many Arabs have been asking themselves more and more questions these days. They have been asking whether the Arabs are people who can only applaud their leaders whether they are right or wrong, who can enjoy talking about their past civilization or conquers, and who can yet scream against real or imagined enemies. They also wonder whether they can look forward toward their objectives, rather than backward at their achievements, because if they keep looking at the past, they will never advance. They see many Arab governments sending their students to be educated in the West, to only add to the suffering of the Arab nations: either such governments don't want their students to come back home, or they don't plan for their students' return to certain jobs, fearing what their Western education might bring to their leadership. Perhaps, more than anything else, the Arab governments are afraid of their students' learning to be free to express themselves and that such students might want to play an effective role in the political affairs of their own countries. For instance, during this war on Iraq, many educated people, like my Iraqi friend Ali, found that they are free to share their opinions concerning the war, but many more found themselves compelled not to declare a position. The major reasons for Ali's feeling free was, first, Ali's sheer distance from Iraq and, second, Ali's assurance that Saddam Hussein would be gone after the invasion is over; but the other educated Arabs were either living in their own countries or were torn between the conflicting realities of declaring any political opinions and criticizing the emotional outbursts of their own compatriots.

Furthermore, Urayyid (2003) mentioned that educated Arabs have been torn by the complexities of this war on Iraq. They understand that their leaders are weak and cannot enter into confrontation with the United States and Britain, nor do they have the armies or weapons to win. But, then, should they rejoice at being freed from Saddam or ashamed that they have had the worst dictator in recent memory? Iraqis may be happy that Iraq is freed from the horrors of Saddam and that they can go from their diasporas to visit their families and friends, but they would be sad to see the destruction and devastation of their country.

Finally, there may be hope that the change in Iraq would remove the blinders from other Arabs' sights so that they can see that there is no future until they cut free from the trap of their past. There is no hope of continued survival for any Arab regime or government that deprives its own people of the ability to critically think and act so that they may add to the growth of human progress. No matter how much Arabs brag about their ancestors' past and hear speeches or poems about it, they will not regain their respect in the eyes of the world community as long as they allow their leaders to control their free mind and keep doing to them what the leaders have been doing for so long (Urayyid 2003).

CONCLUSION

For the sake of peaceful relations among various cultures, the Arab–Israeli conflict must be solved on the basis of equality and fairness. It is widely believed that this conflict has been quite costly to the world community and thus deserves more attention. Therefore, the time has probably come for the United States to step in and seriously help the Arabs and the Israelis reach a comprehensive settlement. After more than a decade on the disintegration of the Soviet Union and several Middle Eastern regional wars, the United States is believed to be the only major player in the Middle East. However, many people doubt that the United States can do it alone, due to its enormous financial, political, and diplomatic support of Israel. Because of this support, the United States has been seen as a partner with Israel and thus responsible for Israeli actions. Otherwise, how can anyone explain the United States' behavior of forcing certain nations to comply with UN resolutions but of failing to even ask Israel to comply with at least one of successive UN resolutions? As long as the Arabs continue to perceive the United States' policy as uneven in the Arab–Israeli conflict and as long as Israel's compliance with UN resolutions does not materialize, the Arab–Israeli conflict is not going to be solved soon. Therefore, the United States will have to maintain a sizable force in that region, accept Muslim animosities around the world, and become ready to receive many more terrorist hits resulting in more American casualties.

By the same token, the entire Middle Eastern region should undergo some serious reforms, and Middle Eastern leaders should bare the responsibility for those reforms. For those reforms to be homegrown, Middle Eastern leaders should make some sacrifices and involve their own people in their own decisions. However, those reforms will need the help of the international community, without appearing as being channeled from outside sources. The challenge is how to move from wars, anarchies, dictatorships, and other forms of Middle Eastern governments to democratic, inclusive, and representative systems in the region? Good will and sacrifice on the part of everyone can lead reforms on the right track, the same way things have happened somewhere else.

REFERENCES

Arjomand, Said Amir. n.d. *Can Rational Analysis Break a Taboo? A Middle East Perspective.* New York: Social Science Research Council.

Fandy, Mamoun. 2003. "Perceptions: Where Al-Jazeera and CO Are Coming From?" March 30, B01. Retrieved from www.washington.com.

Friedman, Thomas. 2003. "Raising Adopted Baghdad Will Be a Mammoth Task." *Gulf News,* United Arab Emirates, May 5, 9.

Hashem, Mahboub E. 1993. *The Middle East and U.S. Foreign Policy: What Are We Doing in the Persian Gulf Region and Why?* The Docking Institute of Public Affairs International Security Speakers Bureau. Hays, Kans.: Fort Hays State University.

Kadhim, Habib. 2003. Quoted in "Iraq and the West: A Report," produced by Herman G. Abnayer and Richard Klug. Broadcast June 6 on World Link TV.

Kawach, Nadim, and Sheerina Nowais. 2003. "Media Coverage of Iraq Flayed." *Gulf News,* United Arab Emirates, May 8, 4.

Munif, Azza. 2003. "U.S. Uses Powell to Tame Syria, Lebanon." Gulf News, UAE, May 9, 8.

Pitt, W. R., and S. Ritter. 2002. *War on Iraq: What Team Bush Doesn't Want You to Know.* New York: Context Books.

Riker-Coleman, Erick B. 1999. "Middle Eastern Civil-Military Relations in Global Perspective: Antecedents and Implications of Militarization." Retrieved from www.unc.edu/-chaos1/mideast.pdf.

Solomon, Norman. 2003a. "American Media Dodging UN Surveillance Story." March 6. Retrieved from www.accuracy.org/media-beat/030306.html.

———. 2003b. "Media and the Politics of Empathy." April 17. Retrieved from www.fair.org/media-beat/030417.html.

———. 2003c. "Introspective Media Not in the Cards." May 8. Retrieved from www.fair.org/media-beat/030508.

Urayyid, Thurayya. 2003. "Iraqis Hoping against Hope." Translated from Arabic by Amin Bonnah to *Los Angeles Times–Washington Post* News Service. May 12, 10. Also in *Gulf News,* United Arab Emirates.

Zarif, Javid. 2003. "Iran's Vision of a New Peaceful Iraq." *Gulf News,* United Arab Emirates, May 12, 10.

Zogby, James J. 2003. "U.S. Media Dances to White House Tune." *Gulf News,* United Arab Emirates, May 5, 9.

17

Iranians and Media Coverage of the War in Iraq: Rhetoric, Propaganda, and Contradiction

Naiim Badii

On March 19, 2003, when President Bush ordered the "decapitation attack" on Iraq, Iranians were preparing themselves for the Iranian New Year celebrations, which start on the first day of spring. Ironically, most Iranians were not only cheerful for their New Year but were also for the war waged against the brutal Baath regime on their western neighbor, Iraq, headed by Saddam Hussein. At the same time, others were worried about the postwar changes, particularly the balance of power in the Middle East.

The prewar anxiety started weeks earlier in London, Tokyo, Washington, Cairo, and elsewhere. While the prewar demonstrations in cities around the globe were organized to protest the looming American–British war against Iraq, in Iran the atmosphere was relatively calm and anticipatory. In fact, an antiwar demonstration organized by a conservative faction in a small square in Tehran known as Palestine Square, where a few people gathered and shouted anti-American slogans, was largely ignored by most Iranians.

For the majority of Iranians who had resisted and experienced the imposed eight-year war with Iraq, from 1980 to 1988, which resulted in at least three hundred thousand deaths, five hundred thousand casualties, and more than $150 billion in damages, the news of war on Iraq was cause for national jubilation. Even the daily conversations in taxies, city buses, and daily gatherings were in support of the pending war against Saddam Hussein, whose atrocities against the Iranians will be forever etched in the memories of those who witnessed eight years of pain, suffering, and destruction. They could hardly forget Saddam's use of chemical weapons on the Iranian soldiers and even on his own citizens, mainly the Kurdish people. When Iranians were watching the televised antiwar demonstrations being held around the globe, they would often comment that "these people know nothing about Iraq and Saddam's brutality."

IRAQ CRISIS AND ISLAMIC GOVERNMENT

The Islamic government's policy toward the war and Iraq was dual and paradoxical. From the viewpoint of the reformists who control the Foreign Ministry, the policy toward Iraq was "active neutrality." Meanwhile, the conservatives were seemingly in support of Saddam Hussein, with the pretext of supporting the Iraqi people, and they widely expressed their opposition to the war in various tribunes. The political behavior of the Islamic Republic was in line with the view that the world opinion would never believe in its "active neutrality" policy. The support for Iraqi people believed to be a twist toward siding with Saddam Hussein. The old proverb prevailed: "The enemy of my enemy is my friend." In reality, it was not the Foreign Ministry who designed Iran's foreign policy; it was the conservatives who directed it. Conservatives believed that the international opposition to the war was in essence against the United States and the coalition forces, and if Iraq is attacked and occupied, then the entire region will become destabilized and threatened by the invading forces.

On February 26, 2003, during the Non-aligned Movement conference in Malaysia, Kamal Kharrazi, Iran's foreign minister, told Reuters news agency, "It is the Iraqi people's natural right to determine their own future and they should be supported. The change of regime in Iraq with the help of a foreign country is not acceptable." In time, the dual and paradoxical foreign policy toward Iraq actually dismantled Iran's "active neutrality" policy in favor of political rhetoric.

Meanwhile, the foreign minister's doubt in the matter prompted him to announce the "referendum plan" for Iraq. In a political scene, Kharrazi's statement was regarded as "interfering in Iraqi affairs." Hence, in a press conference on March 5, 2003, he stated, "The idea for referendum in Iraq and national reconciliation was offered to prevent the war." In this Tehran news conference, Kharrazi said, "The war against Iraq is not a simple matter and Americans should know that Iraq is different than Afghanistan."

Skepticism, confusion, and doubt in foreign policy, and the fear of the United States' presence in Iran's western border, led Iranian politicians to a number of assumptions and predictions. Conservatives in different forums stated openly that the aggressive Americans will undoubtedly be drowned in this lagoon (Iraq) and that the war will speed up their failure in global domination. They believed that those who support Americans would in the end damage themselves.

MILITARY TEMPTATION

From the military point of view, the Islamic Republic's arm forces were in the state of alert along the one-thousand-kilometer border with Iraq. The Badr Corps, the military arm of Iraq's Supreme Islamic Revolutionary Majlis (SIRM), consisting of ten thousand exiled-Iraqi opposition forces, started creeping into southern Iraq. The Iraqi-exiled Mohammad Bagher Hakim, who presided over the Iraq's SIRM for twenty-two years, was ready to enter Iraq from Iran. Shortly after returning to Iraq, he was assassinated.

The United States had warned Iran, before the war on Iraq, to prevent the Badr Corps from entering Iraq during the military operation; nonetheless, they did so and occupied the border city of Yagubeh. The Badr Corps later entered Karbala and Najaf and started demonstrations and anti-American slogans. They stayed in these cities until Hakim arrived, and under pressure from the coalition forces, they surrendered their weapons.

ISLAMIC REPUBLIC MEDIA AND THE WAR

When the first missile hit Baghdad at 5:30 AM on March 20, 2003, in an attempt to kill Saddam and other Iraqi leaders, Iranians were waking up to celebrate their New Year Day, which coincides with the first day of spring, with holiday festivities continuing until the fourteenth day of Farvardin (the first Persian month, equivalent to January). Tehran newspapers had closed their shops on this day; hence, the people's only domestic source of news was the conservative-controlled Islamic Republic of Iran Broadcasting (IRIB). Nevertheless, on the Iranian New Year Day (March 20, 2003), of the thirty daily newspapers in Tehran, only the morning newspaper *Entekhab* published a four-page extra and continued publication until the end of holidays. Other newspapers, such as *Iran* and *Touseeh,* published extras three days after the war had started but had difficulties with distribution due to holidays. In recent years, most newspapers do not publish until the end of holidays.

A few hours after the war had started, IRIB launched its news policy with the conservatives' diplomacy. Imitating satellite television networks such as CNN, FOX News, BBC, and the Qatar-based Al-Jazeera, IRIB put a slogan in Persian language at the corner of the screen: "Jang-e Solteh," meaning "War of Domination."

IRIB selectively broadcast the news of attacks by the coalition forces on Basra and Baghdad, showing damaged buildings, women, children, and other suffering civilians. IRIB reporters and editors based in the television and radio studios in Tehran tried to portray the war in accordance with their own visions.

After the third day of the war, the "lagoon theory" became active in the Islamic Republic media. The anticipation was that the invading forces would sink in the Iraqi lagoon. When coalition forces were behind the gates of Basra, Faw, and Umm Qasr, radio and television news stories were focused on "the resistance of Iraq toward the occupiers."

In reaction to the propaganda aired on the Iranian radio and television in support of the Iraqi army, Saddam Hussein, and Baath Party resistance, most Iranians were asking themselves, "Why should we support Iraq, Saddam, and his party?" A decade ago, it was normal to black out news during war or other crisis in the name of national security, but at a time when people have access to other sources of information, such as satellite television networks, international radio broadcasts, and the Internet, the old approach is highly impractical and even counterproductive. Disinformation as well as misinformation not only loses the people's trust in the media, but it also directs the audience's attention toward other sources of information. This is exactly what happened in Iran during the war on Iraq. Despite its prohibition, people set up the satellite dishes on their patios or buildings' rooftops to watch CNN International, BBC World News, FOX News, and many other networks based outside Iran.

The news policy of the Iranian radio and television networks, controlled by the conservatives and inspired by the probable defeat of the Americans and the coalition forces in the war, raised protest in newsrooms and political circles. Elaheh Kolaei, a Majlis (parliament) representative, told *Hamshahri Daily*,

> Contrary to Iran's neutrality policy in the war, from the very beginning, the Islamic republic radio and television supports the brutal regime of Baghdad, while their only task should be to disseminate news objectively and without bias.

Referring to the Iran–Iraq war, another representative, Naser Ghavami, in an interview with *Hamshahri,* stated,

> For eight years, we told our people and asked them to fight with Saddam Hussein, but now we are saying we should support Iraqi people. It was not only Saddam who fought with us, but thousands of Iraqi people were ordered by their brutal leader to attack us, therefore, this kind of support does not coincide with our national interest.

When the voice of opposition to the IRIB's news policy increased, Ezatollah Zarghami, IRIB's vice president for parliamentary affairs, stressed,

> Those who believe that our reporting was in favor of Saddam and Baath Party will not find any evidence to support their claims. The IRIB's news reporting

policy has been approved by responsible officials and has the approval of the War Committee of the Supreme Council of National Security.

Contrary to the above statement, there are many instances that could be cited to disprove Zarghami's claim. In addition to the IRIB's daily statistics regarding the "civilian's deaths," the "daily destruction of Iraqi people's houses," the "killing of women and children," and the "torture of Iraqis," one can site the following cases:

- daily broadcast of Saeed al-Sahaf, Iraq's information minister, interviews and rhetoric on IRIB;
- showing of one or two injured Iraqis, with pictures of bombarded buildings;
- broadcasting pictures of coalition forces' inspecting the Iraqi people's homes, with fabricated news of civilians' torture;
- showing pictures of American army in the deserts of Iraq, with simultaneous news of Iraqi army resistance and defeat of American army;
- showing water shortage in Basra, without showing the distribution of bottled water by coalition forces;
- broadcasting pictures of American soldiers killed by a hand-grenade attack in Kuwait;
- showing previous pictures of Saddam Hussein in streets of Baghdad; and
- ignoring procoalition demonstrations and the Iraqi people's jubilations after the fall of Baghdad.

If one adds up the killing of civilians reported by the IRIB's statistics, the death tolls pass tens of thousands of Iraqis and thousands of American forces. Overall, there had been 224 Americans killed in Iraq since the war began. That includes 77 accidental and other deaths that weren't the result of hostile attacks—two-thirds of them after May 1, 2003. According to the Pentagon figures, the 147 deaths from hostile fire included 32 that had occurred since May 1, when George W. Bush declared that major combat was over.

Note the following news broadcast by the Iranian television on April 6, 2003: "In Basra, British soldiers raided 70 Iraqi homes and captured many civilians, accused of being Baath Party members."

In the original Persian story, the word *Yuresh* was used for *raid*, which has negative connotation and reminds viewers of a Mongolian-style attack, while the word *civilians* stresses "humbleness" and the word *accused* connotes "innocent." All together, the attempt was to show the British violence in the war. The true story, however, was that the people of Basra had given the addresses of some Baath Party members to the British troops who subsequently captured them.

UPHEAVAL IN BAGHDAD: SADDAM HUSSEIN FALLS

On April 7, 2003, a day before the fall of Saddam Hussein, the Islamic Republic News Agency (IRNA) reported of a bloody conflict between Saddam supporters and people of Baghdad. IRNA reported this story from Baghdad:

> For the first time, the arm conflicts between Iraqi people, Baath Party forces and Saddam Hussein supporters which has been widespread in recent days has provided a great obstacle for Baathi forces. In these conflicts, Baathi forces and Saddam Fadaeean (sacrificers) have used light and heavy weapons against people.

Subsequently, satellite television networks such as CNN, BBC, and the Kuwaiti news agency reported the IRNA news story, and FOX News, in particular, announced the upheaval of Baghdad residents and the killing of Saddam Hussein's Fadaeean, as reported by IRNA.

A few Tehran newspapers reported the Baghdad upheaval. Nevertheless, the Iranian conservative-controlled radio and television did not mention the event, and the conservative *Kayhan* newspaper attacked IRNA for reporting this event and siding with the Americans. It should be noted that IRNA is operated by the reformists and has been summoned to the courts many times.

The fall of Baghdad and the end of Saddam Hussein's rule form another example of IRIB's news policy that should be considered. On April 8, 2003, people around the globe spent hours watching CNN, BBC, FOX, Al-Jazeera, and other satellite televisions' video footage of the American forces entering central Baghdad and the Freedom Square to help the Iraqis to pull down a metal statue of Saddam. Interestingly enough, IRIB did not report a single word or picture on its radio and television networks about the fall of Baghdad. On April 8, 2003, on the IRIB's nightly television newscast at nine o'clock, the top stories were devoted to domestic events, and it was fifteen minutes into the program that a brief story about Baghdad was aired without any clarity about whether the city had been captured or not. Ironically, the newscast was still focused on reporting the resistance of the Iraqi army in parts of Baghdad. Apparently, from the IRIB's point of view, the fall of Saddam Hussein and the jubilation of the Iraqi people in the streets of Baghdad were not newsworthy!

AL-ALAM NETWORK

The Islamic Republic's Arabic satellite television, Al-Alam (The World), was inaugurated during the war on Iraq. Although there were earlier reports regarding the establishment of such a television channel, the crisis in Iraq accelerated its operation and twenty-four-hour programming. The government's objective for the establishment of this network was to broadcast various programs to the Arab countries, particularly Iraq. To achieve this goal, the network hired broadcasters with an Iraqi dialect or accent, to attract an Iraqi audience.

During the war on Iraq, news programs of the al-Alam network aired every hour and consisted of stories about dead bodies and about Iraqi civilian casualties in hospitals and other places. Furthermore, its opposition policy to the war was shown with the slogan "Harb al-solteh," or "War of Domination," which appeared on the corner of the television screen in Arabic. During its newscasts, the network routinely referred to the American forces as "occupiers."

Analysts see some similarities between Al-Alam and Al-Jazeera network. When compared to Al-Jazeera, Al-Alam uses similar logo to diminish the Qatari-based monopoly on Arabic language news and information. One of the distinguishing features of Al-Jazeera is that it heavily supports the Arab nationalism and is not a bit concerned about damaging Iran's national interests. For instance, it uses the forged name of "Arabian Gulf," instead of the historically documented "Persian Gulf," in its news and nonnews programs.

KAYHAN DAILY AND THE WAR

During the war on Iraq, *Kayhan*, the second-oldest daily Persian newspaper in Iran and the leading conservative and fundamentalist newspaper, was closely aligned with Iran's conservative-controlled radio and television in its coverage of the war. As a subscriber to the "lagoon theory," it tried to stress the "resistance of Iraqi army" and the "slaughter of Iraqi children and women" to stir public sentiments against the war and to imply that the coalition forces will fail.

Some of *Kayhan*'s front-page headlines, published in April 2003, are as follows:

- "Iraqis and Americans Battle in Baghdad" (April 5)
- "Resignation of Supreme American Commander in Iraq" (April 5)
- "Conflicting Reports from Central Iraq" (April 6)
- "American and British Aggressors Use Forbidden Weapons" (April 8)
- "Baghdad at Threshold of Human Catastrophe" (April 8)
- "Wild Occupiers Sacrifice Children" (April 9)
- "Bush-Saddam Game Is Over" (April 10)
- "Smell of Dead and Looting in Occupied Iraq" (April 12)
- "Suppressing Opposition to Iraq Occupation" (April 13)
- "First Iraqi People Demonstration against Occupiers" (April 14)

- "Iraqi People Want Islamic Government" (April 15)
- "Wide Protest against Occupiers Reach 6 Cities" (April 17)
- "Millions of Iraqis Demand Departure of Occupiers" (April 19)

AUDIENCE DECIDES

Most Iranians are accustomed to the Islamic Republic's media news coverage and policy, particularly radio and television, which tend to be imbalanced and one-sided. They have learned that they cannot rely on the conservative-controlled radio and television networks for accurate and timely news and information. Conservative newspapers such as *Kayhan*, *Resalat*, and *Islamic Republic*, with limited circulation, present the same type of news stories as IRIB. The closure of more than eighty-five publications, since April 2000, by the Iranian judiciary has posed a serious obstacle for the journalists who wish to inform their readers objectively and without bias. Furthermore, the imposed restrictions have prompted people to search for news and information through Persian and English Internet sites; international satellite television networks; and international radio broadcasts in Persian, including VOA, BBC, Radio Farda, and others.

The conservative-media policy makers in Iran have closed their eyes to the realities of the information age. In their so-called media war, they choose the simplest and most outmoded method, which is censorship, through the process of omission and commission, by jailing reporters and closing communication channels.

Undoubtedly, the media policies of every nation around the globe are based on the national interests and on serving the needs of their peoples. Networks such as CNN, FOX News, and BBC reported the war according to their respective countries' national interests. Even Al-Jazeera network tried to stress Arab solidarity and impart a sense of objectivity. But, no one knows why the media of the Islamic Republic of Iran, particularly radio and television, found benefit in misleading audiences by distorting the news of the war on Iraq.

The prevailing media restrictions encouraged Iranians to search for their daily news and information, particularly during the second war on Iraq, through international rather than through the domestic communication channels. To receive war news from abroad, they connected to the World Wide Web, created websites and web blogs, listened to foreign radios in Persian, and mounted satellite dishes on their rooftops—in spite of the dishes' illegality and the resulting hefty penalty imposed by the Iranian government if caught in possession. In essence, people were adhering to an old Persian proverb that says, "One who seeks will find."

18

South Africa and Iraq: The Battle for Media Reality

Arnold de Beer, Herman Wasserman,
and Nicolene Botha

Even before the first bombs were dropped on Baghdad, it was clear that global media battles would be fought along some frenzied and fuzzy lines. The South African (SA) media, being geographically and politically removed from the military actions in Iraq, never became a territory to be fought over by U.S.–British coalition forces or the Iraqi army. This, however, does not mean that there were not a fair number of local media battles taking place over coverage of the war.

For weeks on end television newscasters vied with one another to gain the upper hand in the battle for audiences. In the process, they positioned themselves along various continua of sentiment—whether pro– or anti–Iraq war, or pro– or anti–Iraq invasion—often only to be criticized from opposing sides to be partisan to the "other" cause. Moguls from the media in "coalition" countries accused each other of "gung-ho patriotism," "unquestioning coverage," and "warmongering" for the sake of economic gain, while they themselves were accused, sometimes by their own employees, of subservience, bias, and propaganda.

WHAT KIND OF MEDIA MIRROR DID SOUTH AFRICANS SEE?

From the outset South Africans were in doubt about the American plans for invading Iraq. In a worldwide survey by Marketing Mix,[1] it turned out that South Africans were in line with the rest of Africa, solidly against what was alternatively called a "war" and an "invasion." More than 80 percent of the respondents in Nigeria and more than 70 percent of those in South Africa said they would not support military action. This was in stark contrast with the same survey in America, where 73 percent of the participants said that they would support their country in military action against Iraq.

Though no specific causality can be shown, it has been argued in the past that in the event of war, societies feel uncomfortable when their media displays a view different from their own and perhaps also from that of the government. Like most of the governments and media in Africa, Pretoria wanted a peaceful solution and not a violent overthrow of Saddam Hussein. President Thabo Mbeki has rallied the members of the Non-aligned Movement and most countries in the African Union to concur with his point of view. Mbeki and his government were especially vociferous in their condemnation of any disregard of the UN. Even so, Mbeki made it quite clear that his government would maintain "very good relations" with the United States.[2]

This standpoint, however, did not deter the United States and the United Kingdom to woo Africa for support, even though the African Union has publicly opposed a U.S.-led campaign against Hussein.[3] Part of the African reaction must be seen against the alienation from the United States due to perceived double standards in terms of America's willingness to support Africa when economic and other help was needed.[4]

South Africa differs from most of what is found in Africa in terms of media freedom. The print media was especially free to report on Iraq in the way they saw fit. This situation should be seen against the background of the transformation of the South African media since the demise of apartheid. In 2003 the media operated in an atmosphere where they were free to criticize the government and take opposition against its policies in Iraq. The overwhelming impression was that this did not happen.[5]

THE "UGLY AMERICAN"

The Iraq conflict in 2003 confronted South Africans with the question, How do we perceive America? Were the Americans the "good guys," getting rid of a terrible dictator, or were they the "bad guys," riding slipshod through and over international conventions (UN) as well as international moral standards?

The South African press generally favored the UN approach to seek a peaceful solution and reveled in vilifying the United States as "a nation of twitching paranoiacs."[6] Following the U.S. decision to attack Iraq without UN support, most major newspapers cautioned readers that the "world today is a much more dangerous place."[7] South African Nobel peace laureate Archbishop Desmond Tutu strongly condemned the Iraq War, not only as "unjust" and "immoral," but also as "evil."[8]

The South African media were not the only ones to mistrust American motives, even U.S. media in the aftermath of the war openly called U.S. foreign policy "news management."[9] The *Economist*[10] even suggested that U.S. president George Bush and his staunch ally, British prime minister Tony Blair, had been "wielders of mass deception" who lied to the world to justify military action against Hussein.

LITTLE SYMPATHY FOR ANOTHER VIETNAM OR AFGHANISTAN

Strong misgivings about U.S. competency for its "war against terrorism" led many in the South African media to speculate that the war could be another drawn out Vietnam-type debacle for America.[11] The media focus was, until late 2003, twofold: first, it centered on the continual killing of U.S. soldiers by suicide bombings and attacks; second, it questioned the competency of the United States to establish a workable democracy in Iraq.[12] Others, such as columnist Leopold Scholtz,[13] likened the American/British-led invasion of Iraq to that of Russia into Afghanistan during the eighties. Similar to the Russians, who knew "very little" about the Afghans, the Americans also acted with "dense ignorance towards the Iraqis." "They searched women physically, humiliated the Iraqis, regularly shot civilians without any punitive measures and generally angered the Iraqis, even those who greeted them with joy initially" (translated).

In short, the message of the SA press in general was that the "ugly Americans" were getting their just deserts. After all, it was the United States who supplied Iraq with weapons of mass destruction when the two countries were in alliance against Iran.[14]

THE SEARCH FOR REALITY

Certainly one of the main media issues on Iraq was the public's and the media's often futile grasps at reality. Not only did the initial coverage lead to a discourse of uncertainty about the rights and wrongs of the war, but it was also clear that the media had difficulty pinpointing its own role. This was exacerbated by the apparent lack of "objective reporting" over a range of media channels. For the general consumer of news, it must have been a continual struggle to distinguish between what could reasonably be perceived as "credible" reporting and what should have been dismissed as blatant "propaganda." This was a particular concern in the print media, where readers were by and large used to a broad separation of "news" and "comment." As will be indicated later, weekly newspapers in particular threw caution to the wind, and it became almost impossible to discern "fact" from "propaganda."

In line with French president Jacques Chirac, who called for a stronger French presence in world reporting, president Mbeki campaigned for an all-Africa news agency, to bring a broader perspective to South Africa. As America's Orwellian *newspeak* kicked in, both the South African media and the public became more and more confused by the "noble intentions" of the Bush government and by the "television and print reality" of the shocking results of its mighty military endeavor in Iraq. As famed South African author and vice chancellor of Cape Town University Njabulo Ndebele[15] puts it: "What this war has exposed is a great country that may have reached the limits of its moral imagination." Referring to U.S. governmental and military nomenclature—a newspeak that has been referred to as "collateral language,"[16] such as "Operation Iraqi Freedom," "coalition of the willing," "war and terror," "surgical strikes," "smart bombs" and "embedded journalists"—Ndebele noted:

> It is the language of terse encapsulation that ironically strains towards the economy of poetry but, unlike poetry, yields not insight but cleverness of the kind that supremely admires itself. The expressions underscore the phenomenon of a war without a transcendent goal or cause. It is a war obsessed with its own techniques.[17]

Neither did it help that the South African public was largely exposed to American news channels, be they in the form of CNN or syndicated news from the *New York Times*, the *Washington Post,* and others. What were South Africans to believe about Iraq when that bastion of "all that is fit to print," the *New York Times,*[18] carried an op-ed article with the headline "A Price Too High" and an introduction that stated:

> How long is it going to take for us to recognize that the war we so foolishly started in Iraq is a fiasco—tragic, deeply dehumanizing and ultimately not winnable? How much time and how much money and how many wasted lives is it going to take?

The end result was that South African newspaper readers were confronted with a barrage of headlines in respected publications, ranging from the cynical, sardonic, and sarcastic to the outright blatantly obscene.

From the *Sunday Independent* (South Africa's quality Sunday newspaper, carrying a large number of syndicated articles from quality U.S. and U.K. newspapers):

"US Moral Decline Brings Barbaric Times" (April, 13, 2003, 6)
"So, Where Are All The Weapons? The absence of any 'smoking gun' in
    the form of weapons of mass destruction in Iraq raises questions about

the legality of the invasion" (a special large strap headline and a sub-
headline and an out of the ordinary comment article, instead of a lead
story on the front page; April 20, 2003, 1)

"The Case of the Amazing Disappearing Weapons of Mass Destruction"
(April 13, 2003, 3)

"US Scoops Appliances of Mass Frustration" (May 25, 2003, 14)

"Marine Commander Admits U.S. Intelligence Was Wrong" (June 1, 2003, 3)

"Burning Hatred" (headline for a front-page main picture of a burning U.S.
vehicle in Iraq; August 24, 2003, 1)

"Revealed: Iraq's Weapons of Ass Destruction" (November 11, 2003, 9)

From the *Mail&Guardian* (internationally acclaimed, award-winning,
"anti-apartheid struggle" weekly newspaper):

"Shameful Journalism" (headline for an upcoming editorial: "journalists
have exchanged the sacred truth for propaganda by becoming embedded—a thoroughly filthy word—it signals wholesale journalistic capitu-
lation to ideological interests that it should be the profession's job to dis-
sect, not embrace"; April 11–16, 2003, 28)

"Hollow Victory for the War Whores" (April 11–16, 2003, 28)

From the *Sunday Times* (Africa's largest selling newspaper):

"Iraq Rolls Out the Carpet for Bush" (a cynical headline referring to a carpet being rolled over an image of President George Bush on the floor of
the entrance to the Baghdad hotel where diplomats and news people
have stayed; March 16, 2003, 1).

It was not only in the print media that South African media consumers received divergent and sometimes mixed messages. The television coverage of
the Iraq conflict was also marked by different views of the war, and debates
raged on air about the role of the media in the conflict.

CONTRASTING TELEVISION NEWS SIMMERS ON
THE EDGE OF PROPAGANDA

Television news in South Africa can broadly be divided into two categories.
The first group includes the "open" or "free to air" services that are accessi-
ble to everybody—namely, the three services of public broadcaster SABC, of
which only SABC3 presents news in English; and the services of e.tv, a private broadcaster. The second category consists of news that is broadcast via

satellite and therefore only available to viewers able to afford a DSTV sub-
scription. In addition to SABC and e.tv, the DSTV package offers Sky, CNN
International, BBC World, and at intervals CNBC with NBC evening news.

In the "open" category, a fairly differentiated media picture emerged:
Whereas the public broadcaster tended to portray the Americans more positively, the private station criticized the U.S. harshly. Day after day, e.tv ended
their newscasts with the same remark: "So far," the anchor would say, "the
Americans have not found any weapons of mass destruction." In its discussion of the way the two networks covered the initial phase of the Iraqi conflict, the news-analysis institute Media Tenor[19] remarked that it often seemed
as if they were not reporting on the same war.

A Media Tenor study analyzed eleven programs of eight broadcasters—
namely, that of the British BBC; the American ABC; the German ARD, ZDF,
and RTL; the South African SABC and e.tv; and the Czech CTV. In this
study, the two South African broadcasters came out diametrically opposed in
their position toward almost every issue that was addressed. Both broadcasters obviously focused on the coverage of the military action, the same as Germany and the coalition countries, but the South African news programs (and
that of the Czech broadcaster CTV) stood out in covering the consequences
of war, a category in which ABC came in dead last. Similarly, the South
African and Czech news programs, as well as their German counterparts, predominantly focused on the dead, wounded, and missing on the Iraqi side.

Also, after the war had started, only South African television news still reported rather extensively on topics such as peace, human rights, and weapons
inspections.[20]

Where the SABC generally evaluated American actions with relative balance, similar to the BBC's news presentation, e.tv positioned itself predominantly as critics of all American actions. Media Tenor found that e.tv took a
particularly large interest in antiwar protests and reported much more frequently than did other networks on questions about the legitimacy of the
war; furthermore, they focused on issues such as human rights, weapons,
peace, and terror. As mentioned earlier, e.tv, on a daily basis, pointed out the
United States' failure to verify the existence of weapons of mass destruction.
This broadcaster also extensively covered political background issues.
Though e.tv searched for answers about international affairs and especially
about relationships between various interest groups after the end of the
war,[21] one cannot but rate the presentation of e.tv as bordering on propaganda against the U.S.

Much more than the SABC, e.tv was concerned not only about the emotional aspects of the war for all parties involved but also especially for the
emotional experiences and well-being of the journalists in Iraq. (Remarkably,

American services concentrated on the depiction of emotions on the Iraqi side much more than did most of the other broadcasters.) On the issue of journalists' working conditions, e.tv proved to be far more critical than the SABC, whose criticism was often general and frequently softened by positive statements and evaluations of the problems.[22]

Apparently, part of the disparity of the South African television channels' war coverage stemmed from their uncertainty about exactly what their audience wanted.[23] On the one hand, the SABC/Markinor opinion poll showed that before the outbreak of the war 63 percent of all South Africans were opposed to military intervention in Iraq and 68 percent were against their country's participation in the war.[24] On the other hand, certain newspaper reports alleged that South African society was fairly divided in their views of the war, often along racial lines. In this connection the *Mail&Guardian* wrote:

> In the past six weeks, one has not heard a single black person endorse the United States invasion of Iraq, or seen one black letter of support in the media. Anti-war protests, including a march by 6 000 people in Pretoria, have overwhelmingly drawn Africans and South African Indians. . . . [If] talk shows and letters to the editor are any pointer, the average white South African felt very differently. Perhaps two-thirds of the letters written by whites to the *Mail&Guardian* on the subject of Iraq have been of the flag-waving pro-war variety.[25]

Divisions along racial lines are perhaps not enough to explain the polarization in the presentation of news on the Iraqi War. Both e.tv and the SABC have significant numbers of black senior staff—the former is 80 percent black-owned, while the latter is a state corporation effectively regulated through a pro–African National Congress board, by the black-dominated government of South Africa.[26] The differences in allegiance might be attributed to the availability of material.[27] The SABC was the only South African broadcaster to have reporters in Baghdad, which must have had a substantial effect on the content of their news programs. Furthermore, the SABC's contract to broadcast CNN after its regularly scheduled programming expired on March 31, 2003, and the station chose not to renew it. Despite earlier talks that they would replace CNN with Al-Jazeera, the SABC instead broadcast BBC World at selected times daily for those who wanted to follow the war.[28]

CONCLUSION

In all fairness it should be stated that the media coverage of Iraq in 2003 was not all one-sided and skewed against the United States. Even one of the most critical newspapers, the *Sunday Independent*,[29] published a special series of articles about Iraq, entitled Iraq, Six Months On—A Survey of the Good, the Bad and the Uncertain. It showed, on the positive side, that there was more media freedom in the country; in fact, according to a Gallup poll, 67 percent of Baghdad residents thought that their lives would be better five years post-2003. However, a number of negative issues were then discussed, including casualties and the cost of reconstruction.

But in the end, an article in the Afrikaans newspaper *Die Burger*[30] encapsulated the issue addressed in this chapter. Beneath a caption of "Make or break war—also for the media?" the author describes how the media coverage of Iraq in the South African media varied from the "banal to the absurd."

Perhaps the variety in coverage of the conflict can be read as a positive indication—that the South African media, which has had its own struggle for freedom of expression, now has sufficient freedom to express a spectrum of opinions without experiencing the pressure of external allegiances.

NOTES

The authors thank Heléne Uys, Department of Journalism, Stellenbosch University; and Nicolette de Beer, Institute for Media Studies in South Africa (Imasa), for their editorial and administrative input.

1. Marketing Mix, "A SABC/Markinor/Gallup International Poll on Iraq," press release (Johannesburg: Systems Publishers), January 31, 2003.

2. B. Tromp, "Pretoria Wants a Peaceful Solution, Not an Overthrow," *Sunday Independent*, March 16, 2003.

3. "World Powers Woo Africa," *Sunday Times,* March 16, 2003, 8, foreign desk.

4. C. Prestowitz, "How the United States Cheats the Poor Nations," *Sunday Independent*, June 15, 2003, 9.

5. For an overview of the media in South Africa and the rest of the continent, see M. Ibelema, M. Land, L. Eko, and E. Steyn, "Sub-Saharan Africa (East, West and South)," in *Global Journalism. Topical Issues and Media Systems* (4th ed.), ed. A. S. De Beer. and J. C. Merrill (Boston: Pearson Education, 2004); S. Jacobs, "How Good Is the South African Media for Democracy? Mapping the South African Public Sphere after Apartheid," *African and Asian Studies* 1, no. 4 (2002): 279–302; World Press Freedom Review, *A Special Report* (Vienna: International Press Institute, 2003).

6. D. Bullard, "Out to Lunch. Stand By and Watch as I Plan My Fabulous Life," *Sunday Times*, October 12, 2003, 3.

7. Editorial, "Iraq," *Beeld,* March 8, 2003, 10.

8. "Tutu Says Attack Unjust and Immoral," *Cape Argus,* March 20, 2003.

9. R. Wolffe and R. Nordland, "Bush's News War," *Newsweek*, October 27, 2003, 22.

10. "Wielders of Mass Deception?" *Economist,* October 4, 2003, 13.

11. R. Cornwell, "Americans Fear Sliding into Vietnam-Type Morass," *Sunday Independent*, November 16, 2003, 3; M. Du Preez, "Mother of All Mistakes," trans., *Die Burger*, April 5, 2003; F. Kornegay, "Bush's Forces May Be Lured into Another Vietnam," *Sunday Independent*, March 16, 2003, 15.

12. R. Cornwell, "Shadow of Vietnam Looms over Coalition," *Cape Times*, April 1, 2003; Z. B. Du Toit, "And after the War, President Bush?" (translated), *Rapport*, March 16, 2003.

13. L. Scholtz, "Iraq Might Develop into an Afghanistan for U.S.A.," trans., *Die Burger*, November 7, 2003, 12.

14. Du Toit, "And after the War, President Bush?" 15.

15. N. Ndebele, "A Country at the End of Its Moral Imagination," unpublished public lecture by the vice chancellor of the University of Cape Town, September 9, 2003.

16. See J. Collins and R. Glover, *Collateral Language* (New York: New York University Press, 2002).

17. Ndebele, "A Country at the End."

18. B. Herbert, "A Price Too High," *New York Times*, retrieved from www.nytimes .com/2003/08/21/opinion/21HERB.html (accessed on August 21, 2003).

19. Research results published by Media Tenor (Bonn, Germany; www.mediatenor .com) regarding a content analysis project on media coverage of the Iraq issue. See M. Rettich, W. Schreiner, and Prinsloo, "The War on TV: 'Better' Is Not Good Enough," *Media Tenor Quarterly Journal*, no. 2.

20. Rettich, Schreiner, and Prinsloo, "The War on TV."

21. Rettich, Schreiner, and Prinsloo, "The War on TV."

22. Rettich, Schreiner, and Prinsloo, "The War on TV."

23. I. Glenn, "Media Coverage of the Iraqi War," unpublished paper read at the *Media in Africa Conference* as part or the twenty-fifth-year celebration of the Department of Journalism, Stellenbosch University, 2003. Retrieved from www.sun.ac.za./ journalism.

24. Marketing Mix, "A SABC/Markinor/Gallup International Poll on Iraq."

25. "Black and White Take on the War," *Mail&Guardian,* April 29, 2003, retrieved from http://archive.mg.co.za/nxt/gateway.dll/PrintEdition/MGP2003/3lv00935/ 4lv00936/5lv00945.htm.

26. D. Smuts, "Keeping the Ruling Elite Locked In," *Cape Times*, November 19, 2003, 13.

27. Glenn, "Media Coverage of the Iraqi War."

28. "SABC3 Ditches CNN," Biz-Community, retrieved from www.biz-community .com/Snippet/196/66/1056.html (accessed March 3, 2003).

29. "Iraq, Six Months On," *Sunday Independent,* October 19, 2003, 13–15.

30. L. Rabe, "Make or Break War—Also for the Media?" *Die Burger*, September 14, 2003, 9.

19

The Chinese Watching the Iraqi War with Shock and Awe—As a Spectacular Game

Zhou He

To millions of Chinese in the mainland and Hong Kong, the U.S–Iraqi war in 2003 was an unforgettable and unprecedented experience. They watched the high-tech war through high-tech communication means with shock and awe—as if it were a spectacular game.

The Chinese were unlike their counterparts in the United States, who experienced the Vietnam War as it was delivered to their living rooms by television every night for almost a decade; likewise, the Chinese were also different from many of their fellow dwellers in the more liberal parts of the shrinking global village who saw Desert Storm live in 1991 through CNN. The reason for the discrepancy is that the Chinese did not have the privilege of watching a major ongoing war on television because of the government's tight control over incoming information and because of the lack of cable services that relayed the signals of international networks. The coverage of the U.S.–Iraqi war by a myriad of media channels, especially by television, was the first time the Chinese were exposed to a modern war through the telescope of the mass media.

The buildup of Hong Kong media coverage of the imminent crisis in Iraq started before the breakout of the war as U.S. military forces were gathering around that besieged country. Newspapers significantly expanded their news role and churned up front-page stories of the conflict for days in a row. Television stations devoted almost all of their regular international news slot to the Iraqi crisis. Several reporters were dispatched by various media organizations to U.S. carriers and strategic military locations for battlefield coverage, a rare move for the Hong Kong media that catered to an audience who was usually indifferent to international news. As the war broke out, the coverage intensified with entire newspaper sections and all news slots on television devoted to the war. Some satellite television stations, such as the Phoenix Satellite Television, covered the war almost around the clock, as CNN and FOX did.

The Hong Kong media's intensive coverage was obviously prompted by universally accepted practice of professional journalism, the newsworthiness of the event, and the competition on a free market. One unique feature, however, was that some of the media were compelled to compete for audience in the relatively secluded mainland China. Several Hong Kong–based satellite and terrestrial television networks were granted permission to operate on the Chinese market, especially in the Pearl River Delta area, adjacent to Hong Kong. Among them were the Phoenix Satellite Television, Sun Satellite Television, and Asia Television. All were funded in one way or another by money from China or pro-China capitalists, and all adopted a pro-China editorial stance. Some were even directly established by the Chinese government as joint ventures with friendly overseas allies and staffed by cadres from China, for the purpose of establishing propaganda watersheds outside China. The Phoenix Satellite Television, for example, was such a venture. Its major share of capital was funded from China, and its top management and professional personnel all came from China's Central Television. Ironically, this venture turned out to be a "reimported" service that was meant to operate overseas because its ostensible pro-Communist editorial stance made it unattractive outside China; however, its somewhat more flexible coverage and its front cover of an overseas operation made it popular in China. The service staged a scoop when it covered the September 11 terrorist attacks on New York with real-time footage from other international television networks and simultaneous translation. Millions of Chinese, including the country's top leaders, watched the horror through Phoenix, the only channel available in China that provided instantaneous coverage in a language the Chinese could understand. For the Phoenix station and other, similar media organizations, the Iraqi war stood as another good opportunity to expand their audience base and further establish their niche on the Chinese market.

The mass media in China were slow to react to the conflict in the initial stage, apparently refrained by the government's ambiguous position and afraid of stepping out of the correct party line. Indeed, the Chinese government was caught in a dilemma during the days leading to the war. Traditionally, it never had a close relationship with Iraq despite its growing economic ties with Iraq, which were established as Chinese companies began to get into the Iraqi market, especially the telecommunications market. Strategically and geopolitically, the Chinese government had no real stake in Iraq. The United States was not a close friend either. It had been a traditional foe until China started to embark on economic reforms and subsequently opened itself up to the outside world in the late 1970s. The Sino–U.S. relationship thereafter experienced ups and downs with the period of Bill Clinton's administration being the peak, when China was seen as a "strategic partner"; and with the beginning of George Bush's government being the ebb, when China was regarded as a contestant. Right before the Iraqi war, China had just improved its relationship with the United States, which was made possible by China's joining the Bush-led forces again terrorism in the world, including militant Islamic groups, such as the Eastern Turkestan Islamic Movement in China's border region of Xinjiang, which were deemed "terrorists" by the Chinese government. More important, the United States had become China's largest export market, worth well over $100 billion per year, which China did not want to jeopardize by any means. However, China was seriously concerned with the expansion of the American-led "world order" and customarily harbored an implicit ideological inclination to oppose "imperialist" invasions. To get out of the dilemma of being neither a foe nor a friend to both sides, what China opted to do in the prewar stage was to present a lukewarm opposition to a United Nations–sanctioned military action against Iraq while urging Iraq to "strictly implement U.N. Security Council resolutions," to avoid "the emergence of new complexity with the Iraq issue," as stated by Foreign Minister Tang Jiaxuan. This was an ambiguous diplomatic position, which obviously put the state-controlled Chinese media in a limbo.

After the French and German antiwar alliance, supported by China and Russia, successfully thwarted the U.S. effort to wage a war against Iraq under the name of the United Nations, as in the case of "Desert Storm," the U.S. and British joint forces launched the military campaign on their own, creating a de facto antiterrorism war that the Western and pro-Western world had to accept or live with. As the French and German governments became apologetic about their opposition at the UN Security Council and tried to patch up their relationship with the U.S.–British alliance after the breakout of the war, so did the Chinese government, by adopting a more detached and approving position toward the U.S.–British alliance. This change was immediately taken by the Chinese media as the green light to cover a conflict they couldn't wait to exploit for their own benefit.

To the Chinese media, this first major war of the new millennium came at a right time. After more than twenty years of economic reforms and commercialization, the Chinese media had gradually transformed themselves from a pure mouthpiece, or "transmission belt," of the party to an amalgamation of various identities, including what scholars call a "social knowledge producer," an enterprise in which workers had to improvise and negotiate their ways through confusion and uncertainty; a "Party Publicity Inc." that engaged in promoting the legitimacy of the ruling party while making profit; an industry bewildered by contradictions and ambiguities; a "piper" who played the tune for the party but did not get paid; a "junk food" manufacturer that appealed to the low tastes of the largest common denominator; a "fiddler" juggling between the "party line" and the bottom line; and a "watchdog" on party leashes. Whatever they were termed, the Chinese media had become an industry that was driven as much by the mission of political propagation as by the market impetus of profit making. In this process of transformation, they had obtained, by default or through fight, a fairly large amount of autonomy in their coverage. By the time the Iraqi war was about to break out, the Chinese media had been able to cover almost everything impartially, except for two sensitive subjects: domestic politics and major international issues. As domestic politics remained a taboo within the current Communist establishment, the Chinese media were eager to expand their coverage of international issues to cater to the increasing needs of their viewers and readers for international news, to test new professional boundaries, and to compete with the increasingly threatening international information providers. They needed to respond to the Chinese people's interest in international affairs, which, though traditionally keen owing to the curiosity created by a suffocating information environment, grew significantly as China joined the World Trade Organization and became an active member of the international community, especially in the area of international trade and business. They also had to face serious competition from the international media, whose coverage of international news was out of the Chinese government's control and who could penetrate the Chinese market through a variety of channels, such as through the Internet and satellite television services, despite the Chinese government's relentless effort to curtail undesired incoming information. The Chinese media's immediate competitors included CNN, which could be received in thousands of hotels catering to foreign tourists throughout the country; the Voice of America, which was regularly listened to by at least twenty million people; and a myriad of international news providers on the Internet, which could be accessed through 27.5 million networked computers regularly used by more than sixty-eight million Chinese users. More important, they had to square off against the Hong Kong broadcasting media that entered the Chinese market either as legitimate enterprises or through spillover across the border. In fact, the Chinese national media were extremely embarrassed when they failed to provide timely and adequate information about the September 11 terror attacks on New York while the Phoenix Satellite Television fed the entire nation with simultaneous footage taken from international television networks.

The Iraqi war was also an ideal conflict for the Chinese media. It involved two sides with whom China had no close alliance. In fact, both sides were tacitly regarded by many government officials and by a large portion of the populace as "two evils," despite the government's overt posture that appeared slightly pro-American in the wake of the September 11 attacks and the global antiterrorism alliance formed in Shanghai. Such a conflict afforded the Chinese media an opportunity to provide an extensive, detailed, and somewhat detached coverage that would appeal to the audience and manifest the Chinese media's professionalism and abilities to do what other global media could.

The news agenda in the war coverage by the media in Hong Kong and mainland China was different because of different journalistic traditions and social contexts. Overall, however, it was largely influenced by the footage provided by such Western networks as FOX and CNN.

As Hong Kong had a pluralistic media environment, with media organizations backed up by different political and financial interests, the news agenda varied from one outlet to another. The mainstream Hong Kong media that catered to the needs of the local audience had an agenda similar to that in the West, as their main information and visual footage came from the Western media. They focused primarily on the fight in the UN Security Council between the U.S.–British alliance and the other permanent members, the Bush administration's search for excuses for a war, the high-tech weaponry, the buildup of the war, the detailed war process, and the Iraqi information minister's unashamed press releases. Two themes predominated their coverage: first, that it was a war waged by the civilized world represented by the United States and Britain against barbarianism and terrorism, despite the disagreement among the leading countries on the timing and necessity of the war; second, that it was a lopsided war dominated by the United States' and the United Kingdom's overwhelmingly high-tech weaponry. To localize this global event and to showcase their abilities to cover international conflicts comparable with other Western media, the Hong Kong media highlighted all the stories filed by their correspondents on the battlefield, who were assembled in a rush and had little previous experience in war coverage. As those correspondents were searching for things that were not extensively covered by the Western media, their attention naturally turned to stories that had a universal appeal or were of particular interest to the Hong Kong people. One salient news item in the initial stage of the war was the sufferings of the Iraqi people and their prewar sentiments. Also salient were the correspondents' own experiences on the site: wearing gas masks and gears, boarding a military carrier, holding an M16 machine gun, mingling with refugees, and walking on the street of Baghdad. However, when the war broke out and journalists' access to the military forces and civilians on the battlefield was restricted, the human-interest side of the war quickly gave way to the flexing of military muscles, the war process, and the awe and shock caused by the high-tech weapons, which were the main news diet provided by the Western media.

The China-backed broadcasting media in Hong Kong whose audience was mainly in the mainland had an agenda similar to that of the Chinese national media during the prowar days—an agenda that featured the antiwar sentiments manifested in antiwar rallies, demonstrations, and criticisms of the U.S.–British unilateral military actions by French, German, Russian, and Chinese leaders. They also covered the human-interest side in an effort to compete with the mainstream Hong Kong media and to attract the Chinese audience who did not often see correspondents from the Chinese national media on the battlefield. Phoenix Satellite Television, for example, dispatched several correspondents to Iraq and neighboring areas to cover the war, especially the refugees and civilians. It also mobilized all its twenty-some-strong news anchors to report, interpret, and analyze the war from their own perspectives. The emphasis on human-interest stories, coupled by simultaneous interpretation from anchors who were somewhat bilingual, appeared to attract a large number of Chinese viewers and expanded the niche of the station in its provision of slightly different news from the Chinese national media. After the breakout of the war, the station invited several military experts to serve as spin doctors and help analyze the increasingly baffling war. Because the majority of the footage came from the Western media and because the experts, by training, harbored a penchant for weapons and war maneuvers, most of the discussion panels turned out to be a display of various high-tech weapons and a graphic illustration of actual and speculated military movements on the battlefield. This, in turn, became a constant pattern in the station's coverage throughout the war.

The news agenda of the Chinese national media shifted noticeably from one of criticism of the U.S.–British unilateral military actions in the prewar period to one of excitement in the high-tech war during the conflict. As the Chinese media, particularly the national network of CCTV (China Central Television), geared up their efforts to do a decent job in their first relatively unrestricted coverage of a major international conflict, they made several dramatic innovations in their journalistic practice, including unedited footage directly taken from the Western media accompanied by simultaneous interpretation by professional interpreters; animated illustrations of war movements; satellite telephone reports by correspondents stationed around the world; teleconferences with non-Chinese analysts, such as Russian experts on international relations; and, most noticeably, a large number of domestic experts on military and international affairs and global economics. Although those innovations appeared more technical than editorial, they inflicted a significant impact on the agenda-building and agenda-setting process. The real-time broadcasting of unedited footage from global networks such as FOX and CNN, for example, made the Chinese media play a less-important and less-active role in the agenda-setting and gate-keeping process, which had been carefully protected and performed by previewing, preselecting, and editing footage from international services. The employment of a large number of experts from various institutions and backgrounds also made it extremely difficult to control the agenda and views expressed. A good example was the function of the group of military experts hired by the CCTV as its spin doctors throughout the war. Those experts, who were military officers working in institutions such as the military-run Defense University, provided explanation and illustration of what was going on and what the movements were on both sides, through war maps updated on a daily basis. Incidentally, their expertise and views dominated much of the war coverage. As they stayed in the limelight every day and obtained some stardom, they became part of the news. One widely believed line of thinking in the country about the perplexing nonresistance on the part of the Iraqi army was the "guerrilla warfare theory," advocated by Colonel Zhang Zizhong, a professor from the Defense University and the most outspoken and most influential among the military spin doctors. Colonel Zhang argued in his daily appearance on television that Saddam Hussein was obviously using the guerrilla warfare strategies used by the Chinese Red Army in its fight against a much stronger government military force in the 1930s: avoiding head-on battles and attacking the enemy only after luring it onto the home turf. This line gained much consonance among Chinese viewers because of the long-touted and propagated victory of the Red Army, and Colonel Zhang became a star that a large number of audiences followed on a daily basis. When it emerged that the once-strong Iraqi army did not exist after the U.S.–British military forces took Baghdad, Colonel Zhang turned out to be a target of fury and criticism—and was finally "fired" by CCTV after the war.

It was the opinion leaders like Colonel Zhang who helped to mold the national perception of the war and who contributed to CCTV's unprecedented lead in the war coverage over its competitors. With its monopolistic position in China; its status as the official national television network; its financial resources; and its connections with other national news providers, such as the Xinhua News Agency, who stationed more than four hundred foreign correspondents in about one hundred countries, it beat its closest competitor, the Phoenix Satellite Television, by a large margin for the first time in several years. It also established a precedent it could follow in the years to come, and it changed the media ecology in the Greater China area.

To most Hong Kong residents, who did not watch television in Mandarin despite its availability on the Hong Kong market, the competition among the major players in this sector went unnoticed. What they were interested in and exposed to was the news diet from the mainstream local media. As people who traditionally were indifferent to politics and international affairs, they did not take the war seriously. In social conversations, university class discussions, and even graduate seminars on international communication, they showed little knowledge and interest in the war and the complex international politics behind it. They viewed the conflict as a spectacular—a baffling war game between two sides of which neither was a home team or a favorite. What most of them remembered was Hong Kong correspondents' funny looks in military chemical warfare gears, the expensive cruise missiles, the smart bombs, the bombing of Baghdad, the platoon that was stopped by resistance from a small building, and the fact that U.S.–British military forces did not find any weapons of mass destruction in Iraq. Although many Hong Kongers felt uneasy and unconvinced by the U.S.–British excuse to wage a massive war against Iraq, their pro-West attitude, derived from more than a century of British rule, did not change in any noticeable way. In fact, the performance and influence of elected national leaders, as shown in Bush and Blair's ill-grounded war endeavor, seemed to make them more aware of not only the importance of a democratic system but also the election of a wise leader.

Unlike the indifferent Hong Kongers, the mainland Chinese watched the war with attention and zeal. Almost everything they were experiencing was new, from the large amount of unedited footage from the Western media that covered every step of the war to the meticulous and sometimes misleading analysis provided by an unprecedented number of experts. Naturally, they were attracted by the novelty of the dramatically new practice of Chinese journalism, through which many of their cognitive and psychological needs were gratified. They were interested in watching a modern war unfolding on their television screens. They wanted to know how advanced the U.S.–British weapons were and how the Chinese army, the largest in number in the world, compared with the U.S.–British military forces. They were anxious to see any evidence of weapons of large-scale destruction in Iraq. They couldn't wait to witness some "guerrilla warfare" strategies and tactics on the part of the Iraqi military that would attest to the value of the Chinese Red Army successes. And they involved themselves quite emotionally and personally in the prediction of the outcome of almost every major battle—as if they were watching an NBA game or some other sports spectacle. What they saw on television made them realize the inferiority of their own army, and it deepened the resentment for the United States among many Chinese, who, ironically, were perhaps the strongest tacit admirers of the U.S. democratic system, economic strength, and cultural values during the days when information about the West was scarce and tightly controlled.

The live coverage of the Iraqi war by the local media undoubtedly afforded residents in Hong Kong and China a rare opportunity to experience a modern war firsthand, with relatively unrestricted access. The detailed frame-by-frame game coverage, which was dominated by information and footage from the Western media, triggered shock and awe among many audience members, as they were exposed to a display of high-tech weaponry, the magnitude of destruction, the canny tricks pulled by the Bush administration in finding excuses or nonexcuses, and the specific maneuvers on the battlefield. However, lost in the war-game discursive experience seemed to be a rethinking of the Western values and political system, and the concern for justice and peace. What emerged in the aftermath of the war was a great sense of cynicism and disillusion.

20

The Self-Absorbed Bully: A Brazilian View of the United States at War

Antonio La Pastina

> If there is something I admire in the United States it is that they first think about themselves, secondly they think about themselves and thirdly they think about themselves. If there is any time left, they think about themselves a bit more.
>
> —Luiz Inácio Lula de Silva, President of Brazil

Bullies are quick to make a person feel two emotions: fear of what they might do and anger over what they have done. When a domineering country, the United States, refused to play by the rules of the community—in this case, invading Iraq without the approval of the United Nations—the bullying actions produced fear and anger in a bystander, Brazil.

The extent of the view of a self-absorbed bully was voiced pointedly by Brazilian president Luiz Inácio Lula de Silva in a meeting on progressive governance in London on July 13, 2003. Sitting next to the British prime minister, Lula, as the Brazilian leader is known, critiqued the United States' foreign policy and the war on Iraq, further noting that "since [the United States] has military, technological and economical hegemony, they move away from other nations, fearing that any one that gets closer is going to ask for money" (quoted in Rosa 2003).

The words voiced by Lula from the beginning of the U.S. war against Iraq have been a mixture of reproach for the United States' imperialistic attitude and resentment over the northern neighbor's refusal to work with the international community to avoid the conflict. Like Lula, Brazilians look at the United States with paradoxical feelings. While the United States is seen as a great country and the center of the contemporary world, it also is seen as an imperialist nation, one that is simultaneously envied, idolized, and demonized.

For many of us growing up in Brazil in the 1970s and 1980s, we saw the relationship between the U.S. government and the Brazilian dictatorship as one in which an imperialistic nation was attempting to impose its values and ideologies upon us. At the same time, the United States was the fountain from which we drank every day: We listened to its music, read its authors, danced to its disco beat, watched its television programs, and wore its fashion. Still, empires impose their will, and the conquered often are rebellious. That was the attitude of my youth: We were subjects of the United States Empire, without a formal conquest. This anxiety over the United States' role in our lives and the jealousy over its green lawns, fancy cars, and trendy wardrobes marked the United States in the minds of my generation in Brazil.

We knew more about the United States than we knew about Argentina, our closest neighbor. But this knowledge was as stereotypical as the knowledge most U.S. residents had of Brazil or any other nation, a knowledge mediated by the television programs, news reports, and music we consumed. Television shows such as *Dallas* were as much a marker and an identifier of how people in the United States lived as they were a form of entertainment.

The United States' war against Iraq, which began in March 2003, was the first major U.S. military operation after the Cold War in which that nation did not work with the United Nations. It also happened far from Latin America, unlike the invasions of Grenada or Panama in the 1980s, and it occurred when Brazil and Brazilians were feeling more secure in their democratic process after more than a decade of elected presidents. This war also happened under a left-leaning Brazilian president who had been outspoken against the United States' push for a free trade zone in the Americas. In this climate of democratic stability, central-left politics, and growing economic security, the news of the United States' invasion of Iraq and its disregard for the United Nations Security Council was received negatively. The fears that an imperialistic giant was reawakening were rekindled.

In that light, the Brazilian coverage of the war was symptomatic of the Brazilian attitude toward the United States and of the dependency of developing nations' media on foreign news agencies for coverage of events outside their borders. Still, this recent conflict in the Middle East boosted the role of alternative sources of information. While traditional international news agencies, such as Reuters, Associated Press, French Press, and CNN, maintained a central role in supplying information to Brazilian news organizations, nondeveloped world news agencies for the first time played an important part in the coverage of an international event involving a major world power. The news agency Al-Jazeera, based in Qatar, and the Abu-Dhabi news station from the United Arab Emirates were critical counterpoints in the coverage of the war against Iraq and other events in that region. This reliance on alternative sources, which were closer to the conflict area and offered a voice from a peripheral nation, provided Brazilian media with a venue to question the information and positioning of the United States and coverage provided by the traditional United States and British news agencies.

According to several Brazilian journalists interviewed for this piece, there was a general anti–United States sentiment expressed in Brazilian media during the war coverage, unlike the sentiment expressed during the Gulf War in 1991, when the invasion of Kuwait justified the attack against Saddam Hussein. According to Fernando Rodrigues (personal communication, July 24, 2003), a seasoned Brazilian journalist, "In Brazil, similar to most of Latin America, there is a strong anti–United States bias in the media."

Nevertheless, the Brazilian media did not position itself in favor of Saddam Hussein but questioned the United States' right to invade and depose a leader of another nation based on unsubstantiated claims and without United Nations support. The three periods of the Iraqi conflict—preinvasion, armed conflict, and reconstruction—were covered in Brazil primarily from the view that the actions were unjustified and represented a unilateral decision by the United States. Still, there were a different coverage format and a different focus during the three phases. Before the invasion, Brazilian media relied on Brazilian correspondents stationed in the United States, international news agencies, and Brazilian analysts and government sources. In this phase, the reliance on foreign agencies was not as marked as in the next.

The second phase began with the actual invasion of Iraq, on March 20, 2003. During this period of military operation, which lasted until the U.S. government's declaration that major combat had mostly ceased, the Brazilian media relied heavily on international news agencies. But unlike the first Gulf war, in the early 1990s, this time international news sources included Al-Jazeera and Abu-Dhabi news. That increased diversity showed a desire to use sources of information that could counter the American and European domination in international coverage. Three Brazilian news media sources had correspondents in the Persian Gulf, but only one outlet had staff in Baghdad. Writer Sérgio Dávila and photographer Juca Varela, from *Folha de São Paulo*, were the only Brazilians who worked from Iraqi soil. Peripheral nations such as Brazil have a limited tradition of sending correspondents to cover international events. The coverage is extremely costly, and the financial return is minimal. Prestige is the main payoff, but it is not sufficient to generate financial returns—consequently, the historical reliance on foreign news agencies.

The last phase of the coverage began after May 1, 2003, when U.S. president George Bush announced the end of the combats. That was the period in which the United States government officially declared Iraq freed and began the process of reconstruction, despite localized conflicts with guerrilla groups and a continuing number of U.S. casualties. In Brazil during that time, war coverage relied more on local experts, United States–based Brazilian correspondents, and news agencies. Issues such as validity of the attacks, the motivations for Bush's decision to invade Iraq, the future of the UN, and the implications of the war in an increasingly globalized society returned to the forefront.

Regardless of the type of sources used in the different periods of the war, the Brazilian media maintained a critical stance toward the Bush administration. Based on print media accounts, reports, analyses, and editorials in the Brazilian print media, the coverage seemed to focus on four issues: oil, the United Nations, the United States' imperialistic intentions, and President Bush's character and motive.

IT IS ALL ABOUT OIL

People in Brazil typically saw oil as one of the main reasons for the conflict in Iraq. Even if this were not the focus of coverage by the large news media, opinion polls and letters to the editor showed that Brazilians believed that one of the main causes for the war was the United States' desire to control Iraq's oil reserves. Articles pointed to the U.S. dependency on imported oil and how onerous the high cost of oil was to the U.S. economy. For example, in an editorial in the *O Estado de São Paulo,* Amaral (2003) wrote, "The oil reserves in the United States are the lowest since 1975 and the dependency on imported oil increases yearly. . . . Estimates presented by the Energy Information Administration indicate that by 2020 the United States will be importing 70% of their oil. The Iraq occupation therefore is strategic." But this was not the only way in which oil played a role in the war coverage.

The memory of shortages and the long lines to fuel cars during the first Gulf War in 1991 plagued Brazilians' reading of the United States' second war against Iraq. Officials of Petrobra (Brazilian Petroleum Company) were quoted heavily throughout the media, providing figures to calm the population about the potential impact of the war. In the decade following the first Gulf war, Brazilian reliance on imported oil decreased substantially. By 2003, only 10 percent of the oil consumed in the nation was imported, and of that amount only 27.5 percent came from the Gulf region, compared to 86 percent of the imported oil in 1990. This fact, however, did not calm the population during the war.

THE END OF THE UNITED NATIONS

If oil was the trigger, then the United Nations was the victim. A big emphasis of reporting about the war, especially before the beginning of the conflict and after the cessation of major combat, was the potential impact of the United States' unilateral decision on the fate of the United Nations as a global governing and mediating body. The day after armed conflict began, the Brazilian president criticized the United States in a speech to the nation. In his pronouncement he said he believed he was speaking on behalf of the Brazilian people, who wished to live in a pacific world where the norms of international law were respected fully.

He said he lamented the conflict, particularly the United States' choice to use armed force without the express authorization of the United Nations Security Council. "We do not want to see worsening of the instability in the Middle East, a region where millions of Brazilians trace their roots and a region we are connected by links of friendship and cooperation," he said (quoted in Weber 2003). Throughout the conflict, the Brazilian president and his aides maintained a united voice on the need to respect the United Nations.

For analysts in Brazil, the fear that the United Nations might lose its relevance came at a time when Brazil had been pushing for a permanent seat on the Security Council. The concern was that if the United Nations lost its power as an arbitrating/mediating/governing body, the world would have less chance of controlling developed nations and protecting international law. A discussion about the end of the United Nations, or the reframing of its mission, usually was associated with discussions on the impact of the war on Latin American and the world economy.

Several analysts feared that the war and the reconstruction of Iraq would further diminish the United States' attention toward Latin America and that the conflict would hinder a global economic recovery that would affect Brazil and the region. For Brazil, according to a *Folha de São Paulo* editorial ("Fim da globalização" 2003) three days after the beginning of the war, "the perspective of liberalization of agricultural markets in the United States and Europe will become even more remote" with the rupture of relationships between some European nations and the United States as a result of the war. The overall fear was that the war would drive away the limited resources available in the global market to invest in Latin America because of new opportunities in postwar reconstruction efforts.

THE EMPIRE STRIKES BACK

As mentioned, the war against Iraq prompted many in Brazil to think about the United States as an imperialistic nation. Living in a peripheral country, Brazilians are conscious of the gap between people of the United States and themselves. But they are also sympathetic to other peripheral nations in the world. The Iraq conflict was represented and perceived as a war of conquest, a war that intended to grant the United States control over the second-largest oil reserve in the world. And for Brazilians, that was a marker of an imperialistic nation at work. The United States' unwillingness to work with the United Nations, coupled with the perception that oil was the main trigger for the war, led many Brazilians to read the news media, looking for clues of the United States' imperialistic, militaristic, and belligerent tendencies.

Articles in newspapers and large-circulation weekly newsmagazines discussed the United States' arsenal and its military might, emphasizing the United States' ability to engage in several fronts simultaneously and providing information on the superior arsenal in terms of aircrafts, ships, and trained forces. Another concern associated with this military power was the perceived reliance of the United States economy on arms manufacturing, which created in the eyes of a few analysts the danger of an increasing militarization of the United States and the global economy.

This perception of the United States as a military giant with the economic power to boost its imperialistic potential created a sense of insecurity among Brazilians who saw danger in the United States' seeing not only the rest of Latin America as a new frontier but also the process of southward movement as a manifest destiny.

THE BUSH REGIME VERSUS THE UNITED STATES

A final main thrust of the coverage was its focus on George W. Bush and his administration. A motif of the early coverage was the sense of revenge: the son vindicating the father. There was speculation, not unlike that in the U.S. media, that George W. Bush was using the war to vindicate his father and to deflect attention from domestic problems. But the distinct difference in coverage in Brazil, compared with that of the United States, was that analysts and reporters argued that it was necessary to separate the U.S. government's foreign initiatives and bellicose tendencies from the rest of the nation. Even after the majority of the U.S. population supported the war, according to some polls, Brazilian analysts framed the argument in terms of a government that was acting on behalf of its own agenda rather than to benefit the nation or the world.

Several articles indicated the lack of reliable intelligence that justified the attack. An editorial in *O Estado de São Paulo* ("Mr. Bush" 2003), stated that Colin Powell repeated the unproven accusations that Iraq "helped, harbored and trained terrorists." It continued accusing the United States of attempting to convince the United Nations of its positions, "which are vehemently unsustainable." This framing of the U.S. government's positions as unproven was a continual mark of the coverage. After the combat was over, several media outlets discussed the excess of the footage presented by the United States government, heavily focusing on the rescue of the army private Jessica Lynch and the supposed staging of the event.

George W. Bush was framed as the cowboy president, an arrogant leader who had little respect for the rest of the world. In the Brazilian media, his presidency was marked by his decision to engage in a military conflict in defiance of the United Nations and his unwillingness to work with other nations at a time when terrorism, as stated in an editorial at *Folha de São Paulo,* was no longer based within a nation-state.

A famous Brazilian singer released an anti-Bush song on the day the United States announced the war. Tom Ze, a popular singer whose heyday was during the dictatorship years, still had a following that packed his open-air show in the Parque do Ibirapuera in Sao Paulo on March 15, 2003, when he sang his song for the first time. The lyrics to "Comrade Bush" follow in part in an English translation (available in Portuguese at www.trama.com.br):

> If you already know
> Who sold
> That bomb to Iraq
> Speak up
> I have a feeling it was Bush
> It was Bush
> It was the Bush
> It was the Bush
> Where will there be a way
> to give a slap on the hand
> To comrade Bush?
> Maybe a screw;
> which is missing in his head;
> will better this abuse

Even if not very popular, the song was emblematic of the war's reception in Brazil. It was seen as an initiative of the United States government to gain control over the second-largest oil reserves while finishing the job started more than a decade ago by the father of George W. Bush. The coverage provided by the United States was not trustworthy, leading Brazilian outlets to search for alternative media sources from the region. The war was also indicative of a sense of entitlement and empowerment that led many Brazilians to fear the United States' imperialistic intentions and to get angry at the inability of that nation to work within the international law and respect the United Nations.

REFERENCES

Amaral, A. 2003. "Guerra—onde está a verdade?" [War—where is the truth?] *O Estado de São Paulo,* March 24. Retrieved from www.estado.estadao.com.br (accessed July 22, 2003).

"Fim da globalização" [The end of globalization]. 2003. *Folha de São Paulo,* March 23. Retrieved from www.hts-net.com.br/oemar/guerra_4.htm (accessed July 22, 2003).

"Mr Bush vai para a Guerra" [Mr. Bush goes to war]. 2003. *O Estado de São Paulo,* March 19. Retrieved from www.estado.estadao.com.br (July 22, 2003).

Rosa, V. 2003. "Lula critica EUA e é repreendido em Londres" [Lula criticizes the U.S.A. and is reprehended in London]. *O Estado de São Paulo,* July 14. Retrieved from www.estado.estadao.com.br (accessed July 29, 2003).

Weber, D. 2003. "Lula condena ataque e pede respeito a civis" [Lula condemns attack and asks for respect to civilians]. *O Estado de São Paulo,* March 21. Retrieved from www.estado.estadao.com.br (accessed July 22, 2003).

21

Threat or Ally? U.S.–Latin American Relations and the Middle East Conflict

Kathleen A. Tobin

In the days following the September 11 attack on the United States, Latin Americans looked to the North with compassion. Natural connections in histories and people unified the two continents in what had become a time of uncertain security and global tension. But within weeks, relations became strained as U.S. foreign policy and Latin American reaction seemed to weaken the bonds that had held the two regions together. A complex story began to unfold, as U.S. officials attempted to formulate a response to the attack and justify pending actions in the Middle East, thus bringing issues of drugs, migration, and oil into the picture. Each of these had played important roles in U.S. policy toward Latin America for decades, and each would command new interest as the world watched.

By the outbreak of the war on Iraq, Latin American support of the United States seemed to have vanished, and anti-Americanism swept the region. The invasion was viewed in some respects as parallel to recent U.S. interventions, invasions, and occupations in Panama, Grenada, Haiti, Nicaragua, El Salvador, and Honduras; and in places such as Cuba and the Dominican Republic in earlier decades. The Left, in both the United States and abroad, condemned the U.S. attacks on Afghanistan and Iraq as typical of U.S. foreign policy, using various Latin American cases as examples and criticizing the U.S. media as supporting such policy (Chomsky 2003; "Latin America Wary" 2003; Martin 2003; Morgan 2003). But the Latin American Right was critical as well, citing U.S. failures in years past to support antiterrorist campaigns in Chile, for example (Rohther 2003). By acknowledging this history alone, Latin American concerns regarding intensification of U.S. foreign policy seemed justified. But new policies toward Latin America evolved in the two years following the 9/11 attack, setting officials throughout the region on edge. A complex web of U.S. interests would involve Mexico, Colombia, Venezuela, Brazil, Cuba, Chile, and various Central American nations in one way or another, as media attention centered on the Middle East (Manwaring 2003; Youngers 2003;).

Beginning on September 11, 2001, the State Department immediately worked to solidify alliances with Latin American nations. Secretary of State Colin Powell was in Peru at the time of the attack, meeting with newly elected president Alejandro Toledo and representatives of the Organization of American States (OAS) to implement the Inter-American Democratic Charter, a fact that was used repeatedly in State Department press releases and press briefings to place Latin America in a place of immediate significance at that point in history. Within his first words following the attack, Powell (2001c) attempted to strengthen the bonds:

> A terrible, terrible tragedy has befallen my nation, but it has befallen all of the nations of this region, all the nations of the world, and befallen all those who believe in democracy. . . . They can destroy buildings, they can kill people, and we will be saddened by this tragedy; but they will never be allowed to kill the spirit of democracy.

Upon his return to Washington, D.C., Powell reiterated his position before the OAS, noting that twenty-nine OAS nations were represented among the victims in the World Trade Center tragedy. He defended the invocation of the Rio Treaty, which designated the attack against the United States as an attack on the entire hemisphere, and he called for the strengthening of the OAS Inter-American Committee against Terrorism. He made references to the "hemispheric community," reminding his audience that he "sat at breakfast with President Toledo" when he was notified of the attack on the World Trade Center.

President George W. Bush continued this portrayal in subsequent months. In remarks to the World Affairs Councils of America, Bush (2002a) noted:

> In September of last year, I welcomed my friend the president of Mexico to the White House. Standing together on the South Lawn, President [Vincente] Fox and I spoke of building a hemisphere of freedom, prosperity, and progress. That was five days before terrorists attacked the peace and security of the world — murdering thousands of citizens from over 80 nations, including almost every nation in this hemisphere.

In this speech, Bush promoted "democracy" and "political freedom," made promises of additional monetary aid and trade agreements, and with broad strokes painted a picture of overall hemispheric solidarity. However, he hinted at issues in a way that would begin to divide sentiments in the Americas. His recommendations regarding the Colombian drug war and the Argentine economic crisis suggested that those countries could not solve their problems without the help of the United States, reinforcing a sense of U.S. hegemony. More specifically, he suggested that Canada, the United States, and Mexico work to build "smart borders" that "ensure safety for ordinary people and trade, but filter out terror and drugs."

The linking of migration to terrorism would cause significant damage to U.S.–Mexican relations during the Bush and Fox administrations. In the days before September 11, Bush and Fox appeared to be reaching an unprecedented agreement on more open borders and humane treatment of migrants. In a luncheon toast to President Fox, Secretary of State Powell (2001a) declared: "We are going to march together as partners and friends, doing everything we can to benefit the people of our two great countries." However, within weeks, the *Houston Chronicle* was describing this "extraordinary political opening" as a casualty of the terrorist attacks. But reporter Michael Riley (2001) expressed no sympathy. Rather, he appeared to defend the shift in policy from "immigration" to "security." Riley described fears that large numbers of terrorists were escaping the United States across the Mexican border and that in Tijuana alone, "between 50 and 60 people of Middle Eastern origin" had been detained for questioning as they crossed the border. He also reminded readers that enemies of the United States used Mexico as a "base for espionage and other operations against the United States" during both World Wars and the Cold War.

By October, the positive relationship between Bush and Fox appeared to be disintegrating. Lino Gutierrez (2001), acting assistant secretary of the Bureau of Western Hemisphere Affairs, attempted to depict an atmosphere of continuing cooperation, in his remarks to the Immigration Subcommittee of the Senate Judiciary Committee, but stated:

> The Mexicans have made progress in certain areas, particularly on their southern border, with stemming the flow of immigrants transiting Mexico to the U.S. While the overwhelming majority of those who attempt to enter the U.S. do so for economic reasons, we have insisted that Mexico do more in this area to ensure that potential malafide migrants do not take advantage of alien smuggling networks to enter the U.S.

In subsequent weeks, Americans would come to fear that terrorists were making their way into the United States through porous borders, thus justifying tighter border controls. The fear was exacerbated by media reports, editorials, and talk shows suggesting that any degree of openness along the Mexican border be blamed for the presence of terrorists in the United States (Ling-Ling

2002). In numerous speeches, President Bush (2002b, 2002c) used a folksy approach, referring to "la frontera," in his appeals to the Mexican government and the Mexican-American community for support of border policy. But his repeated focus on terrorists in discussions of the border helped to create deep divisions between the two nations.

Mexican border fears intensified easily in the United States because anti-Mexican immigrant sentiment was already strong. But the State Department also pointed to terrorist/border problems further away. The "triborder area" (connecting Argentina, Paraguay, and Brazil) had commanded the attention of U.S. government officials for some time, as here they saw a direct connection between Latin America and the Middle East terrorists. The careful, diplomatic choice of words in addressing this region, home to some fifteen thousand people of Middle Eastern descent, became apparent. In an early address, coordinator to counterterrorism Francis X. Taylor (2001) described the situation this way:

> Some of these people are from, or are descendants of persons from countries such as Lebanon, Palestine, and Syria. I applaud the cultural diversity that has been allowed to flourish here. It is no secret that the majority of those persons from that area of the world—an area that is a cradle of religions—follow the Islamic faith. This is a wonderful thing. I applaud your governments for being members of the elite group that believes in, and permits, freedom of religion.

At the same time, U.S. investigative units were examining reports of money laundering and other crimes among the Arab population there, including possible ties to al Qaeda (Bonner 2003).

The issue of terrorism had other implications for Latin America. The war on terrorism gave the United States significantly more power in pursuing "narco-terrorists" in the Andean region. The U.S. media reported accusations that al Qaeda terrorist operations were being funded by the poppy industry in Afghanistan, helping to justify military intervention there. To Latin Americans, the same logic might be used to increase military intervention in Colombia and surrounding nations. The State Department had succeeded in bringing attention to cocaine-industry funding of the Revolutionary Armed Forces of Colombia (FARC), the leading force in the leftist guerilla movement in Colombia. In the name of a "War on Drugs," U.S. aid to Colombia had already been used to weaken FARC, though right-wing paramilitary groups were also funded by the cocaine industry. The shift of attention from a "War on Drugs" to a "War on Terror" could directly affect U.S.–Colombia relations. Critics had long pointed out that the Colombian situation had less to do with drugs than with politics, and perhaps oil, as a notable portion of U.S. aid to Colombia was earmarked for the protection of its oil pipelines.

This paralleled criticism that the conflict in the Middle East had more to do with oil than with terrorism. Within months of the September 11 attack, the State Department tied the issues of drugs and oil in addressing Colombia and the broader Andean region. In remarks at Georgetown University, under secretary for political affairs Marc Grossman (2002) offered continued support in fighting drugs and terror, noting that one of the major reasons "Colombia matters" is that "it is the 9th largest supplier of oil to the United States." However, Venezuela dominates the region in its supply of oil.

Situated in the Andean region, Venezuela would be inextricably linked to U.S. foreign policy that suggested that the drug industry was contributing to political instability throughout the area. The State Department created vivid images of a political crisis in Venezuela that might one day call for U.S. intervention. But it claimed that the presidency of Hugo Chavez was responsible for igniting its social unrest. The democratically elected socialist Chavez was candid in his criticism of U.S. foreign policy, and his reforms threatened a power structure that had protected the elite and the interests of foreign oil.

When an uprising seemed to threaten Chavez's presidency, on April 11, 2002, the State Department prematurely embraced his demise. When it was clear that Chavez had not lost his position, White House press secretary Ari Fleischer (2002) responded:

> The people of Venezuela have sent a clear message to President Chavez that they want both democracy and reform. The Chavez administration has an opportunity to respond to this message by correcting its course and governing in a fully democratic manner. . . . The United States and the world community of democracies will be closely following events in Venezuela.

The White House and the State Department rarely spoke of oil as a vital issue in this critical period and therefore did not publicly link concerns over oil in the Middle East with concerns over oil in Venezuela. Rather, press releases, conferences, and briefings centered on "democracy." The United States continually painted a picture of a world divided into people and nations who supported democracy and those—usually evil tyrants—who did not. This paved the way for the vilification of Saddam Hussein, and supporters of Chavez feared the possibility of eventual intervention in Venezuela.

But in the eyes of the United States, the ultimate antidemocratic figure in Latin America was Fidel Castro. Anti-Castro rhetoric intensified in late 2001, as Americans became increasingly aware of anti-U.S. sentiment abroad, and fears of attacks spread. The placement of hundreds of suspected al Qaeda detainees at Cuba's Guantanamo Naval Base created more tension between the two countries, as Cubans viewed the action as a warning to anyone making a move against the United States. The March 2002 appointment of Otto Reich as assistant secretary of state for Western Hemisphere Affairs further strained relations. The Cuban-born Reich (2002) was clear about his views on Castro in many of his speeches. In his remarks at his swearing-in ceremony, Reich stated, "As most of you know, my country of birth, Cuba, lost its liberty to a totalitarian dictatorship 43 years ago. My family, like so many other nonpolitical families, was in danger simply because of our love of liberty, which ran counter to the communist ideology being imposed by force on that island." He closed his remarks that day by saying:

> As Thomas Jefferson's words remind us, our struggle against tyranny is not finished. Since September 11, exactly 6 months ago today, we are more determined and indivisible than at any time since World War II. Whether they are terrorists in Afghanistan or Colombia, or despots in Baghdad or Havana, anyone trying to impose tyranny over the mind of man has earned our eternal hostility.

Reich frequently spoke of "democracies in crisis," referring to economic and political instability in Colombia, Venezuela, Haiti, and Argentina, and causing Latin Americans to wonder how U.S. foreign policy might evolve. But more important, these early remarks made it clear that the State Department equated Latin America with the Middle East.

Once it became apparent that the United States intended to declare war on Iraq, protests against U.S. policy escalated. Antiwar sentiment proved stronger in Latin America than in the rest of the world, with tens of thousands marching in protest and with criticism emerging in the press (Arthur 2003). Editorials appearing in newspapers across the political spectrum questioned U.S.–British action, referring to it as demagoguery and neo-imperialism. Lima's independent *Correo* warned that this action could have serious implications in South America:

> Sept. 11, 2001 . . . awakened the expansionist goals of the United States. It has . . . taken off its diplomatic disguise and imposed the political and geographic hegemony it holds as a result of the Soviet collapse. . . . Today it is the Islamic fundamentalists' turn. Tomorrow it could be the "Andean narcoterrorists, who are responsible for the moral destruction of the U.S. youth and for the appearance of potential enemies of the free world. . . ." Peru and Latin America must not ignore this . . . as they plan their future. ("The Latin American and Canadian Press," 2003)

The media of Russia and China, whose UN Security Council members opposed the attack on Iraq, reported extensively on Latin American opposition (Etchaleco 2003; "Latin America Continues Slamming U.S.-Led War in Iraq" 2003).

Latin Americans were especially sensitive to the *Guernica* incident. Unnamed United Nations workers covered the tapestry of Picasso's *Guernica* with a curtain during Colin Powell's visit there. The Spanish-speaking world considers the work Picasso's greatest antiwar statement. Rumors varied regarding the intention of the cover-up, some claiming the work was "too busy" for television cameras, while others claimed that it would conflict with Powell's objectives. According to Uruguayan essayist and historian Eduardo Galeano (2003), the move was made so that Powell "would not be put off his bugle calls by such nasty scenes." He went on to say, "What size of curtain will they use to cover up the butchery in Iraq, in the form of blanket censorship imposed on war correspondents by the Pentagon?"

The State Department found itself in a particularly difficult position with Mexico and Chile when trying to gain support for the war in Iraq. Both countries held temporary positions on the UN Security Council, and both opposed the war. Secretary of State Powell worked diligently to gain support by appealing directly to Latin American concerns and promoting the idea of hemispheric solidarity. In a January 2003 address to the National Conference of World Affairs Councils of America, Powell carefully placed concerns over Iraq, North Korea, and AIDS under one large umbrella. North Korea was often linked to Iraq in defining the level of crisis in the world, even if there were little chance of U.S. action there. Mention of the AIDS crisis, however, laid the foundation for what many Latin Americans considered a virtual bribe, as the United States promised $15 billion, earmarked primarily for Africa and the Caribbean. Powell (2003a) noted: "Disease is the enemy of economic growth and development. Disease is the enemy of hope." He also reminded his audience that President Bush's Millennium Challenge Account Initiative would provide additional development assistance:

> Fifteen years ago when I was National Security Advisor, most of the nations of the Western Hemisphere in the southern part of our hemisphere, so many of them were led by generals, tyrants, juntas. And now all of them, except for Castro's Cuba, is on a path to reform and democracy and economic development. They're struggling. They need our help. And we are going to help them with free trade agreements, with formation of the Community of Democracy, with the Free Trade Agreement of the Americas reaching all the way from the top to the bottom of our hemisphere.

By early March, President Bush stated that Washington could take disciplinary action if Mexico and other countries on the council would not support the U.S.-led resolution calling for an attack on Iraq. Chile found itself in a difficult situation: the U.S. Congress had begun negotiations on a trade pact with Chile before Chilean officials publicly opposed the war. In response to the March 2003 report that Washington was decoupling the pact from a parallel

U.S. deal with Singapore, Chilean government officials noted, "The White House no longer considers us an ally" (R. Taylor 2003).

In the weeks before the attack, the U.S. State Department dispatched untold numbers of representatives throughout Latin America to try to win support, but the pressure was greatest in Mexico and Chile. Chilean deputy foreign minister Cristian Barrios told the Reuters news agency, "There is an incessant action by the United States with all the countries that are members of the Security Council. Every time the United States calls, it's to discuss the situation from their point of view. We couldn't pretend neutrality" (Cox News Service 2003). After the war was declared over, the United States and Chile worked to reestablish ties, and once again they discussed a trade pact. When questioned at a press briefing in Santiago regarding Chile's "disloyalty," Powell (2003b) responded:

> Chile is a democracy. It is free to make its own choices. In this case we would have preferred it had made a different choice. But we were disappointed, we take that disappointment and we move on.

The term *democracy* appeared in nearly every State Department address attempting diplomacy following the conflict. It was used to create an image of the United States as a model and supporter for those Latin American nations willing to build and maintain democratic electoral systems. But it was also intended to separate Cuba, and to some extent Venezuela, from the rest of the region because Washington viewed their systems of government undemocratic.

Chile and Mexico had been considered two of the United States closest allies, and the absence of their support forced the State Department to work harder in its "postwar" diplomatic initiative. But the political atmosphere was changing. The unity among Latin American nations in standing up against the United States appeared to provide a solid groundwork for acting in their own best interests in the future and for not succumbing to U.S. wishes. In addition, Brazil's newly elected president, Luis Ignacio Lula da Silva, seemed to be effectively unifying the region in a way that would strengthen its position, politically and economically (Gibb 2003). The United States did not attempt to marginalize this leftist president, as it had with Venezuela's Chavez and Cuba's Castro, for Brazil had become one of the world's most influential trading partners.

The State Department connected "democracy" to "free trade" in addressing Central America as well, a region that appeared more open to diplomatic relations. El Salvador and Nicaragua, both sites of U.S. intervention in recent decades, did join the "Coalition of the Willing." However, the region became a pawn in the battle for allies. Critics of U.S. imperialism cited the cases of El Salvador and Nicaragua frequently. But the State Department catered to them in its attempts to continue relations after the war. Daniel W. Fisk (2003) of the Bureau of Western Hemisphere Affairs reported to the Center for Strategic and International Studies:

> Central America has made great progress. Twenty years ago, thousands of people were dying in the region's conflicts each year. Arms were flooding in from all over the world. International enmity and internal strife were the order of the day. Peace and democracy were fervently sought after but seemingly distant. . . . Today, we are working toward a regional free trade agreement that includes the United States. Throughout Central America, political power flows from the ballot box, not the barrel of a gun. And Central American countries are valuable partners not only in inter-American efforts to combat threats to the region, but also specifically in the global war against terrorism.

Such statements contributed to increasing cynicism throughout the region.

But U.S. efforts to develop hemispheric bonds continued. Though the major conflict in Iraq was declared over soon after it began, the violence continued and no weapons of mass destruction were found. This weakened the United States' credibility and global position, making a broad military expansion into Latin American less likely. In addition, economic problems, caused in part by the tremendous financial costs of the conflict, have forced the United States to negotiate with potential trading partners in Latin America more realistically and cooperatively. U.S.–Latin American relations acted as an important piece of the geopolitical puzzle before and during the early stages of this Middle East conflict. But as the story unfolded, relations crystallized in ways that were clearly unforeseen.

REFERENCES

Arthur, Charles. 2003. "Iraq and Latin America: Documenting Anti-war Protests." AMERICAS.ORG, May–June. Retrieved from www.americas.org/News/Features/200304_MayJune/Iraq-LatinAmerica2.htm (accessed July 2003).

Bonner, Robert C. 2003. "U.S. Pledges Financial Support to Nurture CICTE Counterterrorism Technology." San Salvador, January 22. Retrieved from www.state.gov/p/wha/rls/rm/16821pf.htm (accessed August 2003).

Bush, George W. 2002a. "The Future of Americas." Washington, D.C., January 16. Retrieved from www.state.gov/p/wha/rls/rm/7344pf.htm (accessed August 2003).

———. 2002b. "President Promotes Secure and Open Borders in El Paso." El Paso, Texas, March 21. Retrieved 8/2003 from www.state.gov/p/wha/rls/rm/8907pf.htm.

———. 2002c. "Radio Address by the President to the Nation," Washington, D.C., March 23. Retrieved from www.state.gov/p/wha/rls/rm/8928pf.htm (accessed August 2003).

Chomsky, Noam. 2003. "Iraq Is a Trial Run." *ALAI, Latin America in Movement,* April 2. Retrieved from http://alainet.org/active/show_text_en.php3?key=3442 (accessed July 2003).

Cox News Service. 2003. "Latin America, Especially Mexico and Chile, Struggle to Find Position on Iraq." Hispanic America Center for Economic Research. Retrieved from www.hacer.org/current/LATAMST.php (accessed July 2003).

Etchaleco, Hernan. 2003. "Latin America Unanimously against the War on Iraq," PRAVDA.RU, February 5. Retrieved from http://english.pravda.ru/main/2003/02/05/42999.html (accessed July 2003).

Fisk, Daniel W. 2003. "Shifting Sights: Adapting Central American Security Structures to 21st Century Threats." Washington, D.C., June 18. Retrieved from www.state.gov/p/wha/rls/rm/21766pf.htm (accessed August 2003).

Fleischer, Ari. 2002. "Statement by the Press Secretary," April 14. Retrieved from www.whitehouse.gov/news/releases/2002/04/20020414.html.

Galeano, Eduardo. 2003. "The War." *La Jornada*, March 19, 2003. Retrieved from www.americas.org/News/Features/200304_MayJune/Iraq-LatinAmerica2.htm (accessed July 2003).

Gibb, Tom. 2003. "Latin America Stands Up for Itself." *BBC News,* June 9. Retrieved from http://news.bbc.co.uk/2/hi/americas/2973274.stm (accessed July 2003).

Grossman, Marc. 2002. "Joining Efforts for Colombia." Washington, D.C., June 24. Retrieved from www.state.gov/p/11498pf.htm (accessed August 2003).

Gutierrez, Lino. 2001. "Effective Immigration Controls and Preventing Terrorism." Washington, D.C., October 17. Retrieved from www.state.gov/p/wha/rls/rm/2001/5445pf.htm (accessed August 2003).

"Latin America Continues Slamming U.S.-Led War in Iraq." 2003. Xinhua News Agency, March 30. Retrieved from www.china.org.cn/english/features/60285.htm (accessed July 2003).

"Latin America Wary of U.S. Military Expansion." 2003. *FinalCall.com News*, May 11. Retrieved from www.finalcall.com/artman/publish/article_758.shtml (accessed July 2003).

"The Latin American and Canadian Press on the War in Iraq." 2003. *World Press Review*, July 28. Retrieved from www.worldpress.org/Americas/1024.cfm (accessed July 2003).

Ling-Ling, Yeh. 2002. "Stop Immigration If We Are to Fight Terrorism," published in *Tuscon Citizen*, September 4. Retrieved www.diversityalliance.org/docs/article_2002sep04.html (accessed July 2003).

Manwaring, Dr. Max G. 2003. "Strategic Effects of the Conflict with Iraq: Latin America." Strategic Studies Institute, March. Retrieved from www.carlisle.army.mil/ssi/pubs/2003/irqlatin/irqlatin.pdf (accessed June 2003).

Martin, Patrick (World Socialist). 2003. "Media Bosses Admit Pro-war Bias in Coverage of Iraq." *World Revolution News*, May 2. Retrieved from www.worldrevolution.org/article/963 (accessed July 2003).

Morgan, David (Reuters). 2003. "U.S.: Critic Accuses Media of Aiding U.S. War Propaganda." *World Revolution News*, May 1. Retrieved from www.worldrevolution.org/article/908 (accessed July 2003).

Powell, Colin L. 2001a. "Remarks with Mexican President Vincente Fox." Washington, D.C., September 5. Retrieved from www.state.gov/secretary/rm/2001/4820pf.htm (accessed August 2003).

———. 2001b. "Remarks to the Special Session of the Organization of American States." Washington, D.C., September 21. Retrieved from www.state.gov/secretary/rm/2001/4997pf.htm (accessed August 2003).

———. 2001c. "Statement at the Special General Assembly of the Organization of American States." Lima, Peru, September 11, 2001. Released on October 5, 2001. Retrieved from www.state.gov/secretary/rm/2001/5256pf.htm (accessed August 2003).

———. 2003a. "Address at the National Conference of World Affairs Councils of America." Washington, D.C., January 31. Retrieved from www.state.gov/secretary/rm/2003/17109pf.htm (accessed August 2003).

———. 2003b. "Press Briefing after the OAS Meeting." Santiago, Chile, June 9. Retrieved from www.state.gov/secretary/rm/2003/21348pf.htm (accessed August 2003).

Reich, Otto J. 2002. "Remarks at Swearing-In Ceremony as Assistant Secretary of State for Western Hemisphere Affairs." Washington, D.C., March 11. Retrieved from www.state.gov/p/wha/rls/rm/8740pf.htm (accessed August 2003).

Riley, Michael. 2001. "Immigration Issues Overshadowed by Terrorism." *Houston Chronicle*, September 20. Retrieved from www.chron.com/cs/CDA/printstory.hts/special/terror/impact/1055149 (accessed July 2003).

Rohther, Larry. 2003. "The Faraway War Set Latin America on Edge." *New York Times*, April 21. Retrieved from www.wehaitians.com/the%20%faraway%w20war%20set%20latin (accessed July 2003).

Taylor, Francis X. (Coordinator for Counterterrorism). 2001. "Seminar on Preventing Terrorism and Organized Crime in the Tri-border Area." Asuncion, Paraguay, December 19. Retrieved from www.state.gov/s/ct/rls/rm/2001/7012pf.htm (accessed August 2003).

Taylor, Robert. 2003. "The Region: Another Battlefield Casualty?" *World Press Review*, June. Retrieved from www.worldpress.org/Americas/1091.cfm (accessed July 2003).

Youngers, Coletta. 2003. "The U.S. and Latin America after 9–11 and Iraq." *Foreign Policy in Focus*, June. Retrieved from www.foreignpolicyinfocus.org/pdf/reports/PRlatam2003/pdf (accessed July 2003).

22

From Propaganda to Public Diplomacy in the Information Age

R. S. Zaharna

After 9/11, the need to "win the hearts and minds" of foreign publics surfaced within American political consciousness as if it were a new phenomenon, when actually foreign information activities have been a critical component of America's wartime strategy since the American Revolution. America's historical record, however, reveals a stop-and-go pattern that appears tied to recycled debates that emerge and submerge with the ebb and flow between war and peace.

The most salient debate is whether government-sponsored information activities are manipulative "propaganda" or valid "public diplomacy." Even during the war on terrorism, the propaganda and public diplomacy are viewed as interchangeable substitutes instead of two distinct strategic tools of persuasion. However, according to global opinion polls, America's post-9/11 public diplomacy appears to be producing more adversaries than allies. It may be time to rethink the old thinking of equating propaganda with public diplomacy in the new information age.

HISTORICAL TRENDS AND DEBATES

Information activities aimed at informing, influencing, and gaining the support of foreign publics are an integral part of American history, from the United States' founding as a nation to its current superpower position. In 1776, Benjamin Franklin actively engaged the French government and distributed pamphlets in an effort to gain the support for American independence. Shortly after the War of 1812, Thomas Jefferson sought to counter the bad press America was receiving in Britain. In 1917, during World War I (WWI), President Woodrow Wilson created the Committee on Public Information, also known as the Creel Commission, to build support at home and promote America's message abroad.[1]

Shortly before the start of World War II (WWII), President Franklin D. Roosevelt established first the Office of Coordinator of Information, followed by the U.S. Foreign Information Service.[2] Radio broadcast to Asia began within days after the attack on Pearl Harbor. Broadcasts in Europe began seventy-nine days after the United States entered the war. Both agencies were absorbed into the Office of War Information (OWI) in 1942, as part of an aggressive domestic and foreign campaign that included Hollywood movies, extensive photography collection, and patriotic posters.[3]

During the Cold War, America's foreign information programs grew substantially. The U.S. Information Agency (USIA), established in 1953, conducted a wide range of information- and cultural-exchange activities. The Voice of America (VOA) expanded its language broadcast, while its surrogates, Radio Free Europe/Radio Liberty sought to break through the Iron Curtain. As Harold C. Pachios, chairman of the U.S. Advisory Commission for Public Diplomacy, noted, "The height of USIA's prestige and acceptance probably occurred in the 1960s."[4] Not coincidentally, this was also the height of the Cold War as well.

In contrast to the steady growth of foreign information programs from the 1950s to the 1980s, the 1990s marked a decade of sharp decline in funds and interest in foreign information programs. Many of USIA's posts abroad were cut back by one-third to one-half.[5] American cultural centers and libraries were closed, while positions dedicated to press and cultural affairs were eliminated.[6] Foreign Service officers practicing public diplomacy dropped 40 percent between 1991 to 2001.[7] The State Department's Educational and Cultural Exchange Programs appropriation declined by more than 33 percent from 1993 to 2001.[8] In 1999, the USIA was incorporated into the State Department, with its budget and resources.

The dwindling resources and programs reflected a distinct historical pattern in American public diplomacy. During times of conflict, information becomes a key component of the war effort—either to win over allies or defeat enemies. Typically, the information campaigns begin with a strong presidential initiative.[9] When the president makes the decision to go to war, the first priority is to mobilize domestic and foreign support. New resources are pooled and funneled into an aggressive information initiative. The more intense the conflict, the more aggressive the information campaign. Often the president creates a new office or agency as well. President Wilson created the Creel Commission, President Truman the OWI, President Eisenhower the USIA.

Then, as each war gradually draws to a close, so does the campaign. The extensive wartime information apparatus is dismantled in the process. The Creel Commission stopped its domestic activities the day after the prearmistice agreement was signed to end WWI and halted its foreign information activities several months later. Within months after the end of WWII, President Truman signed an executive order abolishing the Office of War Information. Similarly, the decline of USIA's extensive programs began soon after the fall of the Berlin Wall in 1989 and the fall of the Soviet Union in 1991, forming the symbolic end to the Cold War.

In keeping with this historical pattern, when President Bush launched the war on terrorism, he spoke out forcefully on the need to "do a better job of making our case" to overseas publics. However, because America had been enjoying a peacetime economy and mood during the period before 9/11, information programs and apparatus had to be reestablished. Congress held hearings and increased funding for public diplomacy. The State Department appointed a new undersecretary for public diplomacy. The president created the White House Office on Global Communication, to help coordinate America's message. A familiar trend.

Another, perhaps less-obvious historical trend is that domestic concerns, rather than foreign policy goals, appear to guide the cuts in overseas information activities. In the case of WWI and WWII, domestic opposition to the war propaganda spurred congressional action to effectively halt war-related information activities, domestic as well as foreign. Americans not only grow weary with war but more so with the aggressive tactics used to sustain support for the war. Indeed, the tactics used during WWI and WWII were particularly aggressive: many of those who were involved in the campaign used their expertise to refine propaganda techniques, while others developed American advertising and public relations practices.[10]

Not surprising perhaps, the Smidt-Mundt Act of 1948, which created the USIA, specifically stipulated that overseas information activities could not be used to lobby the American public. Ironically, many of today's commentators continue the tradition of advocating an aggressive ideological warfare and propaganda abroad yet are outraged if similar strategies are used at home—even though the Internet has made the separation between America's domestic and foreign publics purely theoretical.

A final feature of America's past information activities that appears even today is the competition between government agencies and departments, particularly between the departments of defense and state.[11] Historically, the Defense

Department appears to have taken the lead in initiating the information activities. Logically, this makes sense. Information activities are vital to the war effort because they secure and maintain domestic and foreign support, as well as reduce opposition.

As the duration of the war progresses, the foreign information activities appear to expand militarily, politically, and economically. Other agencies become involved. Competition emerges. Noteworthy, the nature and purpose of information appear to shift in relation to which department has the upper hand. When the Defense Department is actively involved in the overseas information activities, the tendency is toward secrecy, control, and manipulation of information. When the State Department or the USIA takes the lead, the focus is on truth and accuracy.[12]

This historical trend appears to be repeating itself in the current war on terrorism. As David Guth observed shortly after the post-9/11 information campaign began, "The control and direction of U.S. overseas information programs remain as issues at the start of a new century as much as they were in the middle of the last."[13]

PROPAGANDA AND PUBLIC DIPLOMACY
IN THE INFORMATION AGE

Underlying all of these historical trends appears to be an unresolved debate over whether America's information activities should rely on "truth" or "propaganda" to influence publics. John Brown speaks to the surfacing and submerging of the American debate over propaganda.[14] In writing about America's "antipropaganda" tradition, he observed that during times of war, the need to win increases the appeal and acceptance of propaganda. As peace looms near, American suspicions of propaganda resurface with a vengeance. Propaganda again falls out of favor. All government information activity labeled as "propaganda" is summarily curtailed.

Once again, the debate over propaganda has resurfaced in the war on terrorism. Yet this time, the term *propaganda* is being used interchangeably with a new term, *public diplomacy,* to characterize all foreign information activities. Ambassador Richard Holbrooke began his piece in the *Washington Post* with the line: "Call it public diplomacy, or public affairs, or psychological warfare, or— if you really want to be blunt—propaganda."[15] Ambassador Kim Andrew Elliott began his piece in the *New York Times* with a similar line: "Public diplomacy— the current and gentler term for international propaganda . . ."[16]

Interestingly, while Americans appear to be against propaganda because of its content, they appear to define propaganda by its source, or who disseminates it. Coincidentally, the term entered American popular parlance tied to sinister foreign sources: "Nazi propaganda" and, later, "Communist propaganda." This American tendency to define propaganda in terms of its source overlooks the fact that all communication is inherently biased, reflecting the perspective, needs, and desires of the communicator. It also blurs the distinct technical features that make each a strategic tool of persuasion during times of war.

From a communication perspective, several key features make propaganda the tool of choice in certain contexts, public diplomacy the choice in others. Propaganda deliberately manipulates the communication through a variety of techniques so that some aspect is hidden from the audience and so that the audience feels compelled to accept the message. With coercion as the goal, information control and deception are key factors to effective propaganda. The Propaganda Institute identified many of the techniques used to manipulate and control information, such as "name-calling, labeling, bandwagon, etc."[17]

Public diplomacy, by definition, is just that—open public communication in a global communication arena. Because the audience is free to accept or not accept the message, persuasion through coercion or control is not applicable. Instead, persuasion is achieved through gaining audience trust and confidence. To gain trust, public diplomacy must be absolutely credible if the government stands any chance of success. Thus, the persuasive value of public diplomacy is tied to its credibility: the more credible a government's public diplomacy is, the more persuasive it is.

Context and purpose greatly suggest when and where a government should employ public diplomacy versus propaganda.

The technical features of propaganda—secrecy, deception, and coercion—make it a highly effective tool of military operations. During war, military strategy demands secrecy and deception to keep the opponent off guard, demoralized, and confused. Secrecy allows the communicator to retain control over information and manipulate the element of surprise. The need to deliberately manipulate information is what makes propaganda and psychological operations such invaluable strategic tools of warfare.

The technical features of public diplomacy—public, open, interactive global communication—make it a highly effective foreign policy tool for informing foreign publics of a government's policies and intentions and for its gaining their support. However, credibility is vital. In fact, credibility is the most important asset that a nation seeks to attain and preserve. In the international communication environment, the slightest hint of deception or manipulation of information would be fodder for the international media and publics. It is perhaps for this reason that Professor Joseph Nye's prediction that future communication battles will be "a contest of credibility" is so astute.[18] Once a communicator loses credibility, through either inaccurate or contradictory messages, the audience loses trust and confidence in the communicator and discounts all future messages. If the audience feels that its trust has been deliberately violated through manipulation or deception, the audience will be even more hostile, and all future efforts to gain support will produce the opposite effect.

Up until recently it may have been possible to equate propaganda with public diplomacy. However, the dramatic changes in the international arena and the advent of advanced global technologies have crystallized the need to distinguish between propaganda and public diplomacy. In the international political arena, communication and information are used to effectively gain public trust and support for a government's policies. The audience must perceive a nation's public diplomacy as a win-win situation. On the military battlefield, however, communication and information are used to successfully defeat the enemy. It's a win-lose situation. To substitute propaganda for public diplomacy can undermine the effectiveness of each as powerful persuasive tools that nations can use during times of war.

NOTES

1. Much has been written about the U.S. Committee on Public Information, known as the Creel Commission. For an overview of its place in American public diplomacy, see John S. Gibson, "Public Diplomacy," *International Educator* 8, nos. 2–3 (Spring 1998); for an excellent communication analysis of the Creel Commission, see Marion K. Pinsdorff, "Woodrow Wilson's Public Relations: Wag the Hun," *Public Relations Review* 25, no. 3 (Fall 1999): 309; and for an international perspective, see Kazuyuki Matsuo, "American Propaganda in China: The U.S. Committee on Public Information, 1918–1919," *Journal of American and Canadian Studies* (Tokyo, Japan) 14 (1996), available online at www.info.sophia.ac.jp/amecana/Journal/14-2.htm.

2. For a more detailed historical overview, see Daniel Guth, "From OWI to USIA: The Jackson Committee's Search for the Real 'Voice' of America," *American Journalism* 19 (Winter 2002).

3. For historical record of the Voice of America, see its website, www.voa.gov; for anecdotal account, see Alan Heil, *Voice of America* (New York: Columbia University Press, 2003).

4. Harold C. Pachios, "The New Diplomacy," remarks to Woodrow Wilson School of Public and International Affairs, Princeton University, Princeton, New Jersey, April 24, 2002.

5. Fred A. Coffey Jr., "Our Crippled Public Diplomacy," USIA Alumni Association, September 2002.

6. Donna Marie Oglesby, "Dog Food, Diapers, Diplomacy," address to St. Petersburg West Rotary, February 19, 2003.

7. Mike Canning, "New Focus on Public Diplomacy," Friends of the Foreign Service Bulletin, n.d.

8. Harold Pachios, "The New Diplomacy," remarks to Wellesley College, Wellesley, Mass., December 4, 2002.

9. Guth, "From OWI to USIA."

10. Edward Bernays has also written extensively about his techniques, see *Propaganda* (1925) and *Crystallizing Public Opinion* (1923). For analysis of Bernays, see Larry Tye, *The Father of Spin: Edward L. Bernays and the Birth of Public Relations* (New York: Crown, 1998); and Scott M. Cutlip, *The Unseen Power: Public Relations, a History* (Hillsdale, N.J.: Lawrence Erlbaum Associates, 1994).

11. Alvan Synder, "U.S. Foreign Affairs in the New Information Age: Charting a Course for the 21st Century," the Annenberg Washington Program in Communications Policy Studies of Northwestern University, 1994.

12. For example, William Harlan Hale opened the first American-sponsored radio broadcast in Europe, on February 24, 1942, with "The Voice of America speaks. Today, America has been at war for 79 days. Daily, at this time, we shall speak to you about America and the war, the news may be good or bad, we shall tell you the truth."

13. Guth, "From OWI to USIA," 19.

14. John Brown, "The Anti-propaganda Tradition in the United States," *Bulletin Board for Peace*, June 29, 2003.

15. Richard Holbrooke, "Get the Message Out," *Washington Post,* October 28, 2001, B07.

16. Kim Andrew Elliott, "Is There an Audience for Public Diplomacy?" *New York Times,* November 16, 2002.

17. Institute of Propaganda Analysis. *The Group Leader's Guide to Propaganda Analysis* (New York: Institute of Propaganda Analysis, 1938).

18. Joseph S. Nye, *The Paradox of Power* (New York: Oxford University, 2003), 68.

23

Can We Make Them Love Us? Public Diplomacy after 9/11

Geoffrey Cowan

EDITOR'S NOTE: *Geoffrey Cowan, dean of the Annenberg School for Communication at the University of Southern California, presented this speech to the Sunset Club in Los Angeles, California, on February 27, 2002. Though the world and the world's attitudes toward America have changed a great deal in the months since then, the editors have included this speech both for its content and because it offers a perspective on what seemed possible at that time. But much has happened since then, and, according to the Pew Global Attitudes Survey and other studies,[1] world opinion toward the United States has become far more hostile in the two years since this speech was delivered and the time that this volume went to press. Dean Cowan has served as director of the Voice of America, director of the International Broadcasting Bureau, and associate director of the United States Information Agency.*

Thanks for inviting me to make a few remarks about this timely and ever-important topic. In a room filled with leaders of international business as well as several diplomats, including a former Secretary of State, it is a bit daunting to presume to discuss the topic of public diplomacy in the post-9/11 period. But I am more than delighted to do so since it is a matter of singular importance for our country—and one that is particularly close to my heart.

A bit mischievously, I suppose—and a bit provocatively, I hope—I gave this talk the headline "Can We Make Them Love Us?" The title, of course, is designed to play off of another question that has been much in the news, in the headlines, and on our minds—a headline that was crystallized in a *Newsweek* magazine cover story that asked the question: "Why do they hate us?"[2]

In my view, both formulations of the issue raise a series of interesting questions—but, as stated, both are way off the mark.

First of all: who is—or are—"they"? Does the *Newsweek* headline refer to people all over the world? To the terrorists of 9/11? To Islamic extremists?

And who is "us"? Is it America? Is it our government, our people, our companies, our culture? Is it the West? Is it modern society?

And is it accurate to say that "they"—whoever they are—*hate* "us"—whoever we are—in the first place?

When you see pictures of demonstrators at anti-American rallies raising their fists while wearing Dallas Cowboy T-shirts, you know that there is, at the very least, some measure of ambivalence.

In the current *New Yorker* magazine, Joe Klein describes a school teacher in Iran who recalled her horror at the bombing of 9/11 with a delicious brand of American irony. "You know what I was really worried about," she told Klein, pausing for effect. "Woody Allen. I didn't want him to die. I love his films."[3]

And what about the celebrations in Afghanistan that erupted last fall, when towns were liberated; when men were allowed to shave their beards; when people could, once again, listen freely to the music that they love? It may not have been Paris in 1945, but it was close enough.

And, while we all know about the antiglobalization protesters who hate McDonald's, we should also remember that when McDonald's came to Moscow, it was received by the public like a rock star—and, despite the protests, consumers around the world still flock to the golden arches.

Moreover, for many people around the world, American ideals remain an inspiration and a beacon. For millions, we are still revered as a birthplace of democracy, liberty, and human rights. While we have our faults—lots of them—we have many more virtues.

It's much too easy to focus on the protesters—who make good copy for the press and good images for the TV cameras—and much too easy to assume that they represent the society as a whole.

Still, the topic remains of enormous importance. Even if most people don't hate us, we can be endangered by those who do. They are the soil in which terrorism grows. And even if most people don't love us, we can be saved by those who do. Our friends and admirers will help advance our ideals and support our treaties and our products, and they will help our tourists travel and flourish around the world.

But just as it is unfair to posit a world where everyone hates us, it is unrealistic and perhaps not even desirable to dream of a world in which everyone loves us. On this, as on so many other subjects, it is worth heeding the words of Machiavelli: "A prince does not have to be loved by the people," Machiavelli wrote, "but he must not be hated. A prince with virtue may not be loved but he must always be respected."[4]

In the aftermath of 9/11, our country seems to have gained a new appreciation of the dangers of being hated and the benefits of being respected. In my view, it is a concern that we had largely and unwisely abandoned in the years after the Cold War. Too many people believed that America's image in the world could be left to the free market alone. Members of Congress and the press asked why the U.S. government should continue to fund international broadcasting in an era of fax machines and CNN, so the Congress cut back on federal support for international broadcasting, including the Voice of America—the area that I know best—and it reduced funding for the United States Information Agency, which ultimately was eliminated and absorbed by the State Department.

The war against terrorism gives us our current focus. But in my view, all great nations, and particularly ours, as the world's most powerful nation, have a permanent need to be concerned about how they are perceived in the world.

That is a much more difficult enterprise than many might suspect. America's image is, in effect, a Rorschach test with countless images and countless participants. We see ourselves in many ways, of course, as indicated by the wide diversity of American views on every issue. But as a generalization, our view of ourselves is very different from the way we are viewed elsewhere in the world . . . and of course there are countless "elsewheres."

The just-concluded Winter Olympic Games in Salt Lake City offer a remarkable case study. The games offered America a fresh and splendid opportunity to be seen and appreciated and respected—and, yes, even loved—by hundreds of millions of people around the world who could see our dazzling country, be exposed to spectacular displays of music and dance, and witness our incomparable hospitality.

My guess is that most Americans who watched the Olympics on NBC came away with the belief that we had put on just such a display. If asked, they probably would believe that we had won millions of new friends around the world. That view is captured, in a sense, by the front page story in Monday's *Washington Post*.[5]

The headline says, "The Games Full of Good Sports." The subhead says, "Captivating U.S.–Canada Final Concludes a Rousing Olympics." And the story reports that "Americans who settled for silver were consoled by the fact that they concluded the Olympic Games not only with a record medal haul, but also the pride of having been a gracious host."

But, sadly, there is more to the story . . . as there so often is. In the same edition of the *Washington Post*, a column in the sports section has the headline "Peaceful Games, Cold War Sentiment."[6]

Let me quote the second paragraph: "The Winter Games finished sour and ugly, with everything under protest and just about every kind of modern social-ill on parade. There were death threats, computer crimes, defensive and chilling nationalism, and doping. No amount of genteel protocol in the Closing Ceremonies could paper over the fact that the Olympics were an extraordinarily contentious event, hardly a non-political exercise in world peace. And in the end they were an anti-American binge."

An anti-American binge?

And let me quote from an article on the front page of the Sunday *New York Times*. "What began in splendor and spiritual unity at the opening ceremony on February 8 is ending with charges of North American bias wrapped in a vehement anti-American fervor."[7]

A vehement anti-American fervor?

Those phrases seem a bit strong to me. They may sound strong to you. But we were watching the events on an American television network. How were they being treated by the television networks in Russia, which threatened to boycott the closing ceremony; or in South Korea, where fans sent sixteen thousand angry e-mail messages protesting Apolo Ohno's controversial speed-skating victory before they overwhelmed the Olympic Committee's server; or in Lithuania; or in France?

And those countries are our allies.

Or, to offer a different example ripped from the day's headlines, how are people around the world reacting to President Bush's State of the Union message last month—which, like the Olympics, generated major news coverage around the world?

You have all, no doubt, read stories about protests around the world, particularly in Iran and South Korea. To some extent, of course, reports of those protests may be overblown. And they were probably organized by people who did not wish us well in the first place. Still, they are real. And they are not confined to our adversaries. As the *Economist* magazine put it, "The harsh language of George Bush's 'Axis of Evil' speech has alarmed people in Europe and elsewhere."[8] Many are concerned about what they deem a unilateralist foreign policy. Others fear that Bush was signaling his intent to invade Iraq.

Here is one final story from the news of the past few weeks. On Tuesday, February 19, the lead story in the *New York Times* reported that the Pentagon was about to create—or had already created—an "Office of Strategic Influence," to gain support for American interests, particularly in the Islamic world. The office was to be run by General Simon Worden, who, according to the *Times*, "envisions a broad mission ranging from 'black' campaigns that use disinformation [and lie to news organizations around the world] . . . to 'white' public affairs that are truthful."[9]

The reaction was predictable. There was an outcry from those who were horrified that the government would spread false information to allies rather than, as in the past, only to enemies, and worried that the new office would discredit everything positive that the Defense Department and others were seeking to achieve. They worried, with reason, that no one would believe anything they said in the future. By the week's end, the Department of Defense had backed away from the proposal, and the White House had denounced it. But needless to say, it has been spread around the world and has and will be used against us by those who hope to discredit America and the news we transmit.

My point is not to criticize the organizers of the Olympics, the policies of President Bush, or people in the Pentagon. There were plenty of similar periods in the Clinton administration, and, indeed, they are almost inevitable. But I want to use these three events, all of which occurred in the last few weeks, to emphasize how hard it is to make friends in the world—and how easy it is to generate criticism.

To our critics, these three episodes fall into a pattern. As Lynne Cheney explained in a perceptive essay a few years ago, every political campaign attempts to frame issues in its own way.[10] To be simplistic, the 2000 campaign pitted the idiot against the liar. Of course neither description was true, but there were enough data points (some accurate, some manufactured by opponents or the press) for the images to take hold. Seen together, these episodes fall into a familiar, if unfair, pattern. America is an arrogant and powerful nation determined to go it alone and to win at all costs. If you think that sounds far-fetched, listen to this quote from Kim Seong Ho of South Korea's ruling party. In a speech to the National Assembly this Monday, he attacked the judge's Olympic rulings and said, "This kind of American arrogance, which disregards international justice and the pureness of sports, reflects U.S. president George W. Bush's unilateral diplomatic policies."[11]

So what can be done?

We have to begin by being thoughtful, purposeful, and strategic. We need to decide what image—or images—we want to project to the world, and we need to think about the many ways in which we achieve—or interfere with—that goal. That is the function often referred to as public diplomacy.

In a certain sense, we need to think of America as the greatest company in the world. For purposes of what I am about to say, think of it, from a public image standpoint, as "America, Inc." It is far larger and more complex—and much harder to manage—than Ford or Disney or Coca-Cola. But it has some of the same vital and legitimate concerns. It has the world's best brand—most loved, most hated, most admired, most imitated. How do we protect and enhance that brand? How do we make sure that our people and our products and our policies are as well received as possible?

In dealing with that issue, we need to be mindful of our almost endless list of product lines and of the very different ways in which diverse cultures around the world will react to them.

On one level, of course, that is the job of the State Department—and perhaps the rest of the functions I am describing should be in the State Department's domain. The proper location for the nation's public diplomacy functions is an important topic for study. But wherever those functions are situated, we are, in my view, woefully low on both funding and ideas.

To some extent, public diplomacy was the role of the United States Information Agency, or USIA. But even in its heyday the USIA only had limited resources. Today, it is the role, in large part, of the undersecretary of state for public diplomacy, a post currently held by a leading advertising executive named Charlotte Beers. But as Secretary Beers points out, she has only the most limited resources. For example, the USIA used to operate free libraries around the world. Now, to her great disappointment, almost all have been closed.

Here is a more dramatic example. Beers has produced a short film on Muslims in America that she wants to distribute in countries around the world. But, she says, there is today no method of distributing it within the most important countries. But those are only the smallest of examples in a field that needs much, much more support.

In addition to more resources, public diplomacy is a field that needs more thought. Years ago, there were leading scholars who spent a great deal of time thinking about propaganda and ways of influencing world opinion. But it is a topic that needs fresh research and fresh ideas. Those in government can implement good ideas, but it is much harder for them to formulate fresh approaches.

As we think about such approaches, I think we should always have, in the words of the Declaration of Independence, a "decent respect for the opinions of mankind." Whenever possible, we should remember that what we say and do in America will be known and will have an impact on our image throughout the world. It will not, of course, have the same impact everywhere—which makes the task all the more challenging.

During the Cold War, some of our domestic policies were shaped, in an important part, by our concern for their effect on our international image. A fascinating book by one of my colleagues at the USC Law School details the way in which our fight for hearts and minds encouraged America's leaders to support civil rights efforts during the Cold War.[12] We should remain mindful of those concerns today. For it is, above all, our policies—from globalization to the Middle East—that generate reactions around the world.

I don't suggest that we should let world opinion force us to make decisions that are not in our best interests as a nation or that do not accord with our values. But as we formulate and articulate policies, we should keep world opinion in mind.

A number of you are members of the Council on Foreign Relations and may know that it has formed a Task Force on Public Diplomacy. At the first meeting, one of the members made a suggestion that I think is worth repeating. He argued that the Islamic world will be impressed and our image enhanced if the United States truly carries through on its commitment to build Afghanistan into a solid independent state. While we all know that the United States has supported Muslim causes in a number of countries, that lesson has, too often, failed to gain sufficient attention or traction. But, he argued, the lesson of Afghanistan may be different and may send an important signal to the world.

Though there is much more to say about public diplomacy, I want to conclude by saying a few words about international broadcasting and particularly the Voice of America [VOA]. On Monday, I was privileged to join eight other former VOA directors—going back to the Eisenhower era—at an event commemorating VOA's sixtieth anniversary. The event is particularly meaningful for me since my father was the second director—from 1943 to 1945—and my sister wrote the seminal history of the agency's early years.[13] But it was especially significant because we were joined by President Bush, who gave a ringing and eloquent endorsement.

As the president noted, VOA now broadcasts—on radio, TV, and the internet—in fifty-three languages to a worldwide audience of more than ninety million regular listeners, viewers, and readers. It is a lifeline of information for people around the world, especially in countries that have no free press of their own. And it is based on one great idea that was articulated in the first broadcast in 1942. "Here speaks a voice from America," the announcer said. "The news may be good, the news may be bad, but we will always tell you the truth." Ever since, VOA has stood by the notion that its mission is to present a balanced and always accurate and complete story.

Honesty seemed the only way, in the early years, to combat Hitler's lies. The founders of VOA, working in the Office of War Information, knew that if the VOA did its job, it would inevitably broadcast some stories that would be unflattering and even painful for America and for our allies. But over time, they believed, VOA would gain credibility. And that would be its strongest asset.

But they also knew that credibility takes years to develop and only an instant to lose. So all VOA directors, Republicans and Democrats, those who served in war and in peace, have committed themselves to the central mission of telling the truth—and telling it, as USIA director Edward R. Murrow used to say, "warts and all."

And that commitment has served America remarkably well. Consider Afghanistan under the Taliban. According to a study conducted in 1999, 80 percent of adult males listened to at least one VOA broadcast every week—and 60 percent said that they listened everyday.[14]

When the battle started this fall and people rushed to the side of the rebels; when they believed that America came to liberate and not to occupy their country; when they believed that when bombs fell on civilians, it was an accident, not deliberate; and when they turned back to the music that had been banned by the Taliban—but had been broadcast regularly on VOA's Pashto and Dari services—when all of that happened, I could not help but think that VOA deserved some of the credit.

But in addition to reporting the news, VOA and international broadcasting can also help them to respect, admire, appreciate, maybe love, and hopefully not hate us.

To show you what VOA does on a daily basis, let's turn back to the Olympics. In preparing for the Olympics, school children throughout Utah learned about one of the countries that would be at the games. In effect, they adopted that country. And when the teams arrived, many of the children met with the athletes or trainers or their friends. That was not a story that received much, if any, play in the U.S. media. But it was a story that VOA's reporters covered in depth. So, for example, a VOA Russian reporter spent time with students who had adopted Russia. And she broadcast a report on the children and the Russian candy they had made and the dolls they were playing with and the music they were learning—and how much the kids liked Russia and about the time they spent with members of the Russian team. And, of course, the story was carried on VOA's Russian service and broadcast in that country on local FM stations as well as on shortwave and AM radio. It is a small example, perhaps, but an episode that is repeated day in and day out on VOA. Hopefully, those Russians who listened to that story will at least be a little more balanced in their reactions to the treatment in the pairs skating competition.

In the final analysis, public diplomacy can only be as effective as the product that we have to sell. And in my view, we have a remarkable product and a remarkable country. Part of our challenge is to think long and hard about our policies and how they are likely to be seen in the world. Part of it is to invest in an infrastructure capable of the task. And part of it is finding a way to tell the people of the world about the children of Utah.

NOTES

1. Studies and reports citing declines in world opinions about America include the *Pew Global Attitudes Survey* (July 2003); "Changing Minds and Winning Peace"

(October 1, 2003), a report by the State Department's Advisory Group on Public Diplomacy for the Arab and Muslim World, popularly referred to as the "Djerejian Report"; General Accounting Office (September 2003) "Report to the Committee on International Relations, House of Representatives."

2. Fareed Zakaria, "Politics of Rage: Why Do They Hate Us?" *Newsweek,* October 15, 2001.

3. Joe Klein, "Who's Winning the Fight for Iran's Future?" *New Yorker,* February 18–25, 2002, 66–76.

4. "A prince," he wrote, "who has a strong city, and has not made himself odious — that is hated — will not be attacked or, if any one should attack, he will be driven off with disgrace."

5. Liz Clarke "The Games Full of Good Sports; Captivating U.S.—Canada Final Concludes a Rousing Olympics" *Washington Post* (final edition), February 24, 2002, A1.

6. Sally Jenkins, "Peaceful Games, Cold War Sentiment," *Washington Post,* February 25, 2002, D1.

7. Bill Pennington, "2002 Games: Riveting Sport and an Angry Backlash," *New York Times*, February 24, 2002, A1.

8. "Means of Persuasion: How America and Europe, Working Together, Might Get Iran to Do, or Stop Doing, Certain Things," *Economist* (U.S. edition), February 14, 2002.

9. James Dao and Eric Schmitt, "A Nation Challenged: Hearts and Minds; Pentagon Readies Efforts to Sway Sentiment Abroad," *New York Times,* February 19, 2002, A1.

10. Lynne Cheney, *Telling the Truth* (New York: Touchstone, 1996). See chapter 6, "The Press and the Postmodern Presidency," 175–91.

11. Quoted in Barbara Demick, "The World; Many South Koreans See Skating Loss as Part of U.S. Plot," *Los Angeles Times,* February 26, 2002, A3.

12. Mary Dudziak, *The Cold War's Role in Civil Rights: Race and the Image of American Democracy* (Princeton, N.J.: Princeton University Press, 2000).

13. Holly Cowan Schulman, *The Voice of America: Propaganda and Democracy, 1941–1945* (Madison: University of Wisconsin Press, 1991).

14. Nora Boustany, "Sitting around the Radio," *Washington Post,* December 21, 2001, A27.

24

War, Media, and Propaganda: An Epilogue

Majid Tehranian

This volume has presented a variety of views on the role of the media in war and propaganda. It is impossible to summarize these views in a short epilogue. Instead, I offer five propositions with some historical evidence that emerge from most of the foregoing chapters.

THE STRUCTURE IS THE MESSAGE

Contrary to Marshall McLuhan's well-known epigram that "the medium is the message," media messages in wartime situations often closely follow the interests of their owners and managers. Government media toe the government line. Commercial media concentrate on war news as drama and entertainment, the goodies against the baddies. Public media often attempt to appeal to a more sophisticated audience, but their coverage of war news is subject to their sources of funding. Community media often respond to the perspectives of their own constituency and sources of funding.

The first casualty of every war is the truth. There is, of course, no single truth. But the truths of the various contending parties are often turned into blatant propaganda. Ideally, journalists are supposed to call the shots as they see them. But journalists are fundamentally no different from other observers. They are hostage to the socioeconomic and political structures of which they are a part. They can try to be dispassionate in a passionate situation. But they can do so often at the risk of being labeled a traitor and losing their jobs. Courageous journalists are often conspicuous by their absence.

In the present global situation, the commercial media empires generally see their interests as closely tied to an emerging American empire. In framing their international news, they often follow the prevailing ideology of the U.S. government. This could be clearly seen during the second Iraq War, in 2003. For instance both in its news and analysis, FOX News in the United States blatantly supported the Anglo-American invasion. FOX News is part of Rupert Murdoch's media empire that, under the name News Corporation, includes Star News in Asia and Sky News in Europe. The same was basically true of the other eight commercial media empires that dominate the world news (during the 1980s and 1990s, a mad rush into media mergers and acquisitions ultimately created nine media conglomerates).[1]

By contrast, the public broadcasting systems in Europe and the United States treated the Anglo-American rationale for the second Iraq War with skepticism. In France and Germany, where governments had been critical of the United States' unilateral approach, the skepticism was particularly prominent. In the Arab world, where the United States' policies vis-à-vis the Arab–Israeli conflict are perceived as titling increasingly toward Israel, the skepticism assumed critical proportions. Al-Jazeera, the satellite television broadcast out of Doha, Qatar, played a particularly important role in representing the critical Arab views. As the most-watched television news in the Arab world, Al-Jazeera proved itself to be an irritant to the Bush administration before and during the war. Through pressuring Qatar, the U.S. government tried several times to influence Al-Jazeera's news and analysis coverage. But it was faced every time with the idea that Al-Jazeera is an independent medium. By supporting Al-Jazeera's BBC style of independence, small Qatar has gained itself an enviable place in the formation of Arab public opinion. By reaching out to a wide spectrum of opinion, Al-Jazeera thus functioned as a corrective to the U.S. government and commercial media coverage.

U.S. MEDIA HAVE EVOLVED FROM WAR CRITICS TO WAR CAPTIVES

In the last four decades, government–media relations in the United States have gone through significant changes. During the war in Vietnam, as in previous wars, American journalists had relatively free access to the front lines. The diffusion of television sets into American homes during the 1960s consequently brought the war news directly into the living rooms. As the war in Vietnam intensified, the bloody images of war scenes repelled many concerned citizens. As American casualties mounted, that repulsion turned the American public opinion increasingly against the war. Free access by the journalists to the front lines also allowed them to wire reports that contradicted the Pentagon's accounts. Undercutting government propaganda were reports of such incidents as the massacre of an entire village population at My Lai[2] and the Pentagon's fabricated body counts of enemies. A military stalemate in combination with these circumstances led the Nixon administration to reach a peace agreement with the North Vietnamese by withdrawing from South Vietnam.

Following the war in Vietnam, some U.S. generals believed that the United States had lost the war because of media journalists. During the Reagan administration, the Pentagon's media policies changed. U.S. military actions in the 1980s did not allow journalists access to the front lines. In the first Iraq War, in 1991, the Pentagon adopted a new policy. Journalists were kept at bay, in a hotel in Riyadh, where they received Pentagon's briefings. Given that the war against Iraq to liberate Kuwait seemed to be fought under the United Nations flag, the Pentagon's new media policies were not vigorously criticized.

In the second Iraq War, however, the Pentagon moved a step further. Journalists were "embedded" in the advancing U.S. troops. The new policy put the journalists in as much harm's way as the troops. It induced a sense of solidarity among journalists and soldiers. As a result, despite the great controversies surrounding the new war, the U.S. commercial media generally accepted the Bush administration's strategy for the war. Few criticisms were voiced against the administration's unilateral policies that were dismissive of its European allies. The embedded journalists were captive to the fate of the troops. They identified with them and could not act as free agents.

PROLIFERATION OF WORLD NEWS CHANNELS IS CREATING A NEW KIND OF JOURNALISM

For those who have access to Internet or direct satellite broadcasting, world news has entered a new, historic stage. News and propaganda can no longer be totally controlled by particular governments or commercial media. There are literally thousands of Internet and satellite channels of alternative news that can be easily accessed. Such proliferation of news and views is no doubt confusing to the ordinary citizens. In the United States, for instance, 80 percent of the audience continues to receive its news primarily through television. That allows government and commercial media to frame world news without much challenge. However, for the Internet and direct satellite broadcasting enthusiasts, access to variety of news and views has significantly increased. The earlier generations had to resort to shortwave radio to get alternative news. Witness the Germans who listened to BBC World Service during World War II. The current generation of audiences can go to their favorite websites or, better yet, start a site of their own.

The new channels of world news may be enumerated as follows:

- direct satellite broadcasting that allows audiences to access over one hundred channels covering a variety of countries and languages;
- Internet radio that allows audiences to reach many channels—for example, BBC World Service;
- websites that reflect a diversity of ideological perspectives and news coverage;
- Internet listservs that allow a telecommunity of news watchers to monitor particular news topics or world regions while engaging the participants in an interactive discussion and analysis (witness Gulf 2000, an electronic club of over five hundred specialists throughout the world who exchanged news, gossip, and views on the first and second Iraq Wars); and
- subscriptions to Internet intelligent reports that allow access to specialized news and analysis.

STRUCTURAL AND CONTENT PLURALISM CAN COUNTER PROPAGANDA IN WARS

The media revolution of the last few decades has made efforts at media muzzling a self-defeating exercise. With social and political movements, democratic forces have been emboldened by a proliferation of global communication channels through the Internet, by direct satellite broadcasting, and by a global and diasporic media. In cooperation with voluntary associations and electronic communities, interactive technologies have provided a new sphere of public discourse, a new negotiation of reality, and a new democratic will.

However, pluralization of channels without pluralization of structures of media ownership and management has limited the democratic effects of the new media. So long as a single form of media ownership and control dominates a country, the democratic potentials of modern communication will not be fully realized. Global communication has placed the democratic norms of security, freedom, equality, and community on national agendas. The central task of the media in democratic societies may arguably be twofold: first, to allow for the diversity of voices in society to be heard; and, second, to channel that diversity into a process of democratic integration of public opinion and will. Without free and vigorous debate among competing views, no nation can achieve the level of integrated unity and determination necessary for democratic societies to act on public issues. Media pluralism would serve these purposes better than a media system exclusively dominated by state, commercial, public, or community media. However, structural pluralism is hostage to the presence of independent market institutions and voluntary associations (political parties, trade unions, religious and civic organizations). The existence of a strong civil society to counter the powers of the state and the market is therefore a precondition as well as an outcome of media pluralism.

The same principles hold true for global media. Structural pluralism may be considered a sine qua non of content pluralism. To achieve a free and balanced flow of news and information, a serious attempt at closing the digital divide must be made. For peace journalism to take on a sustained life, the voiceless in global communication must be empowered. To do so, it takes more than pious ethical codes or perfunctory international declarations. Major resources must be allocated to the development of the global information infrastructure. The establishment of a Global Media Development Bank (GMDB) as a UN-specialized agency may be considered the first step in this direction. GMDB can be financed out of taxes imposed on the two communication global commons, namely, the geostationary orbit and the electromagnetic spectrum. Current commercial users of these global commons are privileged to use a public resource and should be obligated to contribute toward a more balanced global communication system. The bank may, in turn, provide low-interest loans to media organizations who are

- committed to a peace journalism code of ethics,
- aimed at audiences with low or no access to the media, or
- supporting independent media and interactive communication.

TEN COMMANDMENTS FOR PEACE JOURNALISM[3]

Peace journalism in war situations may be defined as a kind of journalism that knows that when elephants fight, the grass gets hurt. The new guerrilla journalism by independent journalists increasingly allows that. Here are ten commandments that may guide the fearless peace journalists:

1. Never reduce the parties in human conflicts to two. Remember that when two elephants fight, the grass gets hurt. Pay attention to the poor grass.
2. Identify the views and interests of all parties to human conflicts. There is no single truth; there are many truths.
3. Don't be hostage to one source, particularly those of governments that control sources of information.
4. Develop a good sense of skepticism. Remember that reporting is representation. Bias is endemic to human conditions. You, your media organization, and your sources are not exceptions.

5. Give voice to the oppressed and to the peacemakers to represent and empower them.
6. Seek peaceful solutions to conflict problems, but never fall prey to panaceas.
7. Your representation of conflict problems can become part of the problem if it exacerbates dualisms and hatreds.
8. Your representation of conflict problems can become part of the solution if it employs the creative tensions in any human conflict to seek common ground and nonviolent solutions.
9. Always exercise the professional media ethics of accuracy, veracity, fairness, and respect for human rights and dignity.
10. Transcend your own ethnic, national, or ideological biases to see and represent the parties to human conflicts fairly and accurately.

NOTES

1. These currently include AOL-Time-Warner, General Electric, AT&T, Disney, Sony, News Corporation, Viacom, Seagram, and Bertelsmann (for further details, see www.fair.org/extra/9711/gmg.html).

2. On March 16, 1968, the angry and frustrated men of Charlie Company, Eleventh Brigade, and American Division entered the village of My Lai. "This is what you've been waiting for—search and destroy—and you've got it," said their superior officers. A short time later, the killing began. When news of the atrocities surfaced, it sent shock waves through the U.S. political establishment, the military's chain of command, and an already divided American public.

3. Majid Tehranian, "Peace Journalism: Negotiating Global Media Ethics," *Press/Politics* 7, no. 2 (Spring 2002): 80–81.

Suggested Readings

Artz, L., and Y. R. Kamalipour, eds. 2003. *The Globalization of Corporate Media Hegemony*. Albany: State University of New York Press.

Barrett, E. W. 1953. *Truth Is Our Weapon*. New York: Funk and Wagnalls.

Bernays, E. 1928. *Propaganda*. New York: Horace Liveright.

Carey, A. 1997. *Taking the Risk Out of Democracy*. Urbana: University of Illinois Press.

Chomsky, N. 1987. *The Chomsky Reader*. New York: Pantheon Books.

——. 1989. *Necessary Illusions: Through Control in Democratic Societies*. 1989. Toronto: Anansi.

Collins, J., and R. Glover, eds. 2002. *Collateral Language: A User's Guide to America's New War*. New York: New York University Press.

Creel, G. 1920. *How We Advertised America: The First Telling of the Amazing Story of the Committee on Public Information That Carried the Gospel of Americanism to Every Corner of the Globe*. New York: Harper and Brothers.

Debord, G. 1983. *Society of the Spectacle*. Detroit: Black and Red.

Dizard, W. 1961. *The Strategy of Truth: The Story of the U.S. Information Service*. Washington, D.C.: Public Affairs Press.

Ellul, J. 1965. *Propaganda: The Formation of Men's Attitudes*. New York: Vintage Books.

Friedman, T. 2002. *Longitudes and Attitudes: The World in the Age of Terrorism*. New York: Farrar, Straus, and Giroux.

Gher, L., and H. Y. Amin, eds. 2001. *Civic Discourse and Digital Age Communications in the Middle East*. Stamford, Conn.: Ablex.

Ginsberg, B. 1986. *The Captive Public: How Mass Opinion Promotes State Power*. New York: Basic Books.

Herman, E. S., and N. Chomsky. 1988. *Manufacturing Consent: The Political Economy of the Mass Media*. New York: Pantheon Books.

Huntington, S. P. 1996. *The Clash of Civilizations and the Remaking of the World Order*. New York: Touchstone.

Huxley, A. 1965. *Brave New World Revisited*. New York: Perennial.

Institute for Propaganda Analysis. 1938. *Propaganda Analysis*. New York: Columbia University Press.

Kamalipour, Y. R., ed. 1997. *The U.S. Media and the Middle East: Image and Perception*. Westport, Conn.: Praeger.

——, ed. 1999. *Images of the U.S. around the World: A Multicultural Perspective*. Albany: State University of New York Press.

——, ed. 2002. *Global Communication*. Belmont, Calif.: Wadsworth.

Kamalipour, Y. R., and K. R. Rampal, eds. 2001. *Media, Sex, Violence, and Drugs in the Global Village*. Lanham, Md.: Rowman and Littlefield.

Keen, S. 1991. *Faces of the Enemy: Reflections of the Hostile Imagination*. San Francisco, Calif.: Harper.

Kellner, D. 1992. *The Persian Gulf TV War*. Boulder, Colo.: Westview Press.

——. 2003. *From 9/11 to Terror War: The Dangers of the Bush Legacy*. Lanham, Md.: Rowman and Littlefield.

Key, W. L. 1989. *The Age of Manipulation: The Con in Confidence, the Sin in Sincere*. Lanham, Md.: Madison Books.

Mowlana, H., G. Gerbner, and H. Schiller, eds. 1992. *Triumph of the Image: The Media's War in the Persian Gulf—A Global Perspective*. Boulder, Colo.: Westview Press.

Nye, J. S., Jr. 2002. *The Paradox of American Power: Why the World's Only Superpower Can't Go It Alone*. London: Oxford University Press.

Pilger, J. 2002. *The New Rulers of the World*. London: Verso Books.

Pratkanis, A., and E. Aronson. 2001. *Age of Propaganda: The Everyday Use and Abuse of Persuasion*. Rev. ed. New York: W. H. Freedman.

Richmond, Y. 2003. *Cultural Exchange and the Cold War*. University Park, Pa.: Penn State University Press.

Sardar, Z., and M. W. Davies. 2002. *Why Do People Hate America?* New York: Disinformation Company.

Schechter, D. 2003. *Media Wars: News at a Time of Terror*. Lanham, Md.: Rowman and Littlefield.

Schiller, H. I. 2000. *Living in the Number One Country*. New York: Seven Stories Press.

Schwartz, T. 1981. *Media: The Second God*. New York: Random House.

Sifry, M. L., and C. Cerf. 1991. *The Gulf War Reader: History, Documents, Opinions*. New York: Random House.

Snow, N. 2002. *Propaganda, Inc.: Selling America's Culture to the World*. New York: Seven Stories Press.

——. 2003. *Information War: American Propaganda, Free Speech and Opinion Control since 9/11*. New York: Seven Stories Press.

Snyder, A. A. 1995. *Warriors of Disinformation: American Propaganda, Soviet Lies, and the Winning of the Cold War*. New York: Arcade Publishing.

Stauber, J., and S. Rampton. 2003. *Weapons of Mass Deception: The Uses of Propaganda in Bush's War on Iraq*. New York: Tarcher/Penguin.

Streitmatter, R. 1997. *Mightier Than the Sword: How the News Media Have Shaped American History*. Boulder, Colo.: Westview.

Taylor, P. 1995. *Munitions of the Mind: A History of Propaganda from the Ancient World to the Present Day*. Manchester, Engl.: Manchester University Press.

———. 1998. *War and the Media: Propaganda and Persuasion in the Gulf War*. 2nd ed. Manchester, Engl.: Manchester University Press.

Index

About the Contributors

ABOUT THE EDITORS

Yahya R. Kamalipour (Ph.D., University of Missouri, Columbia) is professor and head of the Department of Communication and Creative Arts, Purdue University, Calumet (Hammond, Indiana). A noted international scholar, he has taught at universities in Ohio, Illinois, Missouri, Indiana, Oxford, and Tehran. His most recent books are *The Globalization of Corporate Media Hegemony* (2003); *Global Communication* (2002); and *Media, Sex, Violence, and Drugs in the Global Village* (2001). He is managing editor of *Global Media Journal* (www.globalmediajournal.com) and *Global Media Monitor* (www.globalmediamonitor.com). In addition to several significant awards, numerous media interviews, and invited speeches, Kamalipour's articles have appeared in professional and mainstream publications in the United States and abroad. For further details, visit his personal website at www.kamalipour.com.

Nancy Snow (Ph.D., American University, Washington, D.C.) is assistant professor in the College of Communications at California State University, Fullerton (CSUF), and an adjunct assistant professor in the Annenberg School for Communication, University of Southern California. She is the author of *Propaganda, Inc.: Selling America's Culture to the World* (2002); and *Information War: American Propaganda, Free Speech and Opinion Control Since 9/11* (2003). Her prior government service includes two years in the Presidential Management Intern (PMI) program at USIA and the U.S. State Department. A Fulbright alumna to Germany, Snow served most recently as a public diplomacy advisor to the U.S. Advisory Commission on Public Diplomacy and U.S. Senate Foreign Relations Committee overseeing changes in

U.S. public diplomacy legislation since 9/11. She is coordinator of a working group to establish a Center for Public Diplomacy at University of Southern California, Annenberg, and heads the Center for Global Communications at California State University, Fullerton, to build mutual understanding between nonstate and state actors involved in global communication activities intended to understand, inform, and influence international publics. For further details, visit her personal website at www.nancysnow.com.

ABOUT THE CONTRIBUTORS

Lee Artz (Ph.D., University of Iowa) is associate professor in the Department of Communication and Creative Arts at Purdue University, Calumet. He has written numerous articles on cultural diversity and democratic communication for leading journals. His most recent books include *The Globalization of Corporate Media Hegemony* (with Yahya Kamalipour), *Public Media and the Public Interest* (with Michael McCauley, Eric Petersen, and Dee Dee Halleck, 2002), *Communication and Democratic Society* (2001), and *Cultural Hegemony in the United States* (with Bren Murphy, 2000).

Naiim Badii (Ph.D., Oklahoma State University) is professor of communication sciences in the Department of Communication Sciences at Allameh Tabatabai University, Tehran, Iran. He received his bachelor of science (1973) in journalism and his master of science (1976) in mass communication from Southern Illinois University, Carbondale. His articles on newspaper contents and styles have appeared in *Journalism Quarterly* and in Iranian scholarly journals. Badii is coauthor of the book *Modern Journalism* (2001), with Hossein Ghandi.

Ben Bagdikian is a Pulitzer Prize–winning journalist and former dean of the Graduate School of Journalism at the University of California, Berkeley. He served as assistant managing editor and ombudsman of the *Washington Post,* where he played a role in obtaining and publishing the Pentagon Papers. His classic book *The Media Monopoly* is now in its twentieth anniversary (seventh edition). He is the author of a number of books, including *In the Midst of Plenty: The Poor in America* (1964), *The Information Machine* (1970), and *Double Vision: Reflections on My Heritage, Life and Profession* (1995).

Nicolene Botha is a doctoral student in journalism at the University of Stellenbosch, South Africa. Her studies focus on media coverage of the second war in Iraq.

Naren Chitty (Ph.D., American University, Washington, D.C.) is director of the Centre for International Communication, Macquarie University, Australia; he is president of Global Communication Research Association; and he is a former Asian diplomat for the Reagan administration. His publications have centered on South Asian regional cooperation; media and globalization; and mediated terrorism. He is editor of the *Journal of International Communication.*

David J. Collison is a senior lecturer in the Department of Accountancy and Business Finance at the University of Dundee in Scotland. In addition to the influence of corporate propaganda—both on and operating through accounting and finance—his interests include the implications of accounting practice for sustainability (and vice versa). He has published widely in these areas, and he is on several working parties of professional accounting bodies.

Geoffrey Cowan has been dean of the Annenberg School for Communication at the University of Southern California (USC) since November 1996. Before becoming dean, Cowan served as the twenty-second director of the Voice of America (VOA), a position appointed to him by President Clinton in March 1994. VOA is the international broadcasting service of the U.S. government, broadcasting nearly nine hundred hours of programming in fifty-two languages, to a weekly audience of about one hundred million. He also served as assistant director of the U.S. Information Agency and as director of the International Broadcasting Bureau, with responsibility for WORLDNET TV and Radio & TV Marti, as well as VOA. Cowan is professor of journalism and law in the School of Journalism, and he jointly holds a professorial appointment in the USC Law School. He is author of *See No Evil: The Backstage Battle over Sex and Violence on Television* (1980) and *The People v. Clarence Darrow: The Bribery Trial of America's Greatest Lawyer* (1993).

Arnold S. de Beer is emeritus professor in the Department of Journalism, University of Stellenbosch, South Africa. He is editor of *Ecquid Novi: The South African Journal for Journalism Research* and coeditor, with John C. Merrill, of the forthcoming fourth edition of *Global Journalism*. A former member of the Board of the South African Broadcasting Corporation, as well as the Press Council of South Africa, he is presently serving as a member of the Appeals Board of the South African Ombudsman and as a member of the international council of the International Association for Communication and Media Research (IAMCR), as well as head of the media and society division of the African Council for Communication Education (ACCE). Recent publications and publications at the press include topics such as the Internet in

Africa; the concept news; media, gender, and violence; media and conflict; and media and elections in South Africa.

Mahboub Hashem (Ph.D., Florida State University) is a full professor of communication and chair of the Department of English, Mass Communication at the American University of Sharjah, United Arab Emirates. Dr. Hashem taught as a graduate teaching assistant at Florida State University, Tallahassee for two years. He also taught at the University of Toledo and the Governor's Gifted Institute of Ohio as well as the Fort Hays State University in Kansas. He has published books, chapters in books, articles in professional journals, and entries in the *World Education Encyclopedia*.

Zhou He (Ph.D., Indiana University) is associate professor in the Department of English and Communication at City University of Hong Kong. He has worked for the New China News Agency and the U.S. Catholic News Service; he has taught at San Jose State University; and he has published three books and scores of articles on mass communication.

Dana Hull lives in Oakland, California, and is a reporter at the *San Jose Mercury News*, where she has covered education, the state's energy crisis, and the antiwar movement. She arrived in Baghdad in late May and stayed until mid-July, reporting on the U.S. occupation of Iraq and the lives and daily struggles of the Iraqis. She graduated from American University's School of International Service in 1993 with a degree in international relations and peace and conflict resolution. Dana lived in Washington, D.C., and worked at the *Washington Post* before moving to the Bay Area in April 1999.

Karim H. Karim is associate professor at Carleton University's School of Journalism and Communication in Ottawa. He is author of the critically acclaimed and award-winning *Islamic Peril: Media and Global Violence* (2003, updated ed.). He has also published widely on issues of international communication, globalization, and technology. He recently edited *The Media of Diaspora* (2003).

Douglas Kellner is the George Kneller Chair in the Philosophy of Education at University of California, Los Angeles, and he is author of many books, writing on subjects such as social theory, politics, history, and culture, including *Camera Politica: The Politics and Ideology of Contemporary Hollywood Film*, coauthored with Michael Ryan; *Critical Theory, Marxism, and Modernity*; *Jean Baudrillard: From Marxism to Postmodernism and Beyond*; *Postmodern Theory: Critical Interrogations* (with Steven Best); *Television and the Crisis of Democracy*; *The Persian Gulf TV War*; *Media Culture*; and

The Postmodern Turn (with Steven Best). He has recently published a book on the 2000 presidential election, *Grand Theft 2000: Media Spectacle and the Theft of an Election;* and he has also just published *The Postmodern Adventure: Science, Technology, and Cultural Studies at the Third Millennium* (coauthored with Steve Best). Also recently published are his *Media Spectacle* and *September 11, Terror War, and the Bush Presidency.*

Antonio C. La Pastina (Ph.D., University of Texas, Austin) is a Brazilian-born journalist who now teaches at the Communication Department at Texas A&M University, College Station. His research interests are on the role of media and information technologies among nonmainstream communities in national and global contexts.

Ronald Paul Larson is a California State University, Fullerton, graduate history student who writes for the university's award-winning *Daily Titan* newspaper. In 2003, Larson became the only American university journalist to receive Pentagon credentials to cover the war in Iraq. Larson was embedded with the Army's Thirty-fifth Engineer Group, which oversaw construction of prison camps and other facilities in Iraq. Larson received his bachelor of arts in history and communication arts, with an emphasis in radio, television, and film, from the University of Wisconsin, Madison.

David Miller is author of *Don't Mention the War: Northern Ireland, Propaganda and the Media* (1994), *The Circuit of Mass Communication: Media Strategies, Representation and Audience Reception in the AIDS Crisis* (1998; with J. Kitzinger, K. Williams, and P. Beharrell), *Market Killing: What Capitalism Does and What Social Scientists Can Do about It* (2000; with Greg Philo), and *Open Scotland? Lobbyists, Journalists, and Spin Doctors* (forthcoming; with P. Schlesinger and W. Dinan). He is editor of *War and Words: The Northern Ireland Media Reader* (1996; with Bill Rolston) and *Rethinking Northern Ireland: Culture, Ideology and Colonialism* (1998). He teaches film and media studies at the University of Stirling, United Kingdom.

Asra Q. Nomani (M.A., American University, Washington, D.C.) is a former *Wall Street Journal* reporter and the author of *Tantrika: Traveling the Road of Divine Love* (2003), about her spiritual journey as a Muslim woman born in India and raised in West Virginia. Ms. Nomani reported on the war in Afghanistan for *Salon* and has written about Islam in the *Washington Post.* She is working on a forthcoming book about women in Islam, told through the narrative of the holy Islamic pilgrimage of the hadj. Ms. Nomani lives in Morgantown, West Virginia, with her toddler son Shibli.

Leila Conners Petersen is the chief executive officer of Tree Media Group, a multimedia production company based in Santa Monica, California. Leila is editor at large for *New Perspectives Quarterly,* an international journal of social and political thought and is a member of both the Council on Foreign Relations and the Pacific Council on International Policy.

Danny Schechter is a television producer and an independent filmmaker who also writes and speaks about media issues. He has written five books, including *The More You Watch, the Less You Know*, *News Dissector: Passions, Pieces and Polemics,* and *Media Wars: News at a Time of Terror*. He is executive editor of www.mediachannel.org.

Norman Solomon publishes his syndicated column Media Beat in the United States. He is the founder of the Institute for Public Accuracy, a nationwide consortium of policy researchers. Its mission is to broaden public discourse by gaining media access for those whose perspectives are commonly drowned out by corporate-backed think tanks and other influential institutions. Solomon is the author of many books, including *The Habits of Highly Deceptive Media*. He organized two trips to Baghdad in late 2002, the first with Representative Nick Rahall and other delegates, the second with actor and director Sean Penn.

Majid Tehranian (Ph.D., Harvard University) is an internationally recognized scholar and professor of international communication at the University of Hawaii and director of the Toda Institute for Global Peace and Policy Research. He received his bachelor's degree from Dartmouth College and his master's degree from Harvard University. He has authored more than ten books and about a hundred articles, which have appeared in a variety of scholarly journals and have been translated into French, Spanish, German, Norwegian, Finnish, Polish, Slovenian, Korean, Japanese, Bahasa Malay, Arabic, and Persian.

Daya Kishan Thussu (Ph.D., Jawaharlal Nehru University, New Delhi) is the course leader of the master of arts in transnational communications and the global media at Goldsmiths College, University of London. A former associate editor of Gemini News Service, a London-based international news agency. He is the coauthor of *Contra-flow in Global News* (1992); editor of *Electronic Empires—Global Media and Local Resistance* (1998); author of *International Communication—Continuity and Change* (2000); and coeditor of *War and the Media: Reporting Conflict 24/7* (2003).

Kathleen A. Tobin (Ph.D., University of Chicago) is assistant professor of Latin American Studies at Purdue University, Calumet. She has authored numerous articles on Latin America and a book entitled *The American Religious Birth Control Debate, 1907–1937*. She is currently completing a documentary history on global population policy.

Herman Wasserman is senior lecturer in the Department of Journalism, University of Stellenbosch, South Africa. His current research interests include civil society activism on the Internet and the construction of cultural identity in the media. He is deputy editor of *Ecquid Novi*, and his latest publication is the book *Shifting Selves: Post-apartheid Essays on Media, Culture and Identity* (coedited with Sean Jacobs, 2003). He has worked as a journalist and still regularly contributes articles and reviews to print and online publications.

Rhonda Zaharna (Ph.D., Columbia University), a former Fulbright scholar, is an assistant professor in the School of Communication, American University. Zaharna teaches courses in public communication theory, international public relations, and persuasion strategies and has written extensively on international and intercultural communication and on public diplomacy in the Arab and Islamic world. She holds an undergraduate degree in foreign service from Georgetown University and graduate degrees in intercultural communication from Columbia University.

Barrie Zwicker is a media critic and broadcaster entering his sixteenth season as resident media critic for Vision TV, Canada's only independent not-for-profit television channel. Vision TV is available in eight million Canadian homes via cable and DTH satellite and promotes a multicultural and interfaith perspective in its programming. Zwicker produces "The Eye Opener" for Vision TV's hour-long weekly public affairs program, *360 Vision*. Zwicker has been a reporter on major newspapers, including the *Vancouver Province* and the *Detroit News*. He worked for eight years at "Canada's National Newspaper," the *Globe and Mail*, where as education writer he won all three top awards of the Education Writers' Association of North America.